Sailing to the Edge of Fear

ADLARD COLES NAUTICAL
London

Published in 2000 by Adlard Coles Nautical, an imprint of A&C Black (Publishers) Ltd
35 Bedford Row, London WC1R 4JH

Copyright© Frank Dye 2000

Published in Canada by Nimbus Publishing Ltd., Nova Scotia, in 1999.

ISBN 0-7136-5305-1

A CIP catalogue record for this book is available from the British Library.

Printed and bound in Canada.

Sailing to the Edge of Fear

The water is always changing, fascinating, sometimes incredibly beautiful, and it drowns those who are careless or contemptuous of its dangers. People talk about a 'respect' for the sea but respect is based on fear. Few seafarers have any illusions about the sea–it is impersonal, uncontrollable. It is a passion that draws us back time after time.

While the fascination outweighs the fear I sail on.

When the balance changes it is time to stop.

- Frank Dye

This book is dedicated to the other "halves" of the partnership—
Margaret and *Wanderer*.

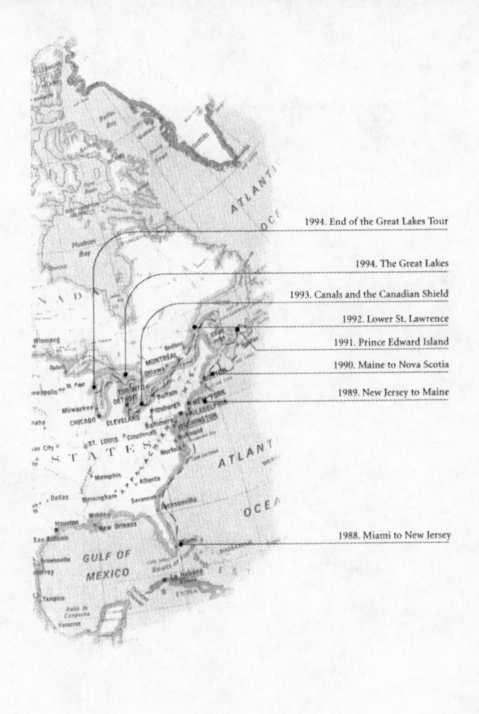

1994. End of the Great Lakes Tour

1994. The Great Lakes

1993. Canals and the Canadian Shield

1992. Lower St. Lawrence

1991. Prince Edward Island

1990. Maine to Nova Scotia

1989. New Jersey to Maine

1988. Miami to New Jersey

TABLE OF CONTENTS

IT WAS DEFINITELY LOVE AT FIRST SIGHT. It was the spring of 1963 and *Wanderer* was sitting inconspicuously in a corner of the Earl's Court Boat Show. Tired of milling between aisles of shiny, faceless GRP boats, I decided to escape and spend the second half of my boat show day in a London art gallery. About to leave by a side door, I walked by this wooden, scruffy 16-foot dinghy. Her varnished decks were salt-crusty and scarred. Inside old stained sails, warps, piles of worn crumbled charts, Wellington boots and anchors lay on her smelly floorboards. On the thwarts sat a small dark-suited man reading a book; he barely glanced up as people crowded around the Wayfarer dinghy-and he answered questions in a shy diffident manner. The publicity, charts, and route maps told of the offshore voyages of this dinghy. I marvelled that so tiny a boat could sail from Scotland to Iceland and across the North Sea to Norway. Eventually, I plucked up enough courage to ask if women crew were ever required. The answer was an emphatic "No."

However, I stayed by *Wanderer* all day, elated by the challenges, toughness, and individuality she and her skipper presented in such an unpretentious manner. By the time I left, I had examined *Wanderer*'s every scar, screw, and piece of equipment in rising excitement. A year later I met Frank again. He was a tutor in an Easter sailing course and I was an elementary student sailor intent on improving my self-taught sailing skills. Although we were born and had lived only 20 miles apart, I had never met Frank, although the headlines that he and *Wanderer* had made on his sailing exploits over the years were well known to me. "Don't sail with that man; he'll kill you," said the instructor of my dinghy course after overhearing Frank's invitation to me to crew him on his Wayfarer the weekend following the course. Fortunately, I didn't even entertain heeding my instructor's advice.

The rest of the season gave me wonderful days afloat in *Wanderer*. I was introduced to day cruising the Norfolk's coast and harbours and I marvelled at the gentle and sharing qualities Frank showed to a completely green crew. Because of my inexperience, I took for granted that whatever Frank told me to do on his boat was normal procedure, and my learning curve was extremely steep. Since he did not complain when we had to reef and unreef half a dozen times in a day's sail, or pull the dinghy over sandbanks because we had missed the tide, or feel our way into an inlet harbour many hours after I thought I should be soaking in a hot bath, I believed everybody else sailed like this and an eighteen-hour day was the expected cruise routine.

One Saturday night we met in a dark North Norfolk sailing club to rig *Wanderer*, having spent a cosy supper evening at my favourite restaurant on the coast. Crossing the bar in an oily darkness and out into The Wash on a balmy warm August night was a new experience to me, and one I enjoyed enormously. About dawn, Frank said, "I've forgotten the anchor. What do you suggest?" So we buried an oar on a sandbank as a makeshift anchor. "I've forgotten the stove, I haven't got any food, and I left the tent behind" were subsequent revelations made in the darkness, but in a happy, hungry mood, I helped Frank use the sails as a shelter and we snuggled down, fully clothed, to await the tide and the light. Shivering with cold and hunger, hours later we got ready to sail on across The Wash. As I struggled to peel off steaming clothes beneath clammy oilskins to 'spend a penny' over the side of the dinghy, I thought, "Funny man. How could he have made so many mistakes when he's sailed to Iceland and Norway, and survived so many sea miles?" The sail back to Brancaster was magical, and I learned later this series of misadventures was Frank's way of selecting his crew.

Over the next few months we talked about sailing to St. Kilda for our summer holiday. Each Sunday we pushed out into the frothing tide, and I became familiar with Frank's sea methods, and *Wanderer*, a 15-foot double-chine wooden open dinghy, became a magical carpet. When we erected the simple canvas tent over the boom, lit the lantern and ate our meal, the materialistic world seemed far away; and no fitted kitchen could have given me half as much pleasure as our small petrol Optimus stove in a plastic bucket with it's watertight lid. Feeling the cold, I experimented with clothing. I was shown how to sew up a quilted tunic and trousers and where to buy layers of fine wool and silk gloves, and hoods, and to learn to walk about in Wellington boots two sizes too large-the theory being that if one capsized, one could kick them off before they acted as drogues.

On the way to St. Kilda we waddled into the boat dressed in more than seven layers of clothes beneath oilskins. I found that washing hair, teeth, or skin was a luxury—fresh water was kept for drinking. One could only carry four gallons on board, and one never knew when supplies could be replenished. Surprisingly, I found one's hair and skin seemed to rectify a natural oil balance after several days without washing, and living in the open air, bodily smells were dissipated anyhow. Rubbing skin with meths before a cruise prevented pressure boils.

Feelings of nausea and sea-sickness plague us both at sea and food had to be selected in light of limited space, life span, weight, and durability. Cooking meat was too much of a procedure and it could not be kept for long, neither could salads and soft fruits. Eggs were packed in plastic containers and shock-corded beneath the side decks-oranges seemed to travel better than most fruits, and powdered milk, soups and drinks were practical to carry, provided that fresh water was plentiful or could be replenished. Bread went mouldy after several days, so biscuits were found to be a good substitute. Cheese, dried fruit, nuts, boiled sweets, apples, and oranges were some of our favourite foods. Breakfast usually consisted of a hot drink, banana sandwich, and porridge. Lunch might be a similar meal, or a sardine sandwich, and supper might be a hot soup, tinned stew, and fruit. Snacks of dried fruit, nuts and biscuits were eaten whilst sailing throughout the day. Frank had welded up a stainless steel oven with two shelves for two ex-army mess tins. The stove swung on gimbals beneath the thwart and it could be used in reasonably settled weather whilst sailing.

"You've done well," said Frank, after a long night sail from St. Kilda. "Stay in bed and I'll make you breakfast." Laying in bed (a sleeping bag on an airbed laid out alongside the centreboard) on the floorboards, I dozed listening to the preparations. Breakfast was served-in an insulated mug and two courses together-green pea soup and scrambled eggs. Not the best menu for a sea-sick crew!

A year later we married, and towed *Wanderer* down to Devon to share our honeymoon. It was December, and the sailing was good, but never before had I known what it was to be so cold. On the last night, we sailed to a waterside restaurant for dinner. We were dressed in many layers of clothes, and as I struggled into oilskins at the end of our banquet, a fellow diner leaned over to me saying, "I'll drive you home. Let your old man sail his own boat home!" But that night, we had the most wonderful moonlit sail down the estuary, phosphorus dancing from every wave, and a silence rarely enjoyed in this noisy, busy world.

Being a self employed businessman, Frank took only two weeks holiday annually. Sundays were free for sailing, providing a customer did not require attention. In such limited leisure many of the British rivers and estuaries were explored in our Wayfarer dinghy in day sails which often meant hitch-hiking home overnight. Being back in the firm on Monday morning at 7:30 A.M. was the golden rule never to be broken.

I have been privileged to crew Frank and *Wanderer* for over 25 years, and the happiest and most hellish times in my life have been spent afloat with them both. Yet, I have no real idea of the compulsions which drive Frank to continue year after year, to make these wonderful, dangerous, and rewarding dinghy cruises. Thirty years on I finally left *Wanderer* 900 miles into this present cruise. I had lost all joy and willpower, and sadly realised that a devoted partner of three decades was simply not good enough to crew such an amazingly determined seaman with such driving ambition. Now we single-hand our own dinghies and still find dinghy cruising the best occupation, religion, obsession, and pure delight that has come our way.

When this world gets too much; when noise, materialism, or sadness threaten to defeat us, we can quickly retreat into our memories and find optimism, fun, and faith in life again, and are ready to plan the next sail.

Luckily, one soon forgets the terrors, hardships, and boredom of long sea passages, and the wonderful memories remain most vivid. Times like flying over the waves, deep reefed, before a force 7 wind, sparkling sun, blue waves, white foam, and up on a plane for many hours running along the Outer Hebrides, *Wanderer* going like a train. Times like being enveloped in a warm deep darkness with the constellations sparkling above our heads so brightly that one could almost touch them and pick a star out of the velvet blackness to place on *Wanderer*'s decks as we lay anchored off a creek at Ras Al Khymer in the Arabian Gulf separating Arabia from Iran. The starlight patterns on the curling waves, and the plaintive murmur of the prayer call from a far off mosque set in the distant sands beneath the gigantic mountain ranges, was a night never to forget.

Times like Christmas Day spent in Key West, trying to sail around Florida, where we rushed before a fierce northerly having battled into huge, cold, breaking seas as the gale swept in. "Marina full" said the notice as we eased *Wanderer* into a crack between two enormous powerboats, and tied her to a palm tree whipping wildly in the rising storm. An hour later, after a rest and a hot shower, we decorated *Wanderer*'s tent with cards, balloons, and Christmas roses (plastic!), ate nuts, dug our Christmas cake out of wet bilges, and said that this was the best Christmas Day we had ever known. Later, American yachtsmen collected us, gave us battery "winking" haloes and we joined in the carol singing to each yacht.

Every night after the labours of the day, with the tent secure, we would creep into our sleeping bags, lay down on the floorboards and enjoy our home. "Take a last look," Frank would say as he leaned over and turned out the swinging candle lantern tied on to the boom. Then we'd listen to the night sounds—wind in the mangroves or pine forests, hoot of a night bird, call of the seabird or wolf—until we fell asleep.

I have a sad and sentimental memory too of Frank urging me to "take a last look." After 20 years cruising in *Wanderer*, she was a frail old lady, waterlogged and very soft in places. Frank decided we should give her a Viking funeral on Morston marshes, but somehow Greenwich Museum heard of our plans and asked for our beloved boat. I felt that her old age would be a happy one in the company of other boats and so, one cold Easter, we sailed her down the Thames.

On that last night that we slept on board moored off Greenwich. Frank woke me at dawn with a cup of hot tea. "Take a last look" he said, as so many times before. Outside the tent it was snowing, and *Cutty Sark* and *Gypsy Moth* stood silhouetted in the snow flakes in that cold grey dawn. There was great pride that *Wanderer* was to join them but we were swept away in the sorrow of parting.

We took her into Greenwich wearing our sailing clothes, and were rather surprised to find everybody else was in reception suits and frocks, so we slipped off our smelly rubber boots and did full justice to the elegant buffet lunch. I lost my composure when Basil Greenhithe asked me to make a speech as we gave *Wanderer* away. I wept. He comforted me gently, saying, "A boat is an extension of oneself." Frank had bought her in 1959 without even sailing her, using the experienced engineer's maxim, "If it looks right it is right!" It was hard to imagine life without her.

Home is where the heart is. That a small-tented dinghy is our favourite home is no accident of fate. What a wonderful church, travelling companion, magic carpet to foreign cultures, and stimulating friend our dinghies have proven to be: No wonder Frank continues to journey.

CHAPTER ONE

1988. Norfolk U.K. to Norfolk U.S.A.
(Miami to New Jersey)

15th January, 1988. Miami, Florida

For the first time in our lives we could look forward to a holiday of more than three weeks. Marg had retired through an injury at work so I sold my business. "We will sail as long as it is fun," we declared.

January of 1988 found us in sunny Miami. To our dismay we learned that *Star Evita*, the container ship from Felixstowe carrying *Wanderer*, had been delayed in mid-Atlantic by heavy gales. Gloomily, we became unwilling tourists but soon found ourselves overwhelmed by the Southern hospitality for which Florida is well-known. Peggy and Clyde, who had bought our second wooden Wayfarer when we had sailed around Florida during an earlier holiday, invited us to stay at their house, and told us, "Take the spare key and come and go as you please."

Seeing our old wooden *Wanderer* still beautifully maintained in their garden was like meeting an old friend. The fabulous Florida subtropical playground of the azure seas, sandy beaches, tropical botanical gardens, sophisticated shops and restaurants, filled our tourist days quite happily. After visiting Barnacle House, a reconstruction of an early settlement in the Miami swamps, we were invited home for tea by a volunteer guide. 'Home' was a beautiful house set in several acres of private garden overlooking Biscayne Bay. English 'afternoon tea' was followed by a supper of champagne and smoked salmon in candlelight in their sculptured patio garden. With a wave of her hand our generous hostess said, "It is too late to go home tonight. Choose a bedroom." But sensing our reluctance to be house-bound, she asked, "Would you prefer to sleep in our yacht at the bottom of the garden? We returned from the West Indies only last week so everything you need will be on board." So instead of a house, that night we fell asleep in a 40-foot yacht overlooking the bay, and in the morning picked pink grapefruit from the trees for breakfast.

Days later it was a great thrill to be reunited with *Wanderer* in Port Everglades when she finally arrived. In the heat and humidity of the vast harbour, Clyde and Margaret laboured to unpack *Wanderer* whilst I did my best to persuade officialdom to issue a U.S. cruising permit. It appeared that we needed evidence that the boat was British—either a builder's invoice or the Small Ships' Registration (SSR) certificate. Unfortunately, we had neither as our boat was a prototype not fully completed when shipped so there was no time to obtain a SSR certificate, and our invoice was marked "provisional" and, therefore, not acceptable. The custom's officer was sympathetic but adamant and I began to think our cruise was at an end before it began! Fortunately, after I asked his advice his mood seemed to change. He suddenly said, "No problem" and walked through to the inner office where we could see the staff discussing our difficulty. "I was right. There is no way we can issue a cruising permit." Then he grinned and added, "But we can clear your 16-foot sailboat as a British Merchant Ship trading along our east coast. How far would you like to trade?" We drove off with the necessary permission for a British trading vessel cleared to Boston!

Clyde drove us to Stuart, some 60 miles to the north, where we floated *Wanderer* off the trailer at a launch ramp, then helped us unload boxes of groceries and sackfuls of gear onto the beach. By the light of a clear moon we said our thanks and goodbyes to the friends who had made our entry and stay in Miami such a pleasant start to the cruise. Rigging the mast, we threw everything into the dinghy and fell asleep on top of the gear, too hot to bother with the tent. At dawn we woke to the full glory of a pink Florida sunrise and again indulged in fresh pink grapefruit.

12th February, 1988. The Intra Coastal Waterway

The Intra Coastal Waterway (ICW) is an inland route extending from the Florida Keys to Chesapeake Bay, 1000 miles from Miami to Norfolk Virginia. It consists of natural rivers, lakes, estuaries, and sounds linked by man-made canals, and was constructed during the wars with the British to carry barge trade out of the range of the British blockade. It is still a commercial route carrying barge traffic but popular with pleasure craft as it avoids the rough waters of the Atlantic Ocean and the dangerous tidal inlets.

Some of the rivers and sounds are vast, and the tide was accelerating as we approached each outlet to the ocean. At first, we were disappointed. The only boats we saw were large yachts going south under motor. The 'snowbirds' (Canadians and Americans travelling down to Florida to escape the harsh northern winters, returning home in the spring) with their deep keels are restricted to the narrow buoyed channel, have motors, and rarely using sail even with a fair wind, and we soon realise that we have freedom to wander far from the dredged channel to explore the creeks with the help of our centreboard and shallow draft. Sailing north in early February, the locals warn us that we are a month too early. They are right, of course, and we are to find that the next states northward are still in the grip of winter!

Many days with a double reef we beat into wild northerly winds, complicated by fierce tides as we reach the wide sounds of Georgia. The many bridges crossings are less trouble to us than to our fellow travellers in their large yachts. Some bridges open 'on demand' by sounding a fog horn, and there is a short wait whilst the duty bridgeman stops the road traffic to lift the bascule; the busy bridges open only at set times, so the big boats wait for the next time of opening. In *Wanderer* we sail to the bridge, lower mast and sails 'all standing' at the last moment, and let the tide and our speed carry us through, swinging up the mast in the tabernacle. We are sailing immediately. This is beyond the experience of the bridge staff, and a startled bridgekeeper on one of the seven bridges spanning the Daccoter River yells at us "If you carry on like that you'll kill yourselves." We had become over-confident until once, just as I had half lowered the mast and sails, a gale-force squall from astern filled the mainsail and lifted me, and the mast, off my feet. Marg had no room to round up head-to-wind so, with the wind ballooning the sails, she grabbed my feet and held me down with one arm while steering with the other, just as the bridge swept above us.

A lifting road bridge on the Intra Coastal Waterway—here, we are approaching the bridge two reefs down.

Despite the increasingly cold and squally weather, sailing along the palm tree-lined rivers, lagoons, canals, and cuts is fascinating. The bird life of pelicans, grey and white herons, and eagles soaring over the vast stretches of forest contrasts oddly with the luxurious mansions set in spotless, weedless lawns, private golf courses, swimming pools, turquoise water-fronted patios, parks of mobile homes, and leisure fishing complexes in pine belts. An especially violent 'northerly' swept south from Canada and we were glad to accept the warm hospitality of the Melbourne Yacht Club.

By now, we have learned to cope with the reactions we invariably get. People watch in disbelief as *Wanderer* struggles in from the thunderstorms, wind, and rain to put the tent up over the dinghy, then as the weather clears they stroll by saying, "Man, that's neat! No leaks?"

March 1st, 1988. Atlantic Boulevard Creek, Florida

At Atlantic Boulevard Creek, approaching Saint John's River, my log records (perhaps a little unsympathetically) Marg's distress at the unrelentingly violent weather:

> Torrential rain and very cold indeed, we were shivering as we sailed. Marg ready to mutiny. We anchor rowed in carefully and the tent was up at 3:30 P.M. then a hot supper before we turn in. Two sleeping bags each, and Marg is fully dressed too. At 8:00 P.M. there is a storm of wind—the tent is flapping and banging—it's unbelievably wild.

The tent will tear at any moment. I tie the skirt down more securely, then forward tent flaps down across the bows and aft flaps under the transom. This reduces the shake by half. It's bitterly cold. At each squall I tell Marg that the rain can't get heavier or colder, but it does! Thank God the anchor is holding. Marg doesn't like it and won't keep quiet about it!

The Saint John's River crossing is going to be tricky and I assess the problems carefully. The ICW crosses the Saint John's River near its mouth where it is at its narrowest. The river discharges a big catchment area, so the downriver currents will be fierce and with strong winds predicted, conditions could not be more difficult—the wind will blow directly downriver re-enforcing the current, *Wanderer* will be swept far downstream without gaining the far shore, and once the ebb starts we get carried out into the Atlantic; the flooding tide running into a near gale will make the river treacherous and a crossing impossible. So the only possibility is to cross at exactly slack water using the last of the ebb to help us out of our creek. We ought to wait for the wind to drop but there is another difficulty—at slack water tomorrow it will be almost dark with no daylight to cope with any gear failure and too dark to find the entrance to the ICW on the far shore or to find a good anchorage. Even worse, the radio announces, "the upper river is in flood and a flood warning is issued for downriver areas."

We are forced into crossing this afternoon. I don't like it. Marg correctly points out that it is 'dangerous' but I point out that we shall lose our protection under the land when the floods arrive and it will be days before we can cross. We are 'on a hiding to nothing.' It needs careful planning.

Sailing double-reefed and short tacking the two miles along the creek, *Wanderer* is spewed out into the river by the last of the ebb, but the ebb reinforced by the river current is still running strongly. The wind drops, the current slacks, we can see the marker on the far shore, and we have a wet but relatively easy crossing. Marg is cheerful now with the crossing behind us as we reach with a force 3 through nice open countryside. We anchor at the island behind buoy 'Red 68' for a pleasant evening, full of light breeze, and sunshine. We watch herons at the water's edge and the small birds flying with lower beaks in the water to feed.

Four closely spaced bridges go well—two courteously open as we approach before we use our foghorn, the others we 'shoot' by lowering the mast and sails all standing. In 12 miles the lagoon narrows into a dredged cut, and the picturesque description of an anchorage in Fox Cut lures us on. The approach is unusually pretty with sandy cliffs, undercut trees, palms leaning drunkenly, and Spanish moss hanging in curtains everywhere. We turn into Fox Cut which is narrow but well-sheltered from the strong wind, and anchor bow and stern. It is a lovely anchorage after 31 miles of hard-wind sailing.

9th March, 1988. St. Augustine, Florida

Another fierce 'northerly' in Matanzas River causes us to dig out our down-filled inner sleeping bags, and go to bed fully dressed in hats, scarves, and gloves.

A pleasant sail along the Matzos River brings us to the town of St. Augustine, Florida which looks interesting so we decide to stay. As we sail to anchor among the other 'transients' in the bay, a man on a large yacht calls to us, "That's a Wayfarer. I sailed one in Canada. Come aboard and we'll fix you a hot drink." A hot drink extends to a chicken dinner and we hear that they have journeyed from the Great Lakes where there are no tides, and on the way they have dragged anchor everywhere and under all conditions. Now they cannot sleep unless one of them is on anchor watch, and probably this is the end of their cruise.

St. Augustine is the nicest town we have yet seen. Originally, it was a Spanish settlement, the oldest permanent settlement on the U.S. mainland, founded in 1565 by Pedro Menendez the Spanish explorer, and it still retains the original Spanish character. It is here that the Spanish explorer Ponce de Leon discovered the legendary Indian "Fountain of Youth" after many years of searching. The well has been restored and I read that the water is guaranteed to restore youth and fitness so I hurriedly take a long drink of the spring water before throwing away my reading glasses and hearing aid. Perhaps I should have checked how long it takes to work.

Sailing away from St. Augustine, we are refreshed and rested, appreciating the real sense of history the place bestowed upon us. Passing a huge gold cross set on the marshes where the Spanish invaders and the indigenous Indian tribes met and battled, we are very sad to leave this beautiful place.

24th March, 1988. The Marshes of Georgia

We have now crossed into the great area of marsh and swamp of Georgia. Enormous wide skies, and we can see the horizon all the way round. The young mosquitoes are just learning to bite and are not very expert yet. I can well believe the statement that "the mosquito is the national emblem of the State of Georgia." It will be a long beat up the Cumberland River, and we plan to cross Cumberland Sound at slack water. The wind is increasing, short seas beginning to break as the tide slackens so we pull down the first slab reef, and fully furl the genoa. We then put in the second reef as the force 7 northeasterly blowing against the weather-going ebb tide is creates a wickedly short sea, and we turn tail and run into Floyd Creek for shelter and a rest.

There are five miles still to go to Cumberland Sound where we expect a pasting and it is every bit as bad as we anticipate. As we come out of Floyd Cut into Satilla River we hit short vertical waves the same length as *Wanderer* and she pitches repeatedly. The weight of gear in the ends of the boat makes the pitching worse and she almost stops. Solid green water over the bows runs aft over the washboards and we have to shake out a reef to keep her moving. Slowly, we work clear and thankfully pump out. Marg is helming and I plot a compass course to take us to the far side of the river as it is impossible to distinguish the channel from marshes at this distance. The northeast wind increases quickly again to force 7 and puts up a very nasty short chop. Into Dover Creek, we furl the genoa, and storm up to windward into the very narrow entrance, only 40 yards wide, of Dover Cut. Here, we get the shelter of the land and have a rather more leisurely flog up to Umbrella Creek.

25th March, 1988. Jeckyll Sound, Georgia

Within a half mile a thick sea mist rolls in, and we are completely alone, no buoys in sight, no sound—nothing. The map shows a big channel joining this sound from the left, the sea is invisible on our the right, and there are various side streams feeding into the sound so there must be strong cross currents. We have no real idea of what the tide is doing. I time each tack and plot a guesswork position, and give Marg a new bearing. Much to my surprise buoy "25" materialises out of the mist 40 yards away on our bows, and we come into Jeckyll Island dock in a thick clammy blanket of sea fog and are glad to be out of it. There is a fish market on the dock where we buy fresh shrimps and boil them for lunch—a meal fit for a king!

The island is beautiful with azaleas, camellia bushes, live oaks draped with moss, and camping at night at the sheltered dock is very pleasant. The cracknels and mocking birds are noisy and the warm winds purr in the pines.

16th April, 1998. Charleston, South Carolina

After weeks of travelling through the marshes of Georgia and South Carolina and North Carolina we come to Charleston, a colourful, flamboyant, friendly southern city, and we tie up at the downtown marina.

Activity is intense at the marina when we return from exploring Charleston. It looks like a disturbed wasp's nest with people dashing about, rowing out, re-anchoring yachts and putting down extra anchors, doubling mooring ropes, putting out extra fenders and lashing down equipment on deck. I stand looking on in amazement until someone shouts to us, "A tornado is headed for Charleston, and it's expected to hit during the early evening!"

I am horrified. We knew that tornadoes are common in the southern states but I had overlooked the possibility of them occurring along the eastern seaboard. I had thought that thunderstorms, cold fronts, or hurricanes would be our lot and now to find that we need to add tornadoes to the list is disturbing.

Marg's log of the incident reflects our feelings of helplessness:

A tornado warning until 10:00 P.M. says a woman at the dock office. It's confirmed by the dock master and we listen to the weather radio to find it's true. Someone takes time to explain that 'twisters' are unpredictable, very local but immensely destructive with winds in the centre reaching 150–200 miles per hour; and although the marina is well sheltered the great danger is a boat breaking away—one rope parts, then the next, she fouls her neighbour who breaks away, then the docks go, and the damage is enormous. We do what we can for *Wanderer*. We double our lines and tie down the tent. There is sudden cloud, no sunset; one moment it is a sunny afternoon, the next we are in semi-darkness. Quickly the sky gets blacker and blacker, the wind increases to 70 knots, the rain is torrential. Never before have we seen such evil purple black skies, nor witnessed such vivid lightning. The wind goes up again. There is roaring, the tent is flapping and drumming—it's very frightening! Then, suddenly, it dies away. The sky is still overcast and ominous. Very heavy rain for half-an-hour, then it alters course and goes out to sea. It has missed us. Later, we learn that the tornado had changed course southward destroying houses and cars, uprooting trees, and killing twelve people.

April 17, 1988. Charleston, South Carolina

The U.S. Customs House is the finest public building we have yet seen, and the central hall is magnificent and we stand and stare. I return in the afternoon to see the customs officer and explain that we are cruising as a 'Merchant Vessel—cleared to Boston' and I can foresee difficulties if checked by the U.S. coastguard who may be unhappy when they find we are a trading ship only 16-feet long, and sailing inland rather than the direct sea route! He grins and says "No problem." The new cruising permit is limited to 12 months and although I had hoped for longer it is the wrong time and place to argue for an extension. At least a 'yacht cruising permit' allows us to explore off the direct coastal route which our previous clearance strictly speaking did not. And we still have the original 'trading permission' as a back-up.

The marshes, swamps, and reed beds of Georgia and South Carolina are vast and lonely; the creeks tortuous and tidal with the main channels occasionally marked by beacons, but it's easy to get lost if we don't keep the position up to date on the chart. I'm writing this at anchor as the sun drops below the edge of the marsh. Suddenly, it's dark but pelicans are still diving into the water for fish.

We hope to arrive at Georgetown tomorrow.

There is a continual stream of big power boats returning north for the summer, all planing and pulling up a big wake. It is always alarming being on a small boat as I am never sure if they are going to slow down, they almost always do—but not always. In Four Mile Creek Canal which is excessively narrow, a power boat planing up from astern comes on us suddenly round a bend, but cuts her throttles back quickly and idles past with a wave. Two more planing powerboats travelling in company throttle down. The first is mystified by a sailboat tacking and I wave him under our stern—another friendly salute. The second doesn't understand and thinks we are baulking him, so he slams his throttles open and passes 'on the right' planing through the narrowing gap between *Wanderer* and the shore and pulling up a great wake. I throw round to avoid a collision and he half swamps us. Pumping out takes a long time.

Minim Creek Canal is narrow, the countryside open breckland, sandy with a few pines, but a tug pushing a raft of barges overhauls us and interrupts our enjoyment, and he fills the channel so we beat into Minim Creek to let him pass.

Crossing Winyah Bay with wind-against-tide is an anxious sail. Double reefed we beat into deep troughs of hissing breaking seas. Marg stood up to take another reef in the mainsail when a wave washed into the boat, and had she not grasped the mast she could have been washed out. Wind force 5-6, short steep seas causing us to surge off the tops.

Anchoring off Georgetown docks we sit out a torrential rainstorm, then as it slackens we row in. We meet Eddy in the next big yacht who calls across to us, "How long will it take to rig your tent?" "Ten minutes," Marg replies. "In ten minutes the kettle will have boiled and there will be a hot meal on your plate. Come aboard when you're ready."

A 40-foot yacht with blown out headsails has just limped into Georgetown. The delivery skipper is taking her north. The gales off the coast have been so severe that he thought he would never survive. He tells us the owner is sueing him for breaking his contract but he doesn't care. He has decided never to go to sea again, and from now on he intends to keep both feet on the ground!

During the next two days the torrential rain shows no signs of abating. Marg spends a long time in the warm dry local library. She tells everyone she is going to give up sailing.

18th April, 1988. Waccamaw River, South Carolina

Marg is delighted with this river. Her log attests to its allure:

> The prettiest river on the Intra Coastal Waterway," says our guide-
> book of Waccamaw River, and we agree. The water turns emerald

green and is lined with thick deciduous trees. Luckily we have fair winds and a favourable tide so we sweep along easily. Enchanted by the quietness of the river I suggest tying up at a small bankside marina and walking. Before we had finished tying up, Ron and Don two local sailors came to talk "You must spend a day at Brookgreen Sculpture Gardens," says Don.. When I ask whether we can walk, he says, "It's too far to walk to but I have my car here and I will drop you off and pick you up later." The spacious grounds of the old plantation home were taken over in 1931 and turned into a garden museum of American sculpture. Rarely have our senses been more sumptuously pleased. Beneath the cloudless blue sky avenues of live oaks, palm trees, dogwood, and flower beds set off the magnificent sculptures, many world famous. Towards evening, Don came to collect us. "We are going home for supper," he said. So once again we experienced home life in an American family. Their easy hospitality and superb food and conversation was a delightful contrast to our normal boat life. Once again back in our dinghy at 10:00 P.M. we found a heavy dew had saturated all our gear. Putting up our tent was a damp affair. It still is bitingly cold at night.

20th April, 1988. "The Rock Pile"

Today summer arrived. Swallows, bees, and osprey nests become a common sight along the waterway. We are sailing in almost gale conditions as we approach "The Rock Pile," a very deep, rocky, narrow 27-mile land cut. If we wait for the wind to die we risk a head wind which will take days to beat through, so we decide to make good use the stern wind— a gale though it be. (Before entering the rock pile section, boats are expected to use their VHF to call forward to check that no tugs are entering the far end of the cut as the barges completely fill the channel. We do not carry VHF.)

Gybing violently at each bend and taking care not to broach into rocks either side of the 20-foot wide channel, we have time to watch golf courses cut into virgin land with overhead cable cars for the golfers crossing the river. Beyond the cut is the Hurricane Marina and we are tired so, for once we are glad to tie up in a marina. We have logged 37 miles in five hours. Later, the manager tells us that a twister has passed over killing four people, wrecking many homes, and sinking a fishing boat trying to enter nearby Newall Inlet. All local boat trips in the vicinity have been cancelled today.

The manager of the Seapath Marina has agreed to store our spare sails until needed—a great relief to get the excess weight out of the our bows.

Sailing to the Edge of Fear

29th April, 1988. Beaufort, North Carolina

Beaufort, North Carolina, is a pretty little town with an exceptionally fine maritime museum where staff have a reputation for making visiting yachts welcome. It has excellent exhibits, a fine reading room, and the staff offer us the use of a guest car for our stay. For the first time we come across other small boat travellers like ourselves, so we linger for a few days enjoying their company. Lance, a professional guitarist, is single handing his 18-foot catboat from Maine down to Florida and back, whilst Pierre and his girlfriend are returning to Canada from the Caribbean after a cruise round the North Atlantic in their 24-foot wooden folkboat. It's Margaret's birthday so Pierre has arranged a party on a neighbouring catamaran and Lance is giving her a recital of classical guitar music as a birthday present.

We return to *Wanderer* tied against the piles in the small boat section of the marina and lay out our meal. Fresh melon slices lie in a can on the thwarts, but first we are enjoying a bowl of boiled shrimps when Marg says, "Look at the way that cloud is building up across the

A power boat that cut a corner.

creek." Before we finish the shrimps, the wind hits us, beginning with a light breeze and building to a full force 8. Within 10 minutes, waves are piling across the bay, then the anchor drags and we drive under the side of the dock with the tent up. Marg strips off the tent whilst I hold the boat off the jetty. It is suddenly very serious; it is taking my full strength to hold the boat off with the tent broadside to the wind and if *Wanderer* goes under the jetty we shall lose our mast. Eventually, the wind drops a bit, and we row across to tie to a pile, tidy up the shambles, then re-anchor, and re-rig the tent. Several yachts on the other side of the creek have dragged, started their engines and are resetting their anchors.

8th May, 1988

We have travelled 550 miles of the ICW since launching at Stuart in Florida, and there is another 345 miles to Norfolk, Virginia. When we launched we planned to arrive at Norfolk by the beginning of June so we can have six weeks in Chesapeake Bay before the excessive heat of mid-July and August. So far we are on schedule.

We have decided to detour through Pamlico Sound and along the inside of the coastal islands of the Outer Banks which should be a much more interesting route than the restricted channels of the ICW. It is a vast area of shallow water contained between the mainland and a long line of low narrow barrier islands sheltering it from the Atlantic. There are a few small settlements on the bigger islands; the 'inlets' have a ferocious reputation and God help any boat trying to run the racing tides through these narrows in bad conditions. Halfway along the islands is Cape Hatteras where the prevailing southeasterlies change to prevailing southwesterlies so we can expect a 'soldiers wind.' From the chart, it appears to be ideal for what the Americans call 'gunkholing'; being shallow it is probably much less used by power boats which pull up such dangerous wakes in restricted water if they don't slow down; if we go through Thoroughfare Canal we join the ICW to Bellhaven with a 30 mile crossing of the exposed and often rough waters of Albermarle Sound instead of the 10 mile crossing from Roanoke.

14th May, 1988. Oracoke Island, North Carolina

The wind has been increasing all day with the seas building up steadily astern and becoming unpleasant in this shallow water. But we are happy with this is the type of sailing compared to our sailing in the shallows of the North Sea. In the middle of this foam flecked waste of water, the only break is Wainwright and Harbour Islands disappearing astern, no sign of the mainland to the west or the string of barrier islands to eastward. At a lonely marker we gybe behind the invisible underwater Hodges Reef and, immediately under the shelter of the reef, the seas flatten. Twenty minutes later the low line of the outer banks' lift above the horizon; then we reach across the sound and along Teache's Channel to Ocracoke under genoa only.

We reach Ocracoke Island which is a remote outer banks settlement, with a large natural harbour almost totally enclosed, and its only connection with the mainland is by ferry. It's a pleasant village which has grown up round the waterfront.

In the evening I walk to the British cemetery. It is here that *HMS Bedfordshire*, one of 25 submarine hunters with British crews loaned to the U.S. in the Second World War, was torpedoed just offshore and some of her crew were washed up and buried here. As I walk back someone asks, "Are you British? Come back at 11:00 A.M. tomorrow; it's the annual Ceremony of Remembrance." What an amazing coincidence that our visit should coincide with the anniversary. After supper, I get out a white shirt, dark tie and my best trousers for the service.

Margaret is returning to England for a rest, exhausted by the violent weather, and by the vast size of this country where many rivers and sounds are so large that it is impossible to see the far shore. Then she will rejoin me at Washington, the nation's capital, way up the Potomac River.

15th May, 1988. Ocracoke Island, North Carolina

Clouds are building across the sound. We turn in early; it's a still night. Half-an-hour later the wind comes out of nowhere—a vicious squall howling round the masts and whining through rigging; it eases slightly and then returns with torrential rain (the crew on board the two neighbouring yachts said next morning that they registered 45 knots). Glad we were alongside a floating dock using our boat rollers as fenders as we would have had hull damage had we been tied alongside the piles.

We inquired about travel to the mainland for a flight back to England for Margaret but the ferry goes in the wrong direction, and without car transport it was looking impossible. We asked the help of the postmaster who, fortunately, replied, "I can get you a ride on the postal van if the driver agrees. I'll phone him this evening." So, by courtesy of U.S. Mail, Marg sat on the mail sacks and the driver kindly delivered her to the bus station for a bus direct to the airport at Norfolk.

It is only when she telephones to say she had arrived at the airport safely that I begin to think of the problems of single-handed sailing: steering, reefing, lowering mast, navigating, night sailing.

Low-laying Ocracoke disappears quickly as I sail across Pamlico River to the mainland with a light southwesterly course due north magnetic—ideal, easy sailing. Surprisingly, the church tower does not silhouette against the skyline as I had expected but the village water tank gives a fine back bearing of due south so navigation is easy. As the wind falls, I start rowing and immediately meet the first difficulty of single-handing—it is impossible to keep a course single-handed with a cross swell. I rig a steering line from tiller to my foot—a crude method but it works although I realise there is a penalty. Normally, if I go overboard *Wanderer* will heave-to and wait for me, but if a line is on the tiller she will sail away so I make up a life line, a bowline over my head, snap-shackle round my chest, and tie this to the thwart.

On landing, I ask a local fisherman about church services as I like to go to church on a Sunday when cruising. He directs me to the local Baptist church where I arrive in time for service on Sunday.

As in England, the Baptist service tends to be 'revivalistic' in the Southern States. The minister is standing on the church porch greeting the congregation as I arrive and I ask if I might attend: "You are welcome here, brother. Everyone is welcome provided they believe in the word of Our Lord." He steps up to me and gazes deep into my eyes—"Brother, have you received The Word of Our Lord?" I am not used to declaring my faith in public and certainly not with members of the congregation listening so I hesitate. "Well, brother?" he challenges, "Father, I'm sailing a small open boat along the coast and I have always believed that no one can sail a small boat at sea and be an atheist," I reply. It was a friendly, sincere service. The item "greet thy neighbour" surprises me: everyone mingled with their neighbours and shakes hands as it is suddenly announced, "Today we have a visitor from England. Frank Dye—please stand up."

Many of the congregation join in with an "Amen" whenever they agree with a particular point in the readings from the gospels and the sermon. The sermon is on "The Difficulty of Communication" and when the minister mentioned that his brother has recently sent him a parcel from Florida and "it was a long, long way from Florida to North Carolina." I feel sure that Margaret would have added her own heartfelt "Amen" in agreement.

18th May, 1988. Engelhard, North Carolina

8:00 A.M.: Light rain begins.

8:30 A.M.: Heavy rain like in England.

8:45 A.M.: Torrential rain, lightning continuous and thunder two miles away and getting closer and I rig my lightning jump leads.

9:00 A.M.: Unbelievable rain—someone now is throwing it down with a bucket.

Within half-an-hour, I am standing in rainwater already well above the floorboards, and I pump it out as continuous lightning is directly overhead and I don't want to have my feet in water if it strikes down the mast.

The lightning is so vivid that I drop the mainsail and sit as far away from the boom as possible. The breeze goes round to the north which means I have to beat all day to get anywhere. Visibility is 50 yards. The rain and thunder slack off so I put up the mainsail, but both return even more violently so I drop it again, and have to pump out as the water is already over my feet. I despair of ever finding the outer marker for Engelhard in this storm as I have been wandering about under the genoa only and I am completely lost. I am sodden down my neck and chest in spite of oilskins and am feeling badly scared. Rain and lightning stop suddenly and visibility is sparkling clear and I can see the edge of the world—and the marker is in front of the bow less than one quarter mile away.

The Americans I have met have been so hospitable and this occasion is no exception. I was welcomed at the marina, my clothes washed and dried, invited to dinner, and taken out hauling and re-baiting crab pots the next day. The marina has a full-size wooden owl to keep off the seagulls which make such a mess and I asked how effective it is. "They soon got used to it and now they sit on its head, although first day I had it I found my neighbour stalking it with a net!" I laughed, thinking maybe gulls are more intelligent than neighbours.

25th May, 1988. Engelhard, North Carolina

I have had five days tied up here and the weather has been poor and getting worse. It's eight in the evening and a tornado watch has been issued. There is a probability of hail and damaging wind for all the sounds and I have changed my mind about leaving. Heavy tornado clouds are building rapidly to the west. *Wanderer* is the worst place in the marina where the gap between the buildings will funnel the wind onto the boat but there is too much wind from the south to move safely round under the buildings. I put out a heavy rope to a post upwind, and ropes from all four quarters so I can swing her to meet any wind, tidy the inside of the boat, fix the tent skirt with ropes under the hull, cleat the stern rope so I can adjust it from inside the boat, oilskins to hand.

Now the sky is black to the west, and overhead, looking very ominous. A sandstorm drives down through the town on 50-knot winds and I don't have time to blink before it fills my eyes and ears. *Wanderer* is beam on, rattling sand, slamming, banging—I must pull her round or I'll lose the tent. I uncleat the bow rope to pull round on the piling and it almost cuts off my fingers and I pull round until 20 degrees to wind, then slack off the stern line. Ferocious conditions, *Wanderer* is laying a little better but heeling badly so I move my bedding so my weight is up to windward. I turn in expecting a long hard night but at midnight I fall fast asleep.

27th May, 1988

A bad northerly front came through yesterday and a yacht and a big catamaran ran back from Albermarle Sound with rigging damage and one was jury-rigged. The seas were appalling, they said.

The ice cream is superb, and the parlour is just at the end of the dock which makes life tolerable.

Daily now, the mosquitoes are biting harder and the temperature is climbing.

28th May, 1988

Today, yet another storm. At midnight it's blowing hard and increasing in force. The tent is flapping badly at rear end. At 2:30 A.M. the is wind even stronger, shrilling in the rigging and roaring round the mast. I check for dragging, but both anchors are holding well and in the same position.

3:10 A.M.: The wind is roaring, tent drumming, and *Wanderer* is rolling a little but well sheltered from the waves by the island, although there are no trees to break the wind. Another lesson learned—a tree wind-break is required when the weather is bad. It's a long night and I wake exhausted.

The daily temperatures are now reaching 90–95°F daily and the mosquitoes are causing me great discomfort. I look back at my recent sailing with real pleasure. I have enjoyed enormously the shallows of Currituck, Roanoke, Pamlico, and Core Sounds.

The wind holds at force two for me while I round the headland, anchoring at 7:00 P.M. The fish are jumping all around me. I am very tired and making mistakes, but I cannot resist getting out the rod to make a few casts—no luck and I fall into bed exhausted. Mosquitoes aplenty so I have to get up to rig the mosquito net. The tent is too hot so I open the end flaps. Too tired to sleep until after midnight.

2:00 A.M.: *Wanderer* is rolling quickly and the wind is now southwest with a four mile fetch. At 4:00 A.M. the rolling makes sleep impossible. I realise I could use this fair wind to advantage but I can hear mosquitoes whining angrily outside the net so I don't.

5:36 A.M.: Daylight and I cannot stand the rolling. Very tired but I am up, breakfasted and away by 6:15 A.M. The forecast predicts head winds.

Norfolk next and I put away the charts and guides "Jacksonville to Norfolk" and "Pamlico Sounds." A thousand miles of hard sailing have passed under *Wanderer*'s centreboard. It is understandable but a pity Marg had not enjoyed it. She did not realise the great distances—and Chesapeake Bay is enormous too but I want to reach the bay before the real heat of summer in upon me.

7th June, 1988. Norfolk, Virginia

My first tidal water sailing for 200 miles and I am nervous. The river is industrial with a lot of commercial traffic, a major naval base, numerous bascule bridges, and three great lift bridges—clearance is 140-feet up, seven feet down—within one mile . The guide says all road bridges open promptly on a sound signal (one long and one short blast) and to monitor VHF; the railroad bridges are left open unless a train is expected, then a wait of up to 30 minutes.

There are warnings that the tide runs strongly and I time my arrival carefully for slack water. The three great lift bridges look enormous even from a mile away, but as I beat up to them the first railroad bridge lowers in front of me. I hove-to for 10 minutes expecting the usual half-mile long freight train, and watch in disbelief as a small hand-operated repair trolley trundles across and this enormous span raising itself back to 140 feet.

The naval base is full of warships, including the battleship *Iowa*, as well as cruisers, submarines and supply ships, fortunately few of them are moving, but numerous launches are scurrying about. Unbeknownst to me, Norfolk is holding its annual Harbour Festival on the river, and I try to sail through the middle, much to the annoyance of the U.S. coastguard who had closed the river to all traffic. A loud hailer booms across the water, "The river is closed to all traffic." I assume they mean commercial traffic and carry on. "To the little sailboat fooling around: The river is CLOSED!"

I book for one night at the Norfolk Sailing Club, a magnificent club but not a friendly one. I was not sorry to leave next day but there is much heavy traffic of tugs, workboats, naval launches, and in the northern naval docks aircraft carriers, submarines, frigates, cruisers are all mothballed.

9th June, 1988. Chesapeake Bay, Virginia

Now I am officially in Chesapeake Bay. There are long white beaches sparkling in the sun which are a great pleasure after the interminable marshes of the Carolinas and there are sharp changes of coastal direction which makes for easy navigation. The wind is off the land and I am close-hauled. Soon I pull down the first reef. The tide is flooding into the wind making a short chop. The wind becomes gusty, and I pull down a second reef.

One mile out, crossing the bay there is a lot of spray flying so I don my oilskins. A tall lookout tower reminds me of the 'danger zone' marked on the chart, so I keep well offshore. There is a vicious gust and *Wanderer* is over-canvassed even with two reefs tucked in and no genoa and I have to take great care, both luffing and freeing the mainsheet in the squalls, to prevent a capsize. I begin to wish that I had run back for shelter although I always object to forfeiting ground. The low laying marshes are not seen so easily as the bright sand beaches so I tack in occasionally to check the back bearing along the shore.

11th June, 1988. Back Creek (off York River), Virginia

I spent a day sheltering in Back Creek off the York River, a pleasant sheltered spot with a yacht club but there is no one about so I tie to their jetty and go for a long walk. The next morning the forecast warns of bad weather, so I decide to snatch a passage up the York River. I pull down a reef and am beating out when a man working on his yacht calls out to me, "It will be rough outside. If you decide to come back you can tie to my dock."

It was far rougher than I expected with wind against tide so I did as he suggested and had a very pleasant two days ashore. John Hanna is a Chesapeake Bay ship's pilot and a yachtsman so I got an excellent description of the bay, places to visit, and things to look for. Like a good tourist, I visit Yorktown which is the site of the last battle of the War of Independence and a British defeat. I join a guided tour of the battlefield—it is well done. The guide makes no secret of the fact that the battle was largely fought by the French, especially the naval side, who provided the siege artillery and professional troops. He is most tactful—he makes me feel almost proud to be British and defeated!

12th June, 1988. Mobjack Bay, Virginia

My host is taking part in a race across Chesapeake Bay so I heave-to at the end of the start line to see him off, then free off myself to cross the wide York River and the even larger Mobjack Bay. The ideal weather forecast of a 15 knot westerly turns out to be a very unpleasant northwesterly of 25 knots and gusty by mid morning.

Wanderer gets a real dusting crossing Mobjack Bay. The shallow water and northwesterly wind soon builds up a short vicious sea on the 14-mile fetch. Even with two reefs down, *Wanderer* is over-canvassed, and several times I run water over the lee gunwale in the squalls but fortunately without capsizing. If I had not had a great deal of experience in the short seas of The Wash in England I would have be acutely frightened. Even so, I am very nervous as I ease *Wanderer* up each wave, luffing the breaking crests. Much to my relief, I get into the lee of Point Comfort, anchor on top of the sandspit, have a cup of tea and go to sleep until the wind drops.

My log book records my difficulties and feelings:

Several squalls, too much sail and more water over the gunwale. This is getting risky and I scramble in another reef. There is a long fetch, seas steep and nasty. Too much sail but the only way I can reef further is by a couple turns of gooseneck although I haven't the weight to hold Wanderer up while doing it. Seas becoming hollow, steep, and very nasty. This wind is far more than the forecast, and must be 20–25 knots. The seas are running the whole length of Mobjack Bay— at least 10 miles. The wavetops are breaking and waves are crashing down; some I have to luff. It gets very nasty, easing the boat over each wave in turn. There is a run of several short steep seas together and I think Wanderer must put her bow down under as she drops off the first but just manages to climb it in time—what a magnificent sea boat!

The waves are increasing, white horses everywhere. The only sails I can see are upwind under the shelter of the land. I can see the old lighthouse beach at the headland glistening brightly in the sunshine. With the fierce ebb tide and seas I am being set down 20 degrees. I consider turning back—it is getting hairy. Now the next wave needs all my attention, then the one beyond, and only then can I look at the next. Slowly, and dangerously we creep closer, pointing high and edging across gradually. Once in the lee of the land I am going to anchor and have a cup of tea! A couple of times the gunwale has water over but she comes up—I dare not lose speed in these vicious short waves. Thank God I am not going to be out here when the flood begins to run against the wind.

13th June, 1988. Rappahannock River, Virginia

The voracious mosquitoes seem to have disappeared over the last few days but they have been replaced by biting flies which are even worse although the bites don't swell up. Recently, there has been no wind until mid-morning, then light five to ten knots fading away at tea time. It's hot and humid. Chesapeake Bay is notorious for thunderstorms—usually in the late afternoon or evening. They can be violent with 40–50 knot winds, torrential rain, lightning and thunder. Thunderheads build quickly above them to 30,000 feet but fortunately they are very localised and quickly over but dangerous if a yacht is caught with sails up. It is general practice is to be anchored before 4:00 P.M. I have also been warned to look out for 'nettles' (or 'sea nettles') but forgot to ask what 'nettles' are. I think they must be a type of seaweed that stings, or maybe just looks like a land nettle.

Wanderer has slowed down and is very sluggish. Her bottom is covered with barnacles which have grown to three-eighths of an inch since we scrubbed her at Beaufort only six weeks ago. I should have asked the builder to anti-foul her before we left England.

15th June, 1988. Hunton Creek, Virginia

While I am sailing close along the shore looking for a place to pull *Wanderer* out when I saw this workboat planing at full power towards the beach ahead of me. He makes no attempt to stop and I think, 'he's been watching too many James Bond films—he's going to plane up the beach!' However, the boat suddenly disappears and I discover that he had gone through a narrow channel into the creek beyond, so I follow and ask permission to pull *Wanderer* ashore for anti-fouling the next day.

I dig my big anchor into the top of the beach and use the four-part mainsheet to pull her above high water on a boat roller. Once I master the method it's quite easy, even single-handed. I scrape off the barnacles, mostly one-quarter- to three-eighths-of-an-inch long. I'm stripped to the waist and wearing shorts but the biting flies soon force me into a shirt and long trousers. "The temperature is 104°FF in the sun and 92°F in the shade," a fisherman says, as he brings me a glass of iced tea. In case there is any doubt about just how scorching it is, the tin of etching primer blows up when I try to open it in the sun, soaking my trousers below the waist—thank goodness it didn't go in my eyes! I suddenly realise that my skin is burning so I tear off my trousers, run down the beach and sit in the water, only to get some rather puzzled waves from some fishermen returning to the beach. The centreboard and case are fouled with large barnacles which I prod out with a long screwdriver. I finish anti-fouling at 4:00 P.M., shaking uncontrollably with heat exhaustion, in spite of the frequent supply of iced tea.

I sleep ashore to let the anti-fouling harden and next morning the fisherman's nephew gives me a hand launching, then a tour of the beach to show me the marine and insect life—horseshoe crabs (a type of spider that took to the water eons ago and developed an external shell), fiddler crabs—the males with one great claw for fighting and waving at impressionable female crabs, lizards, and humming birds. I have been invited to a lunch of blue crab but first I phone Margaret to arrange to meet her at Washington Airport for six weeks cruising.

25th June, 1988. St. Inigoes Creek, Virginia

Today, off St. Mary's River, I encounter the worst day's weather I have ever experienced. I'm 110 miles up the Potomac to Washington but I have time in hand so I cross the river at its mouth where its only six miles wide. This stretch of water has a bad reputation but I have no difficulty apart from running down into a patch of rather nasty overfall.

On Sunday evening, a day after I sailed into St. Inigoe's Creek to attend church, a sullen leaded sky quickly replaced the sun and the TV announces a thunderstorm watch with violent winds, heavy rain, and damaging hailstones. I tie *Wanderer* between the piles pointing across the creek and I make what preparation I can by tying the tent skirt rope down, securing all the gear and putting on my waterproofs. The storm suddenly arrives at 45 knots abeam. The lighting and thunder are so loud and continuous it begins to hurt until I construct some earplugs. The rain can only be described as 'coming down in buckets.' *Wanderer* is snubbing violently with the wind on the beam, visibility is only 30 yards and the tent side is bulging, so much so that it looks as though it will split. It lasts 20 minutes, then works its way across the land.

Before there is time to settle in and calm down, Nick Carter, the church warden and a fellow sailor I'd met the previous day, tells me more ominous news: "A tornado has formed and its coming this way. You'd better come up to the house and we'll find an safe inside room." At 7:00 P.M. the sky darkens and suddenly goes black; the wind increases to a violent level (fortunately, from the bow this time); torrential rain falls horizontally while thunder, lightning, and a water mist drives through every joint in the tent and soaks me right though, even right through my oilskins. I am about to abandon *Wanderer* and fight my way up to the house when it suddenly stops—the tornado had altered direction! "They were real bad ones, its a good thing you were tied up," says Nick when I walk up to the house to report that I am still afloat.

The northerly front comes through in the early hours—a full gale, heavy rain with lightning and thunder for over an hour—but it was tame compared to the violence of the afternoon and evening and I turn over and soon go back to sleep.

Later on, Nick sails *Wanderer* to St. Mary's City and I crew. A lovely, fresh morning with an ideal sailing breeze and the sky full of little cotton wool clouds so beautiful after the cloudless heat of the last few weeks. I have been reading the four copies of the English sailing magazines Nick gave me, including a test of an International Fourteen with bowsprit, an enormous asymmetrical spinnaker and twin trapezes. It sounds exciting but it doesn't appeal to me.

4th July, 1988. Fairfax Yacht Club, Belmont Bay, Virginia

July and August is thunderstorm season. Temperatures have been in the high 90s and low 100s for some weeks now. The only relief is in air-conditioned shops and offices. It is the fourth of July—American Independence Day. I came alongside a cruising yacht in Mattawoman Creek to ask for local advice on the upper reaches of the river. I tell them I am heading for Belmont Bay, which is a big sheltered area of water, to spend the night.

The yacht moors at Fairfax Yacht Club and invite me to join them there for their typical American Independence Day celebration complete with a barbecue, a baseball game and fireworks. I accept and they call out to warn me, "Look out for power boats heading for the fireworks in Washington." A moment later, I am in the narrowest part of the entrance when I hear the roar of engines in the distance. As I turn the corner, I see some 40 big power boats coming down the channel all planing at full power, and all pointing themselves at me! I have never been so terrified in my life. I grab the oars and row frantically through a gap in the spoil banks. When I safely arrive at Fairfax, the barbecue, the baseball game, and the fireworks are most enjoyable and the people at the club exceptionally friendly.

8th July, 1988. Alexandria, Washington D.C.

During the last few days there has been little wind, so I have been rowing. It's exhausting with the temperature over 100°F in the shade and even higher on the water. I tie to the public dock here—four dollars for four hours, in order to look round the city. When I come back I find a man has been waiting for me for over three hours. "That's a cruising Wayfarer and you're Frank Dye." He says it as though it's an accusation so I immediately deny it until I discover what I have done wrong. Tom Johnson is a small boat enthusiast and has read every article Marg and I have written for British and American magazines over the years. He quickly produces our two books for autographing. He's an eccentric American, doesn't drive, has two skiffs (one rowing, and one sail with leeboards), and goes out rowing throughout the year.

Two most enjoyable days pass at the Washington Sailing Centre rowing with Tom and sailing with his friend Paul Harris, a civil servant with a nice sense of humour and a small yacht. Washington Sailing Centre is the noisiest anchorage ever. It's at the end of the airport runway with an aircraft landing or taking off every 50 seconds (although they stop at night), the bird scarer bangs every two minutes day and night, a main highway where I can hear the screech of tires as a driver stands on his brakes to avoid back-ending the vehicle ahead, and a rail marshalling yard with the sound of clanging buffers all night.

12th July, 1988. Washington D.C.

It proved fortuitous that I had sailed to Washington to meet Marg who was returning to sail for another month or so, because the stomach cramps that I had suffered for several weeks suddenly developed into kidney stones. By the time she arrived, I was in agony. When we reached the hospital I was asked only two questions before they took me in: "Your name?" and "Can you pay?" We were amused to be told by the doctors that I was being x-rayed on the same machine as President Reagan when he was shot. Washington is suffering from a heat wave of 104° F so while I am recovering we pay daily visits to the magnificent Smithsonian Institute museums to enjoy their air-conditioning.

One of the great pleasures of small boat cruising is meeting local people—a privilege not extended to bigger yachts. Marg's log describes one of the interesting characters we met along the way:

Sailing back down the Potomac river we stop off to see Jack and his skipjack. In his neat little mobile home beside the creek we are immediately offered showers and breakfast. It does not seem at all strange to avail ourselves of hospitality from this fisherman because Jack is rather special. He is the last of a line of fisherman and passionate about keeping the tradition of the sailing skipjacks alive. Sitting beneath the cool pine trees the humming bird feeder swaying in the breeze this knowledgeable friendly fisherman points out his father's and brother's houses across the creek: "Soon the developers will move in here like other beautiful estuaries, build their marinas, golf courses, condominiums, and a generation's lifestyles and skills will be wiped out," he comments without bitterness. He tells of how fleets of skipjacks fishing under sail for oysters in the Bay had dwindled to a few boats and now all were on the west side of Chesapeake Bay. His plans to promote a skipjack tourist attraction and environment school parties to supplement his oyster fishing in the polluted bay was born of a deep belief in the working boat tradition.

"Come and try crabbing tomorrow morning," he says as we enjoy a crab feast supper later that day. This consists of a pan of blue crabs boiled, tipped onto newspaper spread over the table and dipped in white vinegar and spice. Jack shows us the technique for opening the crabs and extracting the sweet white crabmeat. He eats seven large crabs in the time it takes me to eat two. Frank is faster and manages four. It is a tasty supper in a beautiful, quiet place. Just beyond our view lies the 27-foot skipjack *Dee of St. Mary's*, elegant in her long lines, low cut and unique hull shape. Bobbing beside her is *Wanderer*, a full moon shine on both boats all night.

At 4:00 A.M. this morning we join Jack on the blue crab fishing trip. He teaches us how to lay out his two baited lines on a sloping shallow bank and we haul occasionally, scooping the feeding crabs aboard with a long handled scoop before they could drop off, as the still baited line rolled over a drum alongside

In Chesapeake Bay summer caught up with us. Here, it's 104° F and we had to rig a sunshade. Marg is relaxing with a cup of tea.

the boat. Each crab is sorted into different baskets, 'doublers' are mating crabs, 'jimmies' are large blue-clawed males, and 'peelers' are crabs about to moult. At 9:00 A.M. we motor back with four baskets of crabs. Back at his home, he shows us the holding boxes. We are fascinated to see the intricate shells that the 'peelers' had abandoned and are revolted to watch the bigger crabs now hungry eating the smaller ones as they backed out of their too-small shells.

We sail away in *Wanderer* feeling privileged to have met this unique fisherman and his skipjack.

28th August, 1988. Queenstown, D.C.

A very pleasant town graced by fine houses facing the creek with fishing boats and a few small sailing boats on moorings. I sail round a small 17-foot catboat, enormously broad with a tall, unstayed mast stepped right in the bow, a small cabin, delightfully named *Dumpling*. A traditional design from the New England States but strange to my English eyes. "I saw you looking over my catboat, come home and meet my wife—she's English." The friendly greeting came from 'Tut' Tuttle and his wife Pam and we were later to become good friends.

I had been listening to the weather reports of Hurricane Chris, downgraded first to a tropical storm and now to a decayed hurricane. So I anchor at the far end of the creek, luckily in the more sheltered arm. Expecting a bad night, I lie out two anchors quite carefully in a 'v' towards the entrance which is the more exposed direction.

29th August, 1988. Queenstown, D.C.

This morning the roar of wind in the trees is intense. I look out: black storm clouds are racing across the sky with the speed of an express train, trees are bending to the fierce wind, and the noise is truly impressive. The rain begins to come down in sheets and quickly builds until the creek is blotted out. The rain continues, unabated. There are two arms to this creek, and by pure chance I had picked the more sheltered arm, so I am quite protected. But if this is a 'decayed' hurricane, I hope I never meet a real live one!

Today I am having a leisurely breakfast and sailing back to Queenstown when I meet Tut sailing *Dumpling*. He had been concerned— "I thought I'd rig *Dumpling* and come to make sure that you were alright after yesterday's bad weather." I scrub my tent on their lawn using their yard broom (the fabric was beginning to smell with continuous use). Tut and I visit his mother and the reception is not what I expect—she will not even talk to me. After we leave Tut explains, "My mother didn't like you. She doesn't like people with beards. She maintains 'If you've hair on your face there's something wrong with your brain!' I am surprised she didn't tell you so."

Tut is desperately wanting to attend the upcoming catboat rally but neither his doctor nor his wife will allow him to sail the 28 miles single-handed since his recent heart attack. So I volunteer to explore the Wye River, then return to crew for him if he cannot find a crew by the weekend. It is to be a happy choice.

30th August, 1988. Wye River, Maryland

At Wye River I sail into the first creek hoping it's Dividing Creek. The next creek has two beautifully maintained wooden two-masted open sail boats. I follow the main creek round the bend and anchor. There are two houses on the bluff and no others and I am alone.

I am tired, exhausted, and irritable; I pick at my supper and think how welcome a cup of tea would be instead. I am cheered by a beautiful creek which is completely sheltered by trees all round, one jetty but no sight of a house, a small catboat pulled onto the marsh grass. There is a light breeze. A friendly orange sky filters through the trees and colours the whole of the creek-end with warmth, a full moon shines brightly above the trees at the other end: the river is out of sight, round an invisible bend. A fish jumps almost into the boat but falls back and the splash wets the tent, a big blue heron flies over squarking a loud protest but there is no other sound. I sip a cold iced fruit juice and feel the frustration ebb away as I sit on the floorboards and enjoy the cool of the evening. After night falls, I watch the vivid lightning beyond the horizon silhouette the clouds, it's too far away for the thunder to be audible but the scene is pretty.

2nd September, 1988. Chester River, Maryland

I've been racing—not successfully but enjoyably! I transfered my gear onto Tut's catboat, returning after a week exploring the Chester River. She is a nice boat, but not what I'm used to: a Marshall 17 feet by approximately 8 feet beam with an unstayed mast right in the bow, large gaff mainsail, a large cabin with sitting headroom, centreboard case which is not obtrusive, two full length berths, large self draining cockpit, 800 pounds internal ballast, stiff, points well, and ideal for single-handed sailing.

We cross the mouth of the Chester River and anchor overnight in a little cove at the end of Eastern Neck Island where we are joined by another catboat heading for the rally.

5th September, 1988. Fairlee Creek, Maryland

During the 28 miles to Fairlee Creek the wind gradually dies, and we motor and roll through almost continuous heavy wakes from the weekend power boats. The entrance to Fairlee Creek is invisible from the bay but one boat is entering under sail—another catboat with a dark green hull.

"That must be Bruce. He's the only one who can sail through this entrance!" calls out Tut. Five power boats and two yachts under power line up behind us as I stand on the cabin to watch Bruce make a difficult entrance look easy.

Ten catboats of varying sizes are laid off to stern anchors, bows to the dock and everyone is delighted to see Tut after his recent heart attack. (Tut told me that they had given him a new mainsail for *Dumpling* to give him the will to recover.)

We sit down to a superb meal of soft shell clams and crab which I thoroughly enjoy. Only when I have eaten my fill does someone tell me that the clams and crabs are merely 'starters,' and there are pies, meat, vegetables, and fruit to follow!

It is a soft grey morning with a trace of drizzle and delightfully cool when I put my head out of the hatch. "I love these cold, grey mornings," I say, only to be met by an astonished silence from my American audience.

At the prize-giving, Tut receives much good humoured teasing as he is awarded a trophy for coming last in every race. I hang my head in shame—my helmsman was deserving of a better crew—but we'd had a lot of fun.

9th September, 1988. Chesapeake and Delaware Canal

The C & D canal connects the top of Chesapeake Bay with Delaware Bay. Its an old canal some 14-miles long, which has been dredged and straightened to take ocean going ships up to 900-feet long. My waterway guide says that sail boats must use 'auxiliary power.' I don't have an engine so I have been hoping that rowing will be considered (loosely) as being 'under power.' The tides are strong and once committed there is no possibility of turning back, although there is a mooring basin at Chesapeake City, a third of the way through—the only resting place.

I am not too worried about the big ships because their wakes would be long and not too dangerous unless I am forced into the shallows; the thrash from uncovered propeller blades might be difficult if I meet a freighter in ballast. But it was the planing power boats that really scared me with their steep breaking wakes—and I don't imagine that they would slow in a wide channel. My plan is to row through just after dawn, before the power boaters are up!

I pack the tent in pouring rain at 5:20 A.M. and row with the young flood tide under me, hovering in the shallows to let a tug with a raft of barges get clear before I enter the canal at 7:45 A.M. I slip into Cheasapeake City basin just clear of a tug with a raft of nine barges.

Chesapeake City is one of the nicest small towns that I have come across and where I find myself spending three happy days. There is a fine canal museum with the original engine-house preserved and fine models of the canal when it had working locks. The resident engineer shows me round and answered my questions. (I spent several years building up my own business on the English canal system so I found this personal tour particularly interesting). I obliquely inquire if 'rowing' would be accepted as being 'under power' when I pass through the canal? With equal tact, he does not answer directly, but he had been so kind to me that I resolve to take a tow rather than possibly embarrass him when I left. I promise to introduce him to the area engineer of British Waterways who is a personal friend when he visits England. I put up *Wanderer*'s canvas frame tent—I had almost forgotten how large and much warmer it is than the small plastic ridge tent. At night, the town and bridge look beautiful reflected in the water as I drink my mug of tea on deck before turning in—the nicest part of a pleasant day!

10th September, 1988. Greenwich, New Jersey

Delaware Bay has a bad reputation as it is large with tides that run hard, and it kicks up badly in a blow especially when the wind is against tide. It's also shallow and often foggy with a few widely spaced buoys. There are few places for the deep draft yachts to put into, although the Cohansey River, halfway down the north shore, is probably the best. American practice is to pass through it in one day and all the yachts I met were hammering along with a bone in their teeth, full sail and engines at high revs. As soon as I enter Delaware Bay from the C & D canal I feel happy as it has a difficult and more challenging feel, much like the North Sea and it is pleasant to work the tides, instead of the softer easier cruising of Cheasapeake Bay. Certainly for a Wayfarer dinghy with only an eight inch draft, it is a fine cruising ground with many secretive little creeks invisible until almost aground in the marsh. I put into Silver Run and explore to the bridge before anchoring for the night—completely hidden from the bay.

12th September, 1988. Cape May

With regret, I leave the lower end of Delaware Bay. I had found it to be a wonderful cruising area. In a short chop of wind-against-tide I free off through the short canal into Cape May Harbour and I approach the yacht club cautiously. There is an understandable reluctance among yacht clubs to encourage passing yachts, considering the large numbers 'snowbirding' south each fall and returning each spring. Many of the wealthier clubs further south post a 'Private Yacht Club' sign which I have found to be rigidly enforced, (once I was refused drinking water, and on another occasion permission to tie up in an empty corner in order to attend the neighbouring church service). Surprisingly, the yacht club at Cape May sets out to welcome passers-by even exhibiting a 'Transients Welcome' sign on the docks which is a wonderful sight. I soon make friends who help me pull *Wanderer* out on their slipway for a scrub which she badly needs.

Cape May is a colourful, picturesque Victorian seaside town—a pleasure to walk through with its many delightful styles and friendly atmosphere.

23rd September, 1988. Atlantic City (the gambling centre of the east coast), New Jersey

The New Jersey Marshes are beautiful with wide enormous skies; it is possible to see the horizon all the way round. Now there are clear autumn days, narrow channels with strong tides, tidal range about four feet, it's lonely and quiet. I usually find a side creek and anchor about 4:00 P.M. and sit, look, and write up my log book until the dew begins to fall, then put up the tent and heat my evening meal by the light of the pressure lantern. It is so beautiful that a couple of days ago, I anchored and didn't move—just looked. The creeks are too narrow for normal anchoring so I'm using a Bahamian Moor to restrict swinging. On the horizon are the lights of Atlantic City, the gambling centre of the east coast, but I pass by the billboards at the marinas and landings of free transportation to the casinos without regret. It's cold now, frost on the decks in the morning. I'm using two sleeping bags—one inside the other—and keeping my socks on, and feel grateful for my beard.

7th October, 1988. Tom's River, New Jersey

The other evening, I was confronted with northerly headwinds, force 6 gusting to 7, and it was bitterly cold. I beat for some two hours, cold and wet with spray flying as *Wanderer* punches into the short seas. I sailed through a narrow gut in the marsh to Good Luck Point Marina, shivering with cold and asked if I could stay in the office for half an hour to warm up—and I have now been here two days! They are charming people. They insist that I tie up (a full gale was forecast for the next day which I didn't know as my weather-radio would not receive due to low antenna height and interference from the neighbouring ship/shore radio station); they found me a sheltered corner, then took me home for a meal. The son is building an ice-yacht for this winter—an interesting design and exciting to sail providing you don't hit anything at 80 miles per hour.

A neighbour takes me to see the cranberry bogs (they were going to an air display but the gale cancelled it). Harvest had started that morning so I see the

Though the New York skyline is spectacular seen from a small boat, it is harzardous for those without an engine.

whole sequence. The plants are flooded, mechanical beaters thrash the berries off underwater, and they float to the surface where the wind blows then to leeward. It's a fantastic sight to see acres of brilliant scarlet berries floating in one corner of the lake, lifting gently to a slight swell.

New York, New York

New York Harbour is a dangerous place for a small sailboat without an engine, with continuous heavy wash from ships, tugs, ferries, powerboats, and barges. I cross the navigation channels with great care, sometimes sheltering behind an anchored ship until the traffic thins. It's a magnificent skyline, especially when seen from a small boat like a Wayfarer—the photographs don't do it justice.

The Statue of Liberty beyond Wanderer's *bow.*

On the Jersey City shore, the old liner terminals are all derelict and the traffic thins out quickly. I decide to go up the Hudson River to see the autumn colours rather than go through 'Hell's Gate' with its ferocious current to the East River. The Statue of Liberty stands tall above the harbour—a retired tugboat man (at Good Luck Point) told me she is called "Our Lady of the Harbour." He showed me a video of the unveiling after restoration a few years back—it was an emotional occasion with a speech by the president. My host's tug was shown leading a sailpast by the Tall Ships, a great firework display and by the end of the film tears were running down his cheeks. Ellis Island is also surprisingly impressive—it's where the immigrants docked in millions, to be checked and de-loused before being allowed ashore.

Once past the George Washington Suspension Bridge the west shore becomes striking—a rock face rising almost vertically to 300 feet, black and forbidding, and in deep shadow by 3:00 P.M. when I pass up river.

20th October, 1988. Nyack, New York State

I've had two pleasant days tied up to the Nyack Boat Club pontoon a friendly club which welcomes visitors. I rolled heavily all night when the wind went into the northeast with a long fetch across the river. The Palisades Escarpment runs all the way along this shore, massive and spectacular. The autumn colours are wonderful—like our beech woods but on a vast scale with the occasional scarlet of a maple and brilliant yellow lending splendid colour.

I will return south today as I am very conscious that I need two days of northerlies to get back through New York Harbour—it's too risky to tack through against a southerly with all the heavy traffic (north wind forecast today and tomorrow); snow is predicted this afternoon; the river looks cold, grey and uninviting; snow clouds are already building.

I fortify myself with a hot fish sandwich and an ice cream sundae before I leave.

22nd October, 1988. Jersey City, New York State

Wanderer did not carry her tide out through New York Harbour, the wind was light and fickle and south-easterly instead of north-easterly and even rowing it was too late, so I came into Newport Marina to avoid being swept back upriver: $40 for the night!

"You're in New York now," I was told when I queried this charge. The manager drove me to the bank and grocery store then moved me to a sheltered corner behind a big Norwegian fishing boat-type yacht. A gale was forecast "30–35 knots wind, easterly, with two inches rain overnight" followed by a "warning of severe street flooding in urban and city areas as gullies and sewers are already blocked with fall leaves." The forecast was not upgraded to 'storm' until after it arrived. Even being well sheltered, it was nasty.

7:00 P.M.: Breaking seas running down the dock now, but I'm sheltered behind the big yacht. Wind gradually

Running down the Hudson through New York—bad weather is predicted.

       Sailing to the Edge of Fear

builds to a full gale with heavier gusts. The rain is torrential. I pack my down-filled sleeping bag in the stern locker to save it getting wet and crawl into my light terylene sleeping bag fully dressed with waterproofs to hand. Must have dozed for when I wake the tent is slatting and banging—wind is gale force even in this sheltered corner of the basin.

1:20 A.M.: Savage squalls, wind screaming, probably at least force 10. Rain hitting the tent like lead pellets. I wonder if the tent will hold. I block the tiller hole through the transom with my oilskin trousers to keep some warmth in the boat.

1:40 A.M.: The front tent flaps rip open and the rain squalls are now in the boat with me. It takes me less than half-a-minute to close the flaps and fasten the velcro safety tapes to the skirt line (I should have done this last night but didn't). The velcro on the tent flap is worn at the top and needs replacing as soon as possible. Everything inside is wet, so I pull on my oilskins and crawl into my wet sleeping bag.

3:20 A.M.: The wind stops suddenly—I expect a short lull and a vicious renewal but the gale has blown out—to be replaced by the two inches of rain. A long, long night and I remember thinking in an attempt to comfort myself, "Every night must come to an end." I fall asleep and suddenly it's 8:30 A.M.

25th October, 1988. Atlantic Highlands, New York State

It is a rough passage across to Sandy Hook, I pull the first reef down in the lee of an anchored freighter in New York Harbour, and pump out (I had taken a lot of water on board from the heavy wash of passing vessels). Next, I pull down the second slab reef once clear of the shelter of the land. Then I roll another turn round the boom—the deepest I have ever reduced sail on *Wanderer*. The weather has broken now. The storm has stripped the leaves off the trees, and there are five wrecked yachts in the harbour. I've had two surprises recently (one pleasant and I'm not sure about the second!). In Horseshoe Cove, behind Sandy Hook, I was coming in to anchor for the night and put up my hand to a man in a pretty shoal draft 19-foot yacht. "Hi Frank, come aboard for a coffee," he beckoned. "How did you know my name?" I ask. "I read your book. You and Margaret started me small boat cruising two years ago—it's wonderful isn't it!"

The second unexpected encounter occurred when I was chased the length of the harbour by a man in a small yacht's tender. "Please sign my friend's copy of your book." He went on to explain, "My friend is the editor of a yachting magazine in Maine and he always gives me the books he's sent for review. This time he said, 'You can keep all the books except this one; it's a cult book and the Wayfarer is a cult boat—and I want it back.'"

Wanderer is now hauled out and covered up in a friend's garden in Shark River to await the spring. How kind and hospitable Americans are. I cannot think of any better way of seeing a country and meeting its people than in an open-cruising dinghy.

I have always had great confidence in the Wayfarer and after this cruise, some 2,000 miles from Florida, it has increased even more. What a wonderful boat Ian Proctor has designed—she has done everything we have asked of her and far more.

27th October, 1988. Well-next-the-Sea, England

Back in England I have time to consider what I had learned after the first year's cruise.In Britian, we have little experience of continental weather systems with great stable air masses over enormous land areas—bitterly cold in winter, enormously hot in summer.

We had our planning all wrong. Sailing north in February we expected the temperate Florida winter to follow us north slowly turning to spring. Instead, we sailed into the tail-end of winter in the southern states and shivered, despite our warm clothing. There was no gradual dawning of spring—suddenly, it was summer, the days clear, the sun blazing down from a cloudless sky, and a wide brimmed hat and sunglasses a necessity on the water. And Chesapeake Bay was so hot we had to sail under an umbrella for shade, while in Washington life was only bearable in the air-conditioned buildings. No wonder the early European settlers suffered.

The summer weather too caught us out. The light winds of morning slowly increase to force 4 or 5 in the afternoon. In Chesapeake Bay, wise boats are in shelter and anchored by 4:00 P.M. for the heat of the afternoon can bring violent thunderstorms with storm-force winds, torrential rain, and sometimes large hail. When a cold front sweeps south it brings cold northwesterlies and a rapid drop in temperature, and if one of these fronts combines with an afternoon thunderstorm the result can be very rough indeed; but in a few days the continental air mass re-establishes itself and the temperature climbs back to the high 90s and the low 100s F. It is always necessary to keep a keen eye on the weather—thunderstorms give notice by the build up of great vortexing thunderheads and there is usually time to reach shelter—but there is no protection against tornados.

I go over what I have learned from the season but leave the forward planning until I start sailing. This allows the route to be varied according to conditions and weather. Much of the pleasure of cruising is in the unexpected—in exploring unknown coasts and rivers, benefiting from local information, understanding differing customs and outlooks and avoiding preconceived opinions.

My one reservation is that next year I must remember that the hurricane season— July through September— is the time when hurricanes sweep north from the Caribbean, occasionally coming ashore and doing enormous damage. I must clear Cape Cod before hurricane season begins.

1989. Hurricane Hugo:
New Jersey to Maine

June 24th, 1989

On the airplane I study the chart from Sandy Hook to Cape Cod. This year's cruise should take me along the states of New York, Connecticut, beyond Cape Cod to New Hampshire and Maine.

I must be careful of Buzzards Bay, approaching Cape Cod, with its races and overfalls. I hope my cruising permit has been issued otherwise there will be a delay in leaving. I think what I have to do before launching: anti-foul *Wanderer*'s hull, and stock with food, fuel, and batteries, sterilize water containers, and look over my current diagrams.

June 27th, 1989. Shark River, New Jersey

I am up at 7:00 A.M., uncovering *Wanderer* at Shark River, New Jersey. She has come through the winter well. I sponge out and remove all gear, and empty the stern and bow compartments. Sorting out gear takes me all day in temperatures of 85°F and I am exhausted.

Jack, who stored *Wanderer* over the winter, gives me a hand to roll her onto her side and we clean and anti-foul. I pore over the current diagrams for Long Island Sound, Block Island Sound, and especially 'The Race' where the tides run at over four knots with a very short 'slack.' In Buzzards Bay, leading to Martha's Vineyard too, there are strong tides of four knots and the current runs through the Cape Cod Canal at four knots. The whole area requires that care is taken.

From the chart, it appears that there are two routes to Cape Cod. The route to the south of Long Island is exposed, a lee shore with no shelter and a very long haul for a small boat, so instead I have been planning to sail through New York's notorious Hell's Gate into the East River and Long Island Sound. But Jack tells me there is a third route—the small boat channel on the south side of Long Island inside a line of barrier islands. The channel is practical for small boats although it does get shallow in places and is not much used towards its eastern end. This route is much preferable to facing the dangers of Hell's Gate and the East River with its fast tides and heavy traffic. This is wonderful news.

28th June, 1989. Shark River, New Jersey

It's 6:20 A.M. and we are putting *Wanderer* on a flat trailer and towing her down onto the beach when a police car arrives. It is the same policeman who arrived last year when we were pulling out on the same beach. "They called me from the other end of town; said someone who was launching a boat across the beach; told me to come and stop it." He stands on the port side and looks along the sand, then moves to starboard and looks that way. "I sure can't see anything happening. Can

---

you?" We keep quiet. "Don't be too long," he adds as he drives away. "The police are usually very sensible here," remarks Jack.

We roll *Wanderer* into five feet of water, load all the gear as quickly as possible, and anchor off. What a sensible policeman.

1st July, 1989. Sandy Hook, New Jersey

A warm sunny afternoon lazing in the sun, listening with pleasure to my crew playing a selection of popular tunes on his harmonica while we cover the 19 miles of open sand beach to Sandy Hook. At the hook, Jack uses his VHF via the CG to arrange transport home. I decide to stay in Horseshoe Cove over the weekend to avoid the powerboat race. It is soon Independence Day and I certainly don't want to get caught in a narrow channel with holiday-bent powerboats planing all round me. This is a pretty cove and I need a day's rest to settle into dinghy life again.

2nd July, 1989. Horseshoe Cove, New York State

Horseshoe Cove is pleasant and tranquil. The weekenders arrived on Saturday morning. Too many power boats and weekenders to enjoy what is usually a quiet cove, and by mid-morning there are 30 yachts and 150 power boats anchored all round me: hundreds of children too but all well behaved and quiet—it's the adults who are noisy. Sound travels clearly across the water with only the lightest of breezes, and someone has just started playing music incredibly loudly.

On Sunday morning, I could not stand the noise any more. I counted up as I sailed out—67 yachts, almost 200 large power boats, and runabouts and outboards too numerous to count. So I cross to Long Island and anchor in the marshes in a lonely, winding creek off the State Boat Channel. A quarter mile away is a continuous line of big power boats planing along the marked channel and pulling up huge wakes; across the marshes I can see airplanes taking off and landing from New York Kennedy Airport. Its 7:00 A.M. now as I write my log and the temperature is already 70° F.

3rd July, 1989. State Boat Channel to Fire Island, New York State

The State Boat Channel through the marshes between the barrier islands and Long Island is narrow and winding, occasionally marked by a post with an arrow showing which side to take. Of the large number of big power boats, most are weekenders and know nothing of sailboats; all are planing at full throttle and pulling up enormous wakes in the narrow channel—big enough to fill the cockpit of a yacht or swamp a dinghy. Negotiating bridges here is a problem.

The tide under the bascule bridge is ebbing so strongly that I cannot sail or row through against the current even if I had signalled it to lift, so I anchor close to the shore to wait three hours for the tide to turn. I am reasonably comfortable, sheltered from the wind and waves, although the continuous power boat wakes running into the wind make a very confused sea, and after lunching in the sun, I slowly become sea-sick. With an effort, I lower the mast, raise the anchor, and row under the bridge—anything is better than being sick! I should have remembered that sea-sickness is a bad basis for decisions and this proves a grave misjudgement!

Several times the fierce tide nearly sweeps me back under the bridge and I almost lose my mast on the supports. All this, and an hour of exhausting pulling gains me 30 yards. As I experience the full force of wind, the waves cause me to catch an occasional crab, and lose ground. I am exhausted but there is no room to anchor and drop back. There is a little beach 50 yards away and I exert every last ounce of my energy for 20 minutes before I edge in and land.

Tomorrow is American Independence Day and the big power boats will be roaring about, so I need to find a quiet creek until things are back to normal.

The tide is running fiercely towards the next bridge. I gybe out into the main stream to get a straight run at it and lower the mast. As the sail drops, a wind eddy fills the sail and lays the boom on the wrong side of the tiller and jams it. I don't have time to tidy up as the bridge approaches rapidly.

Beyond the bridge I luff into the wind but the mast will not raise—the boom is under the tiller. I move the boom across and try again. The wind catches the sail and the boom locks under the sidedeck and an oar falls overboard. I push away from a jetty and grab the oar, noticing that the ensign and staff is floating alongside but there is no time to grab it as I am drifting onto another jetty. I clear the reef line which has taken a half-hitch round the tiller which I hadn't noticed hidden under the boom and sail.

I up the mast and back away under oars. My 'red ensign' must have fallen overboard and drowned as there is no sign of it but fortunately I have a spare 'union jack' flag which I can use instead of the correct commercial 'red duster.'

I made a mess of passing that bridge! Shooting bridges is going to be one of the problems of sailing single-handed. I never really mastered it last year either.

5th July, 1989

Tide sluicing me towards another bridge. I only just have time to lower the mast as the tide under me is one knot. There is torrential rain, visibility is less than a quarter of a mile, powerboats appear suddenly out of the murk. There is a five mile per hour speed limit but they are ignoring it and doing far more. The rain is cold and the wind makes it miserable. One forgets how uncomfortable dinghy sailing can be when it is cold, wet, and bleak. The rain is torrential.

The weather is appalling; the rain unbelievable. On the weatherbox radio I hear, "A flash flood watch has been issued. Severe flooding at any time. Do not enter any flowing water across a road. If your car is caught abandon it immediately and get to higher ground." Perhaps I am lucky to be in a boat in this weather after all.

8th July, 1989. West Gilgo Beach, New York State

As the tide floods the banks of the boat channel disappear and only the higher tufts of marsh grasses show. There is no shelter here should a gale come in at high water.

Long Cove looks a likely anchorage. The forecast predicts, "a northerly front moving in tonight. Probably thunderstorms, maybe violent." I pass a marina but I prefer to be on my own. I sail into a beach and check my position. I creep into a creek with only two feet of water, and anchor. Clouds are building quickly, black and ominous from the north with the tops back-lit from the setting sun while violent thunderstorms are approaching from the east.

I decide to re-anchor 100 yards further inland where I am more sheltered from the north. I put a plastic sheet under the tent which needs proofing, tie the skirt line securely down, and clip the jump leads on the shrouds, finishing just as the rain starts. The lightning is especially vivid over Nassau County, beyond the horizon with great black anvil-topped clouds swirling madly. I am glad I moved further in—and that I am now safely anchored with both hooks down.

Beyond the horizon is a continual brilliance; here, it is raining heavily, and leaking through the stern flaps. "There is heavy rain, damaging winds of 50 knots, damaging heavy hail," announces the radio so I pull on my oilskins and put away my sleeping bag to prevent it getting wet. The wind is suddenly screaming and without noticing I fall asleep. I wake at 1:20 A.M. to brilliant lightning, deafening thunder, and violent rain. I turn over and go back to sleep.

10th July, 1989. State Boat Channel

East Moriches is a pleasant creek with a lot of small boats moored off the yacht club. I wave to members on the balcony but there is an unwelcoming frostiness and I assume this to be one of the 'private' yacht clubs that discourages visitors so I sail away.

I have a wonderful downwind sail with the wind increasing all afternoon, pulling down the first reef just after leaving East Moriches, another halfway across the open water. It is getting a bit too exciting and I consider dropping the main and running under reefed genoa as I turn north under the land to Shinnecock where the canal connects the boat channel to the Long Island Sound. At 4:00 P.M. exactly I anchor for afternoon tea and listen to the forecast: "A line of severe thunderstorms stretching from New Jersey through New York, Long Island, Long Island Sound, Block Island, Martha's Vineyard, and out to Nantucket. Dangerous lightning, heavy winds and damaging hailstones. Keep away from windows and find cover," says the radio. "A marine warning has been issued for the sound—severe and damaging thunderstorms. Boats should seek shelter."

Back at Long Cove I wasfortunate—the thunderstorms passed on either side of me but both Nassau County on one side, and Suffolk County on the other, were blasted. This line of storms is so extensive that I think I have pushed my luck far enough. It's already gusty, a grey day is becoming darker and threatening; thunder is rumbling in the distance ominously and closing in. I study the Shinnecock Canal entrance through binoculars, pull down two reefs, and wait for slack water before I reach across and row into Jackson's marina. *Wanderer* is allocated a berth where she will be in the lee of a big powerboat when the wind goes into the west-northwest.

The wind is increasing, and there's the rumble of thunder so I tie up quickly, adding springs, a nylon line from the bow to a post to absorb snatch from the wind tonight, and use the mainsheet as a stern line. I put the tent up. The whole sky is a uniformly threatening dark grey. I am glad to be in.

11th July, 1989. Shinnecock Canal, New York State

There was a furious thunderstorm last night just after I tied up, continuous thunder, lightning every eight seconds, torrential rain but the wind was less than the predicted 25 knots. This morning, I was thinking that the forecasters had exaggerated the danger when I switched on the weather radio. "Violent storms spread across the region last night from New Jersey in the East to Rhode Island. In New Jersey over 100 homes were badly damaged in a tornado, cars overturned, 30 homes totally destroyed although unbelievably only one person was injured. Another tornado developed in East Moriches but details not yet available."

"East Moriches!" I almost stopped at the yacht club there yesterday but thank goodness I didn't! This was followed by a coastguard message—"A power boat has disappeared on passage from New York to Rhode Island. It is named *Impossible Dream*. All boats are required to keep a lookout."

Today a disappointment during my walk to Southampton: I wanted to see the old colonial town of Southampton, and to visit their library. When I arrive, I apologize to the librarian for not having read more American classical literature, and ask him to recommend 10 American authors and one book by each, explaining, "I know its a tall order but my storage in a 16-foot sailing dinghy is limited." We spend an enjoyable time discussing American authors but unfortunately he is not a sailing man so no sea stories are included. He takes me down to the basement where there was a book sale I purchase most of the books he recommends at 45 cents each. I have a library of American Classics aboard at bargain prices.

I was striding along the road to Southampton when an MGB GT sports car stopped and the young lady driver asked if she could give me a lift to town. She mentioned I looked 'a most interesting man' and offered to show me round the town after I had been to the library. We had lunch together and she invited "Do come to dinner tonight." I have always been susceptible to good looking young ladies in MG sports cars and accepted immediately, wondering where in *Wanderer* I had packed my best tie, white shirt and jacket. She drove me back to *Wanderer*. "What time for dinner?" I ask "and where do you live?" "Six o'clock. We live on the big powerboat. My husband saw your British flag this morning at breakfast; he said you looked an interesting man and told me to drive you into town and bring you back to dinner as he wants to meet you!" My ideas of a romantic candlelit dinner faded—although it was still an enjoyable evening.

13th July, 1989. Great Peconic Bay, New York State

I am now in a different area. There are sandy beaches and sheltered bays small enough to enjoy. A delightful contrast to the flat marshes and low skylines of Long Island Barrier Islands. A slow drift to Cold Spring Pond for three miles, and drift through the narrow entrance between the houses. I anchor for an hour and doze.

The last 40 miles has been continuous low laying coast backed by great shallow lagoons emptying and filling through narrow entrances where the tide roars in and out. Overfalls and eddies extending up to a quarter of a mile inshore which I sometimes run into unexpectedly and get wet. The overfalls combined with powerboat wakes make a nasty, dangerous and confused sea.

15th July, 1989. Mystic Seaport, Conneticut

I have been recommended by the British National Maritime Museum at Greenwich to visit the Mystic Seaport Museum. It is a private museum geared to displays and popular lectures—whaleboat demonstrations, open hearth cooking, sail handling, but there is preservation and reconstruction behind the scenes but out of reach to the average visitor.

I sail up the river to savour the atmosphere of the museum. There are several square riggers alongside: one the *Charles W. Morgan* the last American whaleship, a big two-masted schooner, and a host of interesting small craft.

I have come 28 miles today, tired from the early start and my nervousness about 'The Race.' I put up *Wanderer*'s big frame tent for the extra comfort as I hope to be here for a couple of days. Unfortunately, tonight is one of those days when living anywhere is uncomfortable—it is muggy and the temperature just not quite right—too hot and sweaty inside a sleeping bag, too cold and on the point of shivering without it.

The dock master has several times suggested that I will be more comfortable in the visitors' docks but I have managed to avoid moving as there are advantages to being tied to the 'work float'—at eight each morning I meet all the museum back-room staff as they arrive by boat, and consequently I am given free run of the museum, and allowed to tour the back-stage preservation and restoration work and even to sail-test their most recent acquisition—a open sailing fishing boat from Northern Norway.

I continue on my way after a very pleasant few days.

24th July, 1989

Now the coast has changed to rocky granite headlands. There are three beautifully situated houses looking out over the sea like the photographs of New England you see in books. The wind is dropping. I check the chart—Sachuest Point is visible and on a close-hauled course and so I harden sheets.

There is a brassy reflection in the sea astern so spectacular that I grab the camera and it is not until I look through the lens that I realise the sun is fuzzy, the sky is clouding over, grey streamers are crossing the sun, and wisps of mist are wrapping round the mast. Fog again. I take a quick accurate bearing on the point and estimate my distance off and hope the wind holds, and the fog lets me get in before it clamps down. I don't want to have to anchor out here all night. I coax *Wanderer* along, around the rocky point as the fog rolls in behind, then bear northeast.

Looking back, the sun has gone. It's grey astern, wispy but rapidly thickening. There are rocks offshore—I could go between them to save time but it is too risky in fog. There are fish traps ahead marked by orange buoys and I almost sail onto a float as I am rolling up the genoa. I catch a glimpse of rocks through the murk, beat out, gybe, and head in again until I can hear the waves on the rocks and come onto a bearing almost due west and now I know that I am in the cove. I anchor, put up the tent and heat my tea.

It has been a long day. I was lucky to get into the coast as the fog closed in. It was a satisfying sail.

26th July, 1989. Slocum River, Massachusetts

I am now in Slocum River. It has sheltered deep water just behind the sand bar, there is a lot of wind and it is a dull overcast day. I have nothing to do now except listen to the wind. *Wanderer* is beginning to roll. It has been a good day. It is always a great pleasure to watch *Wanderer* close-hauled in short seas, rising quickly, lifting to the crest, swinging down, and rarely out of step. Now I work out headings and distances for each day; essential preparation on a day like this.

I wake at 2:30 A.M. not worrying but just enjoying being aboard *Wanderer*. Slocum River is beautiful at night, quite the nicest river I have yet seen in the U.S., I muse to myself. I was pleased with yesterday—it was an enjoyable and successful day—navigating by compass and distance run, mostly out of sight of land, finishing up with this unexpected sail into this very pretty river. I am almost tempted to spend the day here, and I examine the chart by moonlight and I work out the tides from *Reeds' Nautical Almanac*. The passage of the Cape Cod Canal presents problems for the unpowered sailboat going north. It's ten miles before the shelter of Plymouth (and the prevailing southwesterly provide uncomfortable wind-against-tide conditions).

I decide to take the last hour of the tide through the canal, which, in the open water, will provide one hour of weak tide against me before rapidly increasing in rate as I head north. I need plenty of daylight ahead. Monday at 5:00 A.M. is the earliest practical passage unless I can get someone to tow me through against the current. I don't like it, and I have a gut feeling I could get into trouble.

27th July, 1989. Hadley Harbor, Massachusetts

I am woken by the fog—the sudden stillness always wakes me as fog creeps into an anchorage, and blankets sound, including that of the waves.

I wake again in the early hours with an idea: Why not go 'outside' Cape Cod? I check the chart, I check the forecast. It is 40 miles to Chatham at the southeast corner and there are numerous good harbours and creeks. Then there is the possibility of cutting the corner by sailing through shallows between the islands. Once on the Atlantic side it is five miles to Nauset Harbor and another 25 miles to the northern tip of Cape Cod.

A pleasant day idling along the coast. Nice houses, cliffs and small boats but I am tired by this heat. I have done 19 miles when I anchor, with another 20 to go to the end of Cape Cod. I stretch out sweating; it is humid. The tent is shading me from the sun.

A beautiful, soft, sunny evening, the sun is warming, and it is fresh; the humidity has dropped to zero. This is lovely after the recent sweaty days. A completely tranquil night, no voices, no traffic. The boat is quiet, no slapping of halliards, not even the 'slap' of water under the hull.

29th July, 1989. East Bay, Cape Cod (southern shore), Massachusetts

7:20 A.M.: Off Squaw Island, low laying, marshy. I pull down a reef, put on oilskins and replace my lifeline. It is only too easy to go overboard in an unexpected roll and I cannot think of anything more stupid than watching *Wanderer* sail away, especially if the shock cord is on the tiller so she doesn't round up.

30th July, 1989. Crossing Hyannas Harbor, Massachusetts

One large powerboat opens throttles and, as it comes up onto a plane, it pulls up a big bow and stern wave. I cross its stern very carefully only to find that a few minutes later and *Wanderer* is planing on the front face of its stern wave. She rides it for 50 yards, then accelerates down into the trough to overtake the bow wave, running almost 100 yards on this one. I am rapidly approaching the reef (I can see the disturbed water) and I am still riding the power boat wake. I can't drop back, running dead down wind, the boom is right off, *Wanderer* is planing—if I luff we shall broach in the following breaking wake and *Wanderer* will roll over. For a few seconds it is debatable whether we shall outrun the breaker before the reef or if it will tumble as it hits the reef with us on top. I am overcome with relief when we manage to slow, safely out of the danger of the breaker and the reef.

I have time to recover and relax at Bass River which, according to my guidebook, is "the prettiest river on the south coast—with windmills." There are 'No WAKE' signs so the powerboats are not a nuisance here but small yachts are moored everywhere outside the very narrow channel. It's nine miles to the channel through Hardings Beach to Stage Harbor and Chatham. Chatham is at the corner of Cape Cod and I am looking forward to turning north for an easy run of 30 miles along the Atlantic shore.

In the evening, I come alongside an anchored sailboat to ask for local information. The 'pass' out into the Atlantic between Morris and Monomoy Islands which I planned to follow is very shallow and not used they tell me. However, the old submerged jetty has been removed and the 'pass' is probably possible to a Wayfarer; opposite Chatham town a new breach has developed through the barrier island—it is a half mile wide, 22 feet deep, the tides run through the gap at 11 knots, and it is dangerous! They loan me a large scale chart which shows the tricky dogleg in the swatchway through the sands from Stage Harbor into Chatham Harbor.

Sailing to the Edge of Fear

31st July, 1989. Stage Harbor, Cape Cod, Massachusetts

I am up early to catch the tide round to the adjoining estuary of Chatham. Short tacking out against the tide, I stand too far out into the channel and I lose all the ground won, so I close-haul across the shallows. This is the advantage of a shallow draught dinghy: Why stem the tide when I can go across the shallows and cheat the tide?

This passage I come to know all too well. For the next twelve days I travel it each morning, returning each night frustrated in my attempts to get safely out into the Atlantic.

1st August, 1989. Stage Harbour, Cape Cod, Massachusetts

8:00 A.M.: This is my third attempt to sail out of the New Breach. The current gets hold of *Wanderer* and carries her down towards the breach and I take a flying leap ashore onto the last few yards as *Wanderer* is swept past and hurriedly pull her out of the stream and anchor along the shore. The bar is 400 yards away to seaward of the breach and the whole bay is a mass of broken white water. In the breach, the ebb tide is tripping over a slight swell running in from the sea—there's no sign of a safe passage.

Walking back to *Wanderer* I get the binoculars and study the bar carefully all the way across. The 'broken seas' are 'overfalls,' occasionally heavy, and erratic. There is a calmer passage, but as I watch this is rolled over by a series of hollow breaking seas. I decide to have breakfast and examine it again in half-an-hour. I remember the First Principle of Open Boat Cruising I learned (the hard way) many years ago—

Don't Go Near A Breaking Bar When The Tide Is Ebbing! I re-examine through the binoculars: now the tide is flooding, the bar covering, the sandspit is smaller, and the viciousness of the breaking seas is greatly reduced from half an hour ago. *Wanderer* is lifting

Standing waves in Chatham breach. The bar is a quarter-mile out to sea, invisible in the fog; the ebb tide runs at 11 knots.

up the bank as the tide floods. I will sail out to take a look.

9:30 A.M.: The tide is beginning to rise across the bar. Seas much reduced but still nasty. I up sails, and stow my anchor. Water still ebbing round the end of the beach. Close-hauled I get a thumping as I cross the bar, and sail northward along the coast. I enjoy being out here. It was well worth sailing 'outside' Cape Cod rather than taking the more conventional Cape Cod Canal route. Now it is straightforward—five miles to the anchorage at Nauset, and tomorrow catch the north-going tide to Provincetown. There's fog further out, and the wind has headed me—now 15 knots northeast and increasing.

I am not happy—if the wind goes up to 20 knots, I may not be able to get in at Nauset because of the onshore swell. It's not worth the risk. I turn, face the breach, surfing occasionally on the front faces of the seas. There are overfalls just inside the breach, thrown about heavily, trying to keep straight with seas from astern, water breaking every which way at the bows. The fog closes in, and I go up the river with the flood under me and the shore invisible. I edge across, see ghostly shadows of working boats which disappear astern, crab pots breaking surface in the shallows; I turn and gratefully anchor close to two small catboats in thick fog.

I decide that I have learned a great deal about these tides in the last few days even if I haven't achieved a passage through the new breach.

2nd August, 1989. Aunt Lydia Cove in Chatham Harbor, Cape Cod

I wake as the tide turns and *Wanderer* swings. I check that the anchor is not dragging and go back to sleep. At 6:00 A.M. I am woken by the boom of surf beyond the barrier island. I turn on the weather radio: "A Small Craft Warning was issued in the early hours. A heavy swell is running into the coast from the east 14 to 16 feet."

Wanderer dries out at 9:30 A.M. I can't move. I'm about to lift the bows onto the rollers by a rope round my shoulders, when the tide returns. I am afloat and off in another five minutes, stemming the tide across to the barrier islands and beating down river. Big confused seas off the breach. I run *Wanderer* ashore in a little indentation and anchor along the beach. I take my binoculars and walk to the seaward side of the barrier island—the bar all the way across is a mass of breaking white water, the breach a confusion of white, breaking seas all the way across, and standing breakers in the sheltered channel too. I walk to the point—it's far worse than yesterday, and quite impossible. I walk back to *Wanderer* to find she has dragged anchor and so I have to run into the water up to my waist to catch her!

A fisherman tells me that the fogs of Cape Cod are caused by the warm water of the Gulf Stream from the south, meeting the cold water from Labrador, the Grand Banks, and Maine, on the northeast side of the island. I am finding there is nothing more frightening than sailing out in dense fog so I am unable to judge conditions on the bar with a 10 knot current carrying me out to sea and knowing that there is no possibility of returning if I get it wrong.

3rd August, 1989. Stage Harbor, Cape Cod

This is my fifth attempt to sail through the breach. I decide to sail out of the old entrance several miles south, then free off up the coast on passage to Nauset Harbour and Provincetown.

There is not a single boat to be seen. This is a lovely estuary, sand dunes both sides, full of shallows and little crescent shaped bars, the channel wandering all over the place. Several times I lose the buoys; but no matter as I skate over the shallows with the centreboard raised. There is little strength in the tide as most water and current is through the new breach and the old channels soon silt up.

I go ashore and climb a high sandy dune for a photograph. Again, I'm struck by the beauty of the estuary. This corner of Cape Cod has everything for the small boat cruiser. The sun is out, the wind southwest at 10 knots. The pass into the Atlantic is too shallow with surf running in from a long way out so I decide to sail round the islands. Monomoy is a long island, flat with patches of wave-eaten dunes. The island goes on for ever—I tack and tack, then round the southern end of Monomoy and run back to Stage Harbour on a glorious sunny evening.

Despite the natural wonder, navigating this corner of Cape Cod is more gruelling than I had realised.

5th August, 1989. Stage Harbor, Cape Cod

My eighth attempt. No thunderstorms. The forecast reports winds southwest at 10–20 knots. The Small Craft Warnings has been down-graded from 20–25 knots, so I am up at 6:00 A.M. and away an hour later free off down the channel between beds of seaweed.

I am soon 'cheating' the tide over the shallows to catch the last of the ebb tide to the breach, making some steady progress, at long last. Without warning, the mast falls down! Fortunately, I am tacking, so it comes down gently, and in slow motion so I have time to catch it. In another piece of good luck, the anchor is laid out ready in case it was needed at the breach, so I throw it overboard; the rope immediately takes a turn round the centreboard and rudder and *Wanderer* lies across the tide putting a heavy strain on the anchor but it holds. I am still in the shallows.

The forestay had parted at the lower end immediately above the Talurit eye splice where it is invisible inside the tube. I make a cup of tea and sit back to work out how to re-rig. I am finishing my tea and about to get out the spares box, when a Boston Whaler motors up. "I was watching from my house when your sails suddenly disappeared. I thought you had capsized so I came out to help." He offers me the use of his workshop and to drive me to the local yacht yard for a new forestay. I accept enthusiastically. The rigger confirms that this is a fatigue failure and suggests that a long-necked marine-type eye fitting will cure the problem.

Once the work is done, I check the forestay. It is a good job, it will be less subject to fatigue and I am pleased with it. I must advise the builder and designer of the fault—it only applies to boats with a reefing/furling genoa so there are few affected. I don't want it to happen to anyone else: had it parted when I was sailing across a bar, or along a rocky lee shore, it could have been very dangerous.

My ninth attempt. I follow the inside of outer island to the breach rather than sail down the buoyed channel. The fog rolls in and I can see the shore for less than 200 yards. I short tack close in so I don't lose it. There is a chop running in round the point. It doesn't look dangerous but there are big swells cresting and almost breaking further along, so I steer to keep inside them.

Eventually, I pick up Monomoy Beach at the southern end of the breach. I gybe, unroll the genoa to be sure of sufficient speed to keep clear of the breakers. I look at the compass and I am completely disorientated in the fog. There's a gap in the islands but I am convinced it shouldn't be there. I return along the shore until I recognise a headland of dunes. Looking back, the fog seems less dense, and I decide to try again. It will be cold beating into the wind.

For the second time I am defeated by fog and return.

Halfway back, I look astern and the fog has cleared completely. I will make one last try—I am feeling frustrated and will risk it if at all possible. If the fog closes in, I will come back. I follow the buoyed channel, winding and shallow for the south end of the Breach. Crossing the bar the waves are slight, only 10 feet high. I don't even get wet from the spray—and, at long last, I am out! I am now on my own in a grey world. The flash of Chatham lighthouse penetrates the fog and I sail directly for it. But I am almost into a patch of broken water on the shore before I see it. This is no good. I give up and return.

I stand down the old estuary back to Stage Harbor but the fog is so thick I cannot find my way through the channel and go aground alongside a stranded yacht. I am becoming fond of Stage Harbor—it's a week since I arrived and it is beginning to feel like my second home!

I give up—for today, anyway—but I don't regret it, at least I 'had a go.'

6th August, 1989. Stage Harbor, Cape Cod

7:00 A.M. and I am away from Stage Harbor sailing round to Chatham to get through the breach. I anchor off the south spit and walk across with binoculars. Good visibility. Broken water—too heavy for *Wanderer*, but there's a narrow channel close by the land—very narrow, only 30-yards wide, with white water. It is not encouraging but just possible with a bit of care.

No point in delay so I hoist sails and am away. I catch a couple of breakers opposite the spit and get a lot of water aboard but her weight keeps *Wanderer* moving, the second wave almost stops her but I just managed to get moving and free off in time to sidle away from the end of the third breaker. A bit of a splash as we climb up the next few cresting waves and a crash as she falls into the trough. But it's nothing serious.

9:20 A.M.: At the outer buoy. I look back and seas are breaking right across now. It is blowing and I heave-to and put in a reef. A 'long-and-short' up the coast driving into seas now four to six feet occasionally showing signs of breaking.

Blowing hard. Staggering in the gusts—above 20 knots. Heave-to for a second reef. Offshore, I come about too close to the land and as I tack, a sudden gust, and a breaking wave under the bilge, make *Wanderer* heel suddenly. I slip down into the lee bilge, the mainsheet is still in the jamb-cleat and I cannot reach it, the side-deck goes under, and water pours in. I am wet all over but she comes up—unbelievably. I am shaking but the wind moderates and I am gaining ground again.

The houses on a bluff must be Nauset village. I beat past so that I can see back into the cove and heave-to. Through the binoculars I can see swells breaking all the way across the entrance 8–10 feet high. A fishing boat comes out but I cannot see any sign of the channel she is following. She smashes her way through several breakers taking water solidly over her bows. It is impossible for *Wanderer* to get in safely.

2:18 P.M.: I free off back down the coast eight miles for Chatham. I shake out the reef and am running at five knots. Three big cresting swells pass safely under *Wanderer* and break heavily only 50-yards shorewards and I work further out to keep clear. I'll not be able to get safely in at Chatham and will have to run down to the old entrance or even round the far end of Monomoy.

Off Chatham there are heavy breakers all the way across the bar but the little passage I noticed this morning at the south end is still there; the seas are heavier now especially close to the beach, but it is partly protected by the heavy broken seas of the bar to windward. It's narrow but might be just possible if I am careful not to lose steerage way or stray into the breakers on either side. I beat up the shore, throw round, sail almost into the breakers on the bar, a quick tack, almost into the breakers on the beach, tack, tack again and close-haul with breakers both sides, but the heavy seas on the bar are giving some protection now.

Another 80 yards then I can free off (but careful not to broach). A big swell penetrates the bar and it's big and hollow as it rears up. I hold course as I dare not luff it as *Wanderer* would lose steerage way and would be in the breakers when it had gone. She rolls heavily but recovers. I pat her "Only another 50 yards," I tell her. Two more waves break just astern—*Wanderer* has kept moving and left them behind. I have a choice—either a short, quick, confused, nasty leg running behind the spit or a longer passage still nasty (but not confused), into the river. I wonder if I chose wisely as I plane in on the front faces of the waves? I have to run almost the full width of the river before I am in clear water. I talk to *Wanderer* as I usually do—she did well today. I anchor, make a mug of tea, then return to Stage Harbor.

Blast the fog! After 12 days of unrelenting thick fog, I feel defeated and have a boatyard trail *Wanderer* across the narrow neck to the west shore of Cape Cod.

13th August, 1989. Rock Harbor Creek, Cape Cod

I have now trailed across to the west side of Cape Cod from Chatham to Rock Harbor. It's a nice harbour, only possible to sail within two hours of high water. I met a lot of affable people at church this morning; a Unitarian service. Enjoyable, and the minister gave a good sermon, followed by a christening.

I sail tomorrow for Provincetown at the north end of Cape Cod, weather permitting. Whales are 10 miles offshore this time of year and I want to sail out to see them if the weather is settled.

14th August, 1989

Allen and Mary Fristoe, catboat friends from Chatham arrived this morning with a supply of Mexican chili which I had so enjoyed at their house—one imperial gallons (English gallons are considerably larger than U.S. gallons), and I estimate I shall be living on chili for the next five days.

Two ladies from neighbouring boats came to inspect *Wanderer*. One refused to come aboard, saying, "It's too small" but she looked through the tent flap. "Oh, My God. Where do you put the microwave?!" she exclaimed.

In the evening, a power boat returns from a bluefish fishing trip, and invites me to their barbecue, but I had already eaten a large supper of chili. I was reading in bed when there was a knock on the tent door and two ladies handed me a large portion of barbecued stuffed bluefish. "We heard that you don't have a microwave, so we wrapped it in several layers of aluminium foil," they said with grins. Even through the foil it smells lovely so I open a corner just to see if it looks as nice as it smells—and I was lost…I nibbled and nibbled…I slept badly because of indigestion!

21st August, 1989. At Marblehead, the East Coast Yachting Centre

Today the forecast brings the unwelcome, "a small craft warning with 15–25 knots gusting considerably more. Fifty percent chance of afternoon and evening storms with damaging high winds. Tonight northwestly wind; fog; and temperatures 90°F in Boston Harbor." All the things I don't like!

I decide to snatch a passage before the afternoon thunderstorms and before the thick fog blankets over the entrance to the harbour.

29th August, 1989. South of Cape Elizabeth, Maine

I almost went into Kennebunkport where the U.S. Presidential summer home is located. There is a big coastguard patrol ship on duty just off the entrance which warns off boats and yachts that come too close and I am told it stops and takes apart anything unusual—and over here a 16-foot open cruising dinghy flying the Red Duster is certainly regarded as unusual!

30th August, 1989. At sea in Maine

8:06 A.M.: I am at anchor in a little pool just north of Cape Porpoise. This is one of the few harbours not filled with yachts on moorings, but there are an incredible number of lobster pot buoys, almost thick enough to walk across. I was practising my dead reckoning from some miles out as I need to re-learn my fog navigation. It worked well but the wind died 100 yards outside, so I rowed in.

This morning there is a thick Maine fog—I cannot even see the shore which was 50 yards away when I anchored last night. So I am not going anywhere yet—at least not until I can see the entrance.

At last, I am in Maine and it's a big state—I have been told its the same size as all the other New England States put together. I have travelled 600 miles since I rigged the dinghy at Shark River in New Jersey after the winter—a total of 2,500 miles since Florida.

The coast has changed from marsh and sand to granite and so there's no second chance if I make a mistake. It's been cold at night recently (I am now wearing my woolly hat and sweater in bed) and rough weather. There is a definite feel of autumn in the air but the forecast says the late summer weather will return.

Yesterday was one of the nicest days sailing so far, although it didn't seem as promising early in the day. Light wind all day, no more than five knots and mostly less. I rowed out of Portsmouth (New Hampshire), across an oily-flat sea with long gentle swells from the Atlantic, and only occasional wind ruffles on the water.

First, I set course for Brave Boat Harbor expecting to row in as the wind died; next, I risked carrying on for York River, then gradually working offshore for what little sea-breeze there was, but knowing that if it failed I had at least a two mile row, and rounded Cape Neddick by 2:30 P.M. I laid off a course 10 miles across the next bay to Cape Porpoise but it was too much of a risk—a four hour crossing, a light wind likely to die, and the day well advanced—I should be out at sunset with a long row ahead of me in the dark.

Today I head for Perkins Cove, Ogunquit—a lovely little granite harbour hidden under the headland which reminds me of Cornwall, England. There is a high level footbridge over the channel but I am not sure if it opens, so I follow a big yacht through. The owner ferries me ashore to meet the harbour master, then says: "You must try a real Maine lobster." He and his wife take me out for dinner. They recommend 'steamers' which turned out to be soft shell clams which I thought was the main course, but he had ordered 'real Maine lobster' to follow!

31st August, 1989

Twenty-two miles today in thick fog running headland to headland. I am beginning to doubt my position when I hear the roar of engines and a big off-shore speed boat thunders past at the limit of visibility, followed by nine more. I am relieved as they were running from headland to headland on radar, so I must be on course. Ten minutes later I come across a fisherman who asks, "Did you see the president—and his nine Secret Service escorts?" What a pity that a president cannot enjoy an afternoon alone in his boat like the rest of us!

I see the upper part of Wood Island lighthouse for a few seconds through a gap in the fog just long enough to know I am on course. Then nine miles to Cape Elizabeth where the powerful light just pierced the fog but, surprisingly, the fog horn was silent. Suddenly, when the lighthouse is close abeam the horn hits me—like a physical blow—a huge blast that goes echoing round the horizon. Whether the horn was inoperative, or whether it was a freak of the fog I shall never know (Sound in fog is directionally reliable but there are often silent areas where the sound 'bounces').

Further south, I have been clamming and lobstering, but north of here shellfishing is banned because of a Red Tide—a naturally occurring red algae which makes shellfish toxic (we came across a Red Tide in the Carolinas last year). Luckily, it does not last long.

11th September 1989. Caldwell Islands, Maine

I ran out of wind at Port Clyde and rowed back to the Caldwell Islands for the night, a pretty cove inside a ring of little granite islands.

This morning I opened the rear of the tent and looked out. There were no boats except for a few lobster boats out in the sound miles away hauling pots. I watched five seals round up a school of fish, then cut into them for breakfast, a tremendous commotion with fish and seals jumping and cutting the water to foam round my dinghy.

I probably dozed off halfway through my breakfast for suddenly, some 60 feet beyond my bow, I heard a deep and resonant voice. I could not catch what it was saying, yet I was sure I knew it—and yet there had been no-one in the cove! It was coming closer! The hair rose on the back of my neck. It was louder! Now the voice was at my bow, and I caught the drift of what it was saying, "...If the British Empire lasts a thousand years...then let it be said, 'this was their finest hour.'" It was Winston Churchill—and he was alongside my Wayfarer. I wondered for a few seconds if I was still of this world or whether the "old man" had come for me. I sat rigid with shock, then I ripped open the tent flaps to find a lobster boat hauling a pot along-side, drifting downwind, his radio full volume broadcasting a recorded speech by Churchill.

It left me badly shaken.

12th September, 1989. Long Cove, Maine

A feel of autumn; bright sun but a cool day. I am 250 miles from the Canadian border. I have covered 100 miles from Portland, with many more miles exploring the rivers and estuaries. Now I need to push on a bit. The large State of Maine has many attractions. Vinalhaven, Deer Island and Mount Desert Island are all worth seeing.

13th September. Near Long Cove, Maine

A weird experience. Last night I anchored in a small, secluded creek. After mdinight I am restless and make a cup of tea and sit on the bows with my back to the mast absorbing the stillness and silence of the place. It is a dark night, the steep sides around me rising sharply, only slightly darker than the creek itself. It is utterly silent: a sombre, black picture of unbelievable starkness!

A screech owl cries out three times. I step off the boat and walk into the darkness so intense that it really is 'darkness visible.' I feel so certain that at the far end of the creek's bend is a boatman waiting for me and that I shall know him—with his flowing white hair, fiery eyes, unkempt appearance ; it will be Charon the immortal and beyond him the River Styx, waiting to carry me to the hereafter.

Ten minutes later *Wanderer* wakes me as she starts to roam restlessly round her anchor coming to a violent stop at the end of each swing. Surprisingly, there is no wind and I think, "Yes, *Wanderer*, you are as scared as I am!" and it is only by a conscious effort that I prevent myself from pulling up the anchor immediately and sailing away. I lie awake most of the night, hearing no wind. Had I experienced a hallucination? I don't know but when I lift the anchor it is knotted into a great ball of 'knitting'—*Wanderer* had been sailing round all night trying to get away.

It had been a frightening night.

17th September, 1989. Camden Harbor, Maine

At midnight there is heavy rain for 30 minutes. I wake to violent pitching, rolling, and surging into the float. It quickly becomes worse. I assume it is caused by the wakes of powerboats but when I look out, I realise the floating docks are rising and falling. *Wanderer* is light, pitching out of phase with the heavy pontoons, her nylon mooring ropes stretching and snatching her into the docks. If it gets worse, or a roller punctures or rides over the dock, there will be a lot of damage.

Camden Harbor is sheltered from seaward by half-tide reefs, but at high water the reefs flood and a strong onshore wind rolls a heavy sea into the harbour and the present spring tide accentuates the problem. In two hours the reefs will dry but until then I am in trouble. Just as I had feared, it does get worse and I begin to think that I could lose my boat. I pull my oilskins over my pyjamas, jersey, and boots. I rig a second roller. I have got to move!

At one in the morning, a couple return to their yacht. Their boat is rolling too but being deeper and heavier she rolls in phase with the floating docks, while *Wanderer* is moving faster and more violently. It is pitch dark now. I try to pass *Wanderer* outside their yacht and into her lee, but it is no good—the bows hit violently. I shall have to row. The wind is not excessive—probably 20 knots, 25 knots in the gusts. I take off the tent and throw it on the dock and rig oars. The couple give me a shove out, a few quick oar strokes to get clear, then I let *Wanderer* drift downwind, and row into the lee at the end of the docks.

The steady drizzle and spray has wetted everything; tent up and I am soon warm but wet. I sleep in oilskins.

Sailing to the Edge of Fear

18th September, 1989. Camden Harbor, Maine

A dull nagging pain during the evening in my left side. It gets worse until I sweat. Maybe a kidney stone again? Sweating steadily as the ache increases, then reduces. I hope it has passed—I don't want a recurrence as in Washington last year when I was hospitalised. I must drink more water.

19th September, 1989. Camden Harbor, Maine

"A small craft advisory has been issued; north to northeast 20–25 knots and gusty, becoming southeast tonight." Damn it. I shall roll and snatch again at high water when the sheltering reef covers in the early hours. I decide to leave Camden and snatch the passage before the wind increases too much. I row over to a pontoon temporarily to take the tent down and to stow my gear. The dock staff walk over to say, "We are having these floats out in half an hour; end of season." "I'll be gone," I reassure them.

22nd September, 1989. Pickering Island, Maine

The sun is already low behind the trees as I approach Pickering Island. Dew is falling heavily. Overfalls over the sheltering reef but it was only one-and-a-half hours after high water and I risked it as I wanted to get in before darkness—the rudder and centreboard touched on the rocks and kicked up in 18 inches. Boat and equipment running wet and my clothing soaked through with the heavy dew.

The sunset looks beautiful, a vivid pastel orange, the Camden hills a lovely blue against the sun. Mosquitoes and gnats are in plentiful supply. The tent is up and the hurricane lantern lit as it was already dark by the time I had anchored.

I switch on the weather radio: "Hurricane Hugo: A tropical storm watch is in effect from St. Augustine to Myrtle Beach; a hurricane warning to Cape Lookout. Hugo is expected to come ashore in the next 24 hours; water level nine to twelve feet above normal; sustained winds 105 miles per hour." There follows a general warning: "Make every preparation." I sailed up that coast last year and I can visualise it and the people I met—the land is low so I expect they will evacuate to higher ground.

I listen to the local coastal forecast: "A hurricane warning is issued for Fernando Beach to Oregon Inlet, Pamlico Sound, Albermarle Sound, and the Carolinas." Hurricane Hugo, now a category 4 hurricane, will cross the coast between Charleston and the North Carolina border, with four inches of rain, and is expected to be in Rhode Island by Saturday morning. Maximum sustained wind speed now 135 miles per hour.

I have several alternatives:

a) Phone Dave Getchells who I met recently. He is the organiser of 'The Maine Trail' and knows this area like the back of his hand and offered his help if I need it, (and if I can find a phone). We could try to borrow a trailer to get *Wanderer* ashore and into shelter.

b) Find a 'hurricane hole'—Pulpit Harbor (first creek to the right) is said to be good holding ground but there will be a queue of yachts trying to get in to anchor, and find a house for shelter.

c) Pull up a beach here, lower the mast and tie down—provided the beach is suitable. This depends on the extra height of water—predicted to be 12 feet. If Hugo strikes at high water I shall be in trouble. High water on Friday is at 5:25 A.M.

There is nothing I can do until daylight so I settle down to read all I can find about hurricanes, then I do some basic thinking about how to survive...

The rudder touches as the tide drops and I have to paddle out and re-anchor in the dark. I make a mental note of the items to go into a rucksack if it becomes necessary to abandon my boat.

22nd September, 1989. Pickering Island to Swains Cove, Maine

It's 2:30 A.M. and I listen to the forecast while waiting for news of the hurricane: "Hugo came ashore overnight at Isle of Palms south of Charleston. Sustained winds of 135 miles per hour, 12 inches of rain, 10–11 feet above normal tidal levels have been reported locally. Tropical storm warnings have been issued for the coast of Maine." It is very frightening.

I intend to be up at first light, inspect the beaches on the island to see if I can get far enough above high water, to see if there are high trees that may crush *Wanderer*, or if there is a ravine to protect me. Otherwise, I must beat back to Pulpit Harbor to the 'hurricane hole.'

5:00 A.M.: Still dark. A quick breakfast, porridge, and fresh fruit. Might as well eat well with Hugo beyond the horizon and about to devour me! In the pre-dawn light I can feel the thick, dense fog. I can't see 50 yards, let alone the beach. There is no possibility of assessing protection on the island in these conditions. I swear viciously, panicked by the very real possibility that I could lose my boat today!

Hugo is losing strength. Now 85 miles per hour sustained wind speed, but higher gusts reported. Now moving northwest faster, and expected to continue at 30 miles per hour. A tropical storm warning has now been issued for Maine.

Local recommendation is for boats on summer moorings to be lifted ashore this morning.

It is too early to relax as hurricanes tend to regain power as they cross water. Everything depends on the route that Hugo takes—inland or along the coast?

Fog is now 200 yards. I row to the beach to look round. I could beach at high water this afternoon at 5:30 P.M. and pull *Wanderer* on rollers up onto the crest of the ridge, but the exceptional water level would carry her over into the hollow under trees; this hollow has no shelter to the east, north, or west. I row along the shore looking for better shelter but find nothing. Neither shall I be able to find Pulpit Harbor in this fog! The chart shows two possible coves: Swains Cove, one mile northeast with a dock on the south shore so I could tie one rope to the dock and the other to an anchor; or sail to Eggemogin Reach where there appears to be shelter on the north shore. I row to the end of the island in 200 yards visibility. Dead reckoning to Swains Cove is straightforward—45 degrees magnetic, one mile, with time to get settled. If it is unsuitable I will go on or, if the fog clears, beat back to Pulpit Cove.

9:18 A.M.: I up the mainsail—it's a fine reach northeast. The island disappears within a minute and I am alone. One mile on I should pick up the land and follow it to the cove. The fog is disorientating and I concentrate almost entirely on the compass.

9:34 A.M.: Another shadowy island disappears back into the fog, then suddenly land appears ahead. I follow the shore past the little cove—a nice small house, but no shelter. Then I find a narrow entrance to a cove. A lobsterman is ferrying pots from his boat. "May I ask you a few questions?" I inquire politely. "Yes. But I'm not sure what answers you'll get," he grins. "Yes" he confirms, "this is Swain's Cove. It is as good a place as any to shelter from Hugo, but there are no spare moorings. Two yachts came in yesterday and intended to return, but they've gone on hoping to get lifted out. There's reefs and rocks on the north side of the cove—so anchor anywhere in the centre. You'll see at low water." He goes on to deliver more bad news: "There's no landing at the dock; and they won't allow you to tie to it either—they're summer people."

I put down two anchors and row them in securely. Another fisherman, taking his boat ashore to haul out, rows across to say, "You'll be alright there; you're clear of the rocks."

The rain begins and I rush up the tent (with plastic undersheet to cope with the expected torrential downpour) but *Wanderer* is already wet, everything damp and unpleasant, and the fog not clearing at all. The forecast reports that "Hugo is losing strength, now 80 miles per hour sustained winds, and has increased speed to 35 miles per hour north-northwest; it is located in western Virginia. Rain expected to be heavy but little flooding is predicted as Hugo crosses Maine because of the speed it is travelling. It will pass through the state quickly.

Several fishermen are taking their boats off heavy moorings and pulling them ashore. I am surprised as I'd have expected a boat to be safer on a heavy mooring free to swing to the wind, than ashore where the storm can get hold of her. I ask why and I am told impatiently: "Fifteen inches of rain in an open lobster boat and you've got a sunk boat."

4:10 P.M.: I am invited to the home of Charles and Edna Hutchinson for a meal and they offer me the safety of their house and a bed until Hugo has passed. But I prefer to be on board although its but a forlorn hope that I can do anything if *Wanderer* drags onto the rocks.

My surroundings are almost calm as the Hutchinsons row me back after supper. Brilliant phosphorescence at each stroke. I turn in, fully dressed inside my oilskins as there is no point in getting my sleeping bag wet when Hugo hits.

11:30 P.M.: No wind, all is flat and calm, except for the sound of heavy hurricane-generated surf on the seaward side of island.

2:04 A.M.: The wind roaring in the trees like an express train passing just overhead, but the wind doesn't reach to water level. I turn over. The next thing I know it's 6:30 A.M. and daylight. The southerly wind is roaring through the trees. The protection from the high shore is amazing—no wind at water level. Swain's Cove may not be recognised as a hurricane hole but it is an excellent approximation.

The Hutchinsons collect me to see the TV news but few pictures are available from Charleston as the power failed when the hurricane hit. McClellanville, where Marg and I spent three days last year, has ceased to exist. Damage is erratic—a whole end wall of a house has gone but all the furniture inside is untouched, a big single-storey house removed from its foundations and deposited undamaged 250 yards away in the marsh, big fishing boats several miles inland, and the town centre devastated. As well as 135 miles per hour winds there were 22-foot ocean swells running in from the Atlantic.

Local families were evacuated to the area school on high ground, water rose above the floor, and they climbed onto the tables. When the water rose above the tables they put the children into the roof space; the water rose to chest height above the tables—and then went down! The house of Mrs McClellan had completely disappeared, and she is shown collecting the occasional piece of unbroken antique family china from the mud when she was rescued.

27th September, 1989. Approaching Benjamin River and Northwest Cove, Maine

I reach across to the west of the island and square off before the northwest wind on a dead run. The wind is far stronger than expected once we're clear of the land and I have to heave-to on port tack immediately to pull down one reef. *Wanderer* is too close to the land but fortunately everything goes right and I have room to free off, gather speed, and tack (I remember thinking that I had room for one attempt only and reminding myself "make a mess of it and you'll be on the rocks for certain this time Dye!").

We're clear of the land, *Wanderer* begins to plane on the front faces for a considerable distance before dropping back onto the rear face. White horses, seas on the quarter make for an uncomfortable ride as *Wanderer's* stern wave pulls them over to break at the transom. A wild sail—safe but only just as the seas are steepening as they approach the shallows before the bridge. I run down the coast and consider going into Benjamin River which is sheltered beyond the reef, but there are too many yachts. An exciting ride past Center Cove and I turn into Northwest Cove.

Two small yachts are in Northwest Cove on permanent moorings, pitching in the steep sea rolling in. I roar past the yachts and the old lighthouse now converted to a house with picture windows, and round up onto the shore. It's a mussel bed and I flinch as I listen to the sharp shells cutting into the gel coat of *Wanderer's* hull. I get out the weather radio to hear, "A small craft advisory has been issued; wind northwest, dropping overnight."

At the moment, I am well sheltered behind the island but when the wind goes round, the reefs will be the only shelter and, as they will cover at high water anyway, the result will be big swells running into the cove. Obviously, the blasted fellow who recommended this as a good anchorage has only been in here in good conditions—not in a strong northwesterly when the reef is covered—I should have checked the chart myself instead of accepting his advice so unthinkingly. I shall have to get out. The small craft advisory was accurate as the wind is certainly 20–25 knots. I pull down the second reef and then I turn down one roll of sail round the boom as well. I decide to get out over the shallows downwind but there is only a few inches depth and I narrowly miss a rock and I have to scramble over the side to push *Wanderer* round. It was stupid to attempt to sail across a reef in heavy wind and to leeward. Beating out is difficult with the wind and sea funnelling into the cove!

28th September, 1989. Mount Desert Island, Maine

I have to go to windward of an island. It's extremly gusty. The seas are heavy, every second wave hits the bow and comes over as spray, an occasional wave breaks across the gunwale and round my trousers. There is a yellow strip of sand just below surface between two islands; it must be a sand bar but it is too rough to examine the chart for depth. So I ease along the shallows gently and edge across where the water is darker indicating a slightly deeper channel. I heave-to under the lee of the island to examine the chart. I consider another reduction in sail but hope to be in the lee of islands shortly. I may have to drop the mainsail once past the headland and run in under the genoa. The seas are bad.

Reaching, I can spill wind but there is a lot of spray and water slopping aboard. I have to pay contant attention to playing the mainsheet to spill wind. At last, I can look into Bass Harbor. Only one mile to the headland then I can free off. Two lobster boats cross my bow planing fast, and I luff up to meet their wake but the sea is so confused that I don't notice it.

2:00 P.M.: Cresting seas and then overfalls to windward of a reef as the tide tops up the seas. Suddenly clear and into deep water where it is almost flat and I feel deep relief. *Wanderer* is reaching, and with the wind on the beam I can spill the more heavy gusts. I gybe and photograph the Hills of Mount Desert for the first time. A dead run now. Wind increasing, the fetch is longer and seas increase in size, and steepen rapidly as it is the last of the ebb. Planing fast. I look back— a mistake—as I see 'big devils.' It develops into a wild plane to the next buoy, then slightly off a dead run as I alter course.

As I come onto a broad reach the wind pipes up and seas build—now *Wanderer* is quartering down wind and sea, and it is increasingly difficult to hold a course. I discover the rudder blade has worked up because of the speed and I pull it down. Twice I almost lose control as she quarters down into the trough with a heavy gust pushing her; sooner or later she'll broach.

I have held onto the sail for far too long and now there is no way that I can safely luff-up to drop the mainsail. I am in trouble!

Suddenly, the water is flat and I can relax. Even under the land there are still some vicious squalls but I am sheltered. I rest up at the Southwest Harbor town dock with porridge, peaches and cream, and nuts. Then I sail through the island passage into Somes Sound advertised as "the only fjord on the East Coast of the U.S.A." Well into the fjord there is a bay under high cliffs and mountain scenery—this is Valley Cove, a recommended anchorage. A permanent mooring is marked with an unfriendly sign marked, "PRIVATE" so I drop my grapnel anchor further out, but the water is deep, the anchor 'up and down,' so I re-anchor closer to the little boulder strewn beach.

Even here, I have to extend the anchor warp with a nylon lifeline to reach bottom, then set a second anchor to prevent *Wanderer* fouling the grapnel when the wind dies.

It has been an exciting day and it went well but 20 miles in extreme conditions has exhausted me.

29th September, 1989. Mount Desert Island, Maine

Somes Sound, Mount Desert Island is a spectacular cove with almost vertical granite cliffs several hundred feet high.

The sun is shining on the cliffs, trees, and the occasional red maple, and I can look down the fjord for miles. One shore is green and the other in dark shadow—spectacular. Valley Cove is not a good anchorage—overnight wind was forecast 25 knots southwest but it is actually southeast so it blows along up the length of the sound and funnels over the cliffs and 400 feet vertically down into the cove. The wind gusts, roars, and whistles, and *Wanderer* surges about most of the night. Fortunately, I have two anchors down. An uncomfortable night with *Wanderer* heeling to the "williwars" roaring down from the cliffs and shearing about all night.

I spend breakfast waiting for the wind to drop, but instead conditions get rapidly worse as the wind increases. I feel considerable alarm now as it's impossible to hoist the reefed mainsail in this weight of wind roaring down from the cliffs above. I study the open water carefully but there are no white horses out in the open waters of the fiord, so I decide to run for shelter at the top of the inlet under reefed jib only.

Even kneeling on the foredeck, I am risking a capsize as *Wanderer* rolls heavily under the vertical gusts, so I crawl forward to haul in the anchor ropes. I raise and stow the heavy danforth anchor first as the grapnel is much easier to handle in a hurry. The grapnel breaks out immediately, and I haul in hand over hand—and the anchor jams under the bow! Damn it! The squalls are so violent that I cannot free it without capsizing, so I take a couple of quick turns round the mooring cleat and it will have to stay jammed under the bows. I unroll one third of the genoa, *Wanderer* pays off and immediately comes up into a plane.

Clear of the cove, the dinghy accelerates madly. Conditions are indescribable out in the open—the southerly must be funnelling up the fjord to storm force. The wind is so strong that every cresting wave is blown to smoke before it breaks, the surface covered with two feet of spume and I am soaked immediately.

A frightening sail. *Wanderer* accelerates to 20 knots, jumping from the crest of each wave, across the trough, digging her bow solidly into the wave ahead, bursting through, and airborne to the next crest. I am sitting as far aft as possible

---

before *Wanderer* clears the little headland, now I scramble back onto the rear buoyancy, utterly concentrating on keeping the boat square with the waves—any deviation or a breaking crest at the rudder and *Wanderer* is going to roll in.

Twice, I try to free the genoa sheet but as I move forward I can feel the altered trim with the dinghy beginning to bore, and I scramble back just in time to prevent pitch-poling. I look at the point some two miles up the fjord and think: "If I can survive that far maybe I can get a slight lee" but I know with absolute certainty there is no way I could survive for two miles in these conditions. The reefed genoa begins to flog, vibrating the whole boat—just like the blows of a sledge hammer. I watch fascinated, as the mast begins to whip between deck and spreaders. The hull, equipment—everything—is vibrating unbelievably and I dare not move forward to get to the reefing line or free the jib sheet. The luff of the reefed headsail is a blurred vibrating outline. Any moment, I expect the mast to fracture or a shroud to pull out of the deck. I think: "This is it! Of all the sailing I have done I am going to die in sheltered water."

Suddenly, there is a rattle as two fathom of chain whips along the side deck and disappear astern. My two quick turns round the mooring cleat have worked undone, the anchor has come loose from under the bow, and two fathom of chain and a hundred feet of braided terylene warp is whipping out astern. I expect the cleat to pull out of the deck but it holds. There is a 'bang' as the rope tightens, and in an instant all is peace and sanity…except for the scream of the wind! I can't understand what has happened: then I realise that the anchor is acting as a drogue 100 feet astern; speed has dropped to 12 knots, and *Wanderer* is under control.

Still shaking from the trauma and disbelief, I offer up a prayer of thanks; then I put the shockcord on the tiller, walk slowly forward, and roll up the jib—running under the windage of the bare mast.

Ten minutes later I am safe—a thankful and much wiser man!

30th September, 1989. Northeast Harbor, Maine

It is 13 weeks since I left Shark River where I launched in June.

There is now continuous heavy weather and I decide to stay in harbour until it blows out. Last year my worst gale was at the end of October but now I am much further north. I wonder if it might be wise to pull *Wanderer* ashore now at Northeast Harbor. Frustrated, I decide to leave early tomorrow morning with the forecast for "West 20 knots," but now the forecast is updated to "30 knots" and I change my mind. The weather has broken.

2nd October, 1989

Today I set sail again. The colours are spectacular at the waters edge but I don't want to run close under the land just to avoid the 'williwars' and become becalmed. As I leave the harbour there is a lot of weight in several gusts, including a vicious squall as I pick up the wind beyond the coast guard boat. I cross her bows to keep under the land and feel the full force of the wind as I harden in at the gybe mark to free off to Southeast Harbor. The squalls worsen and span the length of the harbour and build a short sea. I raise the centreboard to the minimum necessary to prevent leeway, but even so I am overpowered in the gusts even with two reefs down. It must be blowing 30 knots. I tack quickly between the squalls. It is risky sailing so I shall be relieved to get under the land.

I go to bed at dark as I finish writing in my log. I'm feeling frustrated at the lack of progress. There are gales every day now. I plot the course for tomorrow. Intricate dead reckoning is not possible when beating and single-handed.

13th October, 1989. Green Island, Maine

A beautiful bay. The finest scenery yet. I check compass course to identify headlands. It would be easy to get lost amongst this mass of islands and bays. A rapid is pouring out through a narrow gap, about 30 feet either side of a central boulder, sides of high rock. A torrent with eddies each side. The stream drops two feet. I broad reach, wind freshening and I begin to climb. I make a very quick use of the rudder to avoid being caught in the eddies. I climb to within 10 feet of the level lake; I try and try but cannot get any further against the current. Suddenly, I realise that I can't get out—I cannot spill the wind out of my sails as I am on a broad reach; I can't tack round because of getting caught in a back eddy along the shore, I can't gybe for fear of getting into the eddy behind the centre boulder. For several minutes I continue sailing uphill without moving, hoping there will be a lull and *Wanderer* will drop back. Eventually, I edge across, spin round, gybe so quick that the current carries *Wanderer* down clear of all eddies. I heave-to a few yards from the point so I'll be able to notice if *Wanderer* fore-reaches.

I'm stationary 50 feet off the rocky shore eating my lunch when I look up to see a lobster boat coming across: "You in trouble? I've seen you close to the rocks for a long time." He passes a lobster across, "Have a lobster for your supper." We chat and he recommends the neighbouring cove for the night. Tall trees shelter the cove from the wind but put it in shadow by 4:30 P.M. It's still warm and sunny outside but cold in here in the shade.

I spend the afternoon and evening sewing my sails. I call the lobster "William" after the old Duke of Clarence whose portrait always reminds me of a boiled lobster. He's been hopping about the floor of the dinghy and clicking at me, and I have been chatting to him while I sew. I have become quite fond of him. I have measured him up and he will just fit into the pot if he tucks his feet under him neatly. Its a pity really. I feel like a cannibal!

I have an excellent supper by candlelight consisting of lobster, sweet corn, bread, and tea. I turn in at eight o'clock a little worried that the anchor may tangle round the anchor flukes as the tide turns—there is not enough wind to keep *Wanderer* clear.

The sound of water wakes me as the tide floods and runs over the reef. At midnight there is complete and utter silence. I can see the moon through the fabric of the tent—every detail in the boat is clearly visible. Outside is a mirror reflection, not a ripple on the water, bathed brilliantly in white moonlight. There is absolute quiet: no birds, owls, animals, or wind in the branches. A most unusual night.

17th October, 1989. North Haven, Maine

The weather has broken. There has been a lot of wind in the last two weeks but I intend to sail as long as possible. Then I must borrow a trailer and pull *Wanderer* out.

Perry Cove, Vinalhaven (opposite North Haven), Maine

Rain and the temperature drops. A cold bleak wet afternoon, rain heavy and continuous. Everything I touch is wet. The wind is roaring in the trees, forecast is 30 knots increasing to 35 knots overnight. A front is stationary across Maine with the remains of Hurricane Jerry moving along it.

18th October, 1989

An Inuit hail "Ak-soo-may" from alongside—it comes from a kayaker. It is Geoff Heath who cruised his Wayfarer to Northern Labrador some years before. We had corresponded but never met. I am delighted to see him. He has paddled round to ask if I'd like him to store *Wanderer* for the winter. He says he has a friend with a trailer.

It's cold and I eat my lunch in my sleeping bag for warmth. Geoff returns with a thermos of hot soup and extra warm clothes. How very thoughtful. He comes aboard for a chat. "We'll load you up at 'the landing' at noon," he says. He's going ashore here as it is too wild outside today (at least 35 knots) and he hasn't practised his 'rolling' technique recently!

This is my last night on board and I am sad at the thought. At midnight the rain stops. I get out my down-filled inner sleeping bag, and for my last night I sleep in warmth.

19th October, 1989

We pull *Wanderer* out at the landing. The wind is rising quickly and the waves building, and half an hour later it would not have been possible.

The rain is torrential at midnight. I listen to the roar of wind in the trees, increasing until it is at ground level, and the rain gets progressively heavier. At 2:30 A.M. the wind jumps round 180 degrees and within a few minutes it is blowing across the clearing at 40–45 knots, and the rain is even harder. It is unbelievably ferocious. I hear gusts roaring across the meadow and wait for them to hit, half expecting *Wanderer* to heel and swing to meet them, but the land tent, which Geoff had lent me, stays upright. I am lucky to be ashore. If this gale had caught me afloat I may not have made it through, for few coves offer 180 degree protection. The violence goes on and on, but at last it is dawn and I climb out of a wet sleeping bag into wet clothes. Geoff drives me to the Vinalhaven ferry (to the mainland) but the boat is tied up because of the gales and I am told, "All sailings since last Friday have been cancelled because of bad weather."

The ferries to the mainland are still cancelled because of rough conditions, and over 100 wedding guests are marooned on the island. I spend the time stowing gear and digging boulders from the clearing—a relaxed quiet, enjoyable time in the company of two very nice people who are building their own home. I have always wanted to sail amongst icebergs but never have (I was refused permission to sail in Svalbard many years ago) and to meet Geoff Heath, a man who has actually done so in his Wayfarer, is a great pleasure and privilege.

20th October, 1989

Transport home is easy. Dave Getchell, organiser of the Maine Island Trail for Small Boats and a friend of the Heaths, meets me at Rockland as I disembark from the ferry and calls out: "My neighbours will give you a lift to Boston." Kindly, they deliver me right to the airport with just two hours to wait for the next British Airlines flight to London.

"You'll find no amateurs beyond Schoodic, Frank," warns Dave Getchell as I leave. "It's a different world!" It's a comment that I find intriguing. The newspaper I read on board the airplane tell me that there has been a hurricane in the west of England with winds of over 100 miles per hour; an earthquake in California with a bridge collapsing; the value of the British pound is dropping again

Reflecting on my five month's sail, I can't help but dwell upon how demanding this Atlantic coast is. So many yachtsmen told me "You *must* go through the Cape Cod Canal" that I began to wonder why. I found out—for the coastal passage tested my skill to the utmost.

The strong currents, the meeting of the warm waters of the Gulf Stream with the cold waters from the Labrador Current causing the notorious continuous fogs, and the Atlantic seas on the lee shores, is something I shall remember for a long time.

Schoodic—it is a name to conjure with on the East Coast! Countless locals fishermen and yachtsmen last year had told me not to venture beyond Schoodic— a headland in Maine with great dangerous offlying reefs, while beyond lurked a world of huge tides, tortured currents, hazardous reefs, unpredictable weather, a lonely coast, few people, even fewer fishermen, and almost continuous mist and fog. It was not an area to venture into unless the yachtsman is self reliant—"There is no-one to help if you get into trouble." Certainly it seemed to be the natural limit of cruising for pleasure yachtsmen and all power boaters, and its fearsome reputation gave it a menace that could well come to haunt my sleeping hours.

1990. Maine to LaHave

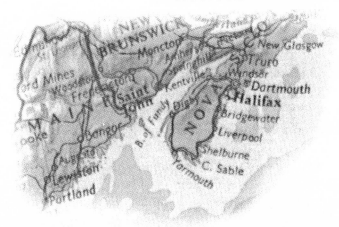

AS I BEGIN MY ADVENTURES aboard *Wanderer* in Maine in early June, a fisherman warns me, "Frank, there are no amateurs beyond Schoodic—there is no-one to help if you get in trouble." It is an almost idenitical warning to the one Dave Getchell gave me last autumn.

Geoff Heath who had stored *Wanderer* over the winter painted a different picture. Before I left, he showed me on a school atlas the coasts of Maine and Nova Scotia, remarking, "It's very pretty with good cruising, particularly Machias Bay in the U.S., and all the south and east shores of Nova Scotia; Cape Breton Island is different—the coast is cold, rugged, and foggy. But there's a canal passage leading to superb sheltered salt water sailing in the Bras d'Or lakes in the interior with rarely a trace of fog; the south side of Newfoundland is high, rugged, spectacular but with little shelter!"

Launching is uneventful. It took three hours to stow gear aboard, then Geoff's father crewed me on a short sail round to Winter Harbor—a warm, sunny day for the first sail. The next day, I set out beating for the high land of Île au Haut on the horizon but the island disappears when I am only three miles out. The temperature drops suddenly and fog clamps down so I run back into Winter Harbor while I can still rely on my back bearing, and feel my way into the cove in less than 100 yards visibility to spend three days in fog and rain.

Early June, 1990

6:15 A.M.: Foggy, no wind. I doze off and it is 7:40 A.M. Some rather unenthusiastic stowing—spare batteries in a waterproof container, and I stick red electrical insulation tape round the container holding the red flares so I can find them quickly by sight or feel in an emergency, then write to U.S. customs at Portland asking for an extension to my cruising permit which soon expires. Today there is non-stop rain, and the temperature has dropped even further. I had forgotten how cold and miserable these foggy, chilly, wet Maine days can be as a northerly front goes through. I add thermaware underclothes and feel warmer.

12th June, 1990. Seal Trap, Île au Haut, Maine

The northerly wind was forecast to swing round to southerly at midday so I leave Winter Harbor, Vinalhaven at 10:00 A.M. A pleasant sail, sunny, but still cold. I cross to Île au Haut and anchor in 'Seal Trap,' a real gem of a cove. I am glad Geoff recommended it. The name is said to be a corruption of the French "ciel" meaning "sky." It is completely sheltered, uninhabited, no visiting yachts, totally hidden—and the mosquitoes aren't biting either. I work steadily all afternoon and almost finish the maintenance jobs left from fitting out last week.

It is a beautiful cove. The sun is behind the trees at 7:30 P.M. It's going to be a cold night. I make a mug of tea to warm up then promptly knock it over. Duck Harbor has just room for three boats to anchor. I climb Duck Mountain—a scramble to 600 feet with several false summits over bare glaciated rock.

It is low water, two feet deep. I hoist the mainsail, put the shock cord on the tiller and leave *Wanderer* to sail close-hauled for the entrance while I tidy things. Glancing up, I see a pinnacle six inches above the water only 10 feet ahead, and snatch the shock cord off the tiller and throw *Wanderer* round. It passes alongside three feet away. It's as close a shave as I ever want. The narrows are now only 40-feet wide at low water with rocks two feet below the surface. Tide is flooding in fast through the entrance as I try to sail out. I am afraid I will get swept back and lose my rudder on a rock so I out oars and row through the narrows.

Outside—fog! I am tired, doubting my ability. My unbrushed teeth taste foul!

18th June, 1990. Merchants Row, Maine

It's one of those days when everything goes smoothly! Yesterday I found my way into MacClathery's Island in fog. Today the forecast at 5:30 A.M. is for "south-southwesterly 10–20 knots, fog clearing in the afternoon, forty percent chance of thunderstorms and rain. Fog reforming and becoming dense overnight," and I return to my warm sleeping bag.

I shall have to get used to Maine fog sooner or later. Visibility less than one-quarter mile, the trees rustling to a fresh breeze when I sail with two reefs down. A lot of wind and some swell through the gaps between the islands. A pleasant day's sail, each island appeared out of the fog on time as I dead reckoned through the islands of Merchants Row, then I turned downwind to run 10 miles along Deer Isle. The disturbed water gives a hint of the dangerous reefs just below the surface and with increasing wind I gybe into Pickering Island for lunch. I listen to the radio, a small craft advisory has been issued during the morning for winds of 20–25 knots.

Now there is open water to windward and swells from the Atlantic are bigger with a nasty cross sea superimposed. An occasional wave is much bigger as several waves combine—what John Buckingham (one of my past crews) would have described as "big sods." Reefs running out from the headland and island cause the swells to top up and crest.

Off Sheepshead Island, I can see calm water beyond and I am glad to reach it. The wind has dropped the last half hour but is building again as I pass between Wagle Island and Dunham Point, staggering as I come close-hauled to beat into the bay even with two reefs down. Camden Hills, blue on the horizon. Surfing on the front faces, I figure that it's best not to look behind. The most recent radio report says that all local places—Rockland, Martinicus, Southwest Harbor—are recording winds of 23–27 knots.

With wind increasing further, the best place for shelter is in Swain's Cove on Little Deer Island (where last year I sheltered from Hurrican Hugo) and even this weight of wind is no problem as I run to Little Deer Island and reach along the coast all in the wind shadow of the island. The last three nights have been warm.. Could it be summer at last? It is fortunate that the weather is colder in Maine so thunderstorms do not generate the violent winds so common further south.

23rd June, 1990. Mount Desert Island, Maine

I spend a whole day rowing down Eggermoggin Reach in torrential rain with lightening sizzling overhead for two hours. I'm cold and wet right through my oilskins as I call at the *Wooden Boat Magazine* and Boat Building School.. The staff there helps me tie up, then insists I join them for a hot evening meal. I am invited to attend lectures and boat building sessions—an invitation that I accept with alacrity. It is wonderful to see the knowledge and skills of a great craft being passed on by dedicated instructors to keen students.

24th June, 1990. Mount Desert Island, Maine

A small pram dinghy rows round the bay and stops for a chat and offers me the use of his mooring close under the shore if I stay. The fog is just lifting off the water but the hills are still shrouded. I make up an O'Brien adjustable knot for the tiller and another for the mainsheet traveller, something I learned from *Wooden Boat Magazine.* and it works well. I blow up my inflatable and row across to a big yacht that has arrived to ask for 'local knowledge further east.' They are not friendly or helpful.

Later, I attempt to tow *Wanderer* to another mooring more sheltered from the swell but I realise I am getting nowhere however hard I row. Each time I pull on the oars, the inflatable stretches then returns to normal as I lift the oars without moving *Wanderer.*

26th June, 1990

I have now cheered up. I had been getting very depressed with the unrelenting fog. Eight hours to cover eight miles today, but I've had a nice meal, quiet and enjoyable on the boat.

After my meal, I spread the chart to prepare for tomorrow and suddenly realise that I'm within 10 miles of Schoodic. The warnings about the place remain vivid in my mind and I study the chart with renewed interest.

A few miles beyond is Correa, perfect for a sheltered night; then comes Petit Manan with its notorious reef rising from a great depth to the surface and extending several miles offshore. Here, three currents meet and it needs care, and the sailing guide make it sound horrific. Surely it cannot be worse than England's Portland Bill or The Binks in the Humber Estuary? The thought cheers me up a little.

I begin to plan my route and timings. Care is needed, especially to avoid any wind-against-tide. My instinct tells me it is preferable to arrive at slack water and carry my tide north—but does slack water coincide with low water? Will the fog give me a clear passage or force me to dead reckon?

I have accepted that fog, strong tides, and Atlantic swells are to be my lot from here on.

Further south, I asked a man from Maine for an accurate description of Maine fog. "What size is your boat?" he inquired looking at *Wanderer*. "It's 16 feet," I reply. "Well, in your 16-foot boat you'll need to walk forward to see if you've set your genoa." I laughed heartily but I am to discover that he was not exaggerating.

27th June, 1990

The wind fills in; it is nice to have steerage way over these swells instead of rolling. Quickly, it increases dramatically and *Wanderer* is overpowered. Waves are cresting and there are all the signs of a lot more to come. I come about and pull down the first reef on port tack, tack and close-haul for Ironbound Island then Winter Harbor. Swells cresting with some weight, getting unpleasant but I decide to free off to run down to the smoother water in the lee of Ironbound. Surging diagonally down the seas, I am soon in smooth water; only one lobster boat on a mooring in Fish Cove, but it is open to the west across to Mount Desert. I heave-to for a bite to eat and to check the chart. My course is straightforward: through the narrows and onto course 160 degrees to windward; I follow the coast inside a green beacon and through the gap in the reef into harbour. However, there is a strong tidal set and I close haul through overfalls to get clear (I try tacking but am swept back each time).

Now there are huge gusts of wind and I am glad of my reef, white horses are everywhere, and I thrash to windward against a racing tide. I had not realised the tide sets so strongly into these long bays. The wind drops and after ten minutes and no renewal, I pull up full sail. Five minutes later the wind is back, and I reef again. The strong tide is sweeping me back, so immediately, I tack out to sea in order to short-tack along the shore. This is a dangerous thing to do as the area is littered with rocks. I cannot afford to lose steerage way; too much wind and stag-gering, and I can't reef any more as I shall lose too much ground. Slowly, *Wanderer* gains ground while I ease her through the squalls.

At last, I gain shelter of two rocky little islets, and heave-to for a second reef out of the tide and wind. Only just in time as it is already a two reef breeze now and increasing. Long and short tacking along the coast; I wave to fisherman and he motions that it is too rough for a small sailboat. I slip through a gap between the islands, tack round, surf down front faces of swells into a big bay. The swells are heavy so I come head to wind to ask people on the dock if there is a more sheltered spot in the harbour. "Around the next headland—a lobster man is harbour master. Follow the yacht now going in, tie up and he'll call," they tell me.

29th June, 1990. Schoodic to Jonesport, Maine

I round Schoodic at 9:15 A.M. and set course across the bay for Petit Manan with its three-mile long offshore reef. I plan to cross the reef at slack low water but the wind dies so I am one hour late; 'the passage' halfway along is narrow, the tide runs very hard through it, so once committed there is no turning back.

The marker buoy is small and I cannot spot it so I play safe and go round the end of the reef. There is no problem but it is still scary. At the end of the reef the tide accelerates suddenly and sluices eastward at two-and-a-half knots (judging by my speed past the lobster floats). I decide to use the whole of the north-going flood tide, and run out of wind and tide 33 miles later as I drift through Jonesport.

I arrive at Moosabec Reach. The town is spread along the north shore and the church spire reminds me that I have not been to church recently. I had considered Norton Island Bay as a possible anchorage but there are so many lobster boats that the wakes will be dreadful as they leave in the morning. The wind dies so that I just have steerage way and a low line of purple clouds are forming across the horizon astern and the sky above is wispy with the sun as a hazy indistinct outline. The wind increases quickly to 15 knots and two lobster boats slow to displacement speed as they cross *Wanderer*'s course and wave, pointing to the clouds astern which I am already watching anxiously. It is going to be a race to get in.

The buoys pass at great speed because of the tide. The tide slackens and there is no entrance visible even through binoculars. The wind dies a quarter mile short and I row in but it looks all wrong and I get out the chart to check bearings. This is Patton Cove and it dries so I row and sail to Bunker Cove; a lovely steep-sided remote-feeling cove with vertical rock walls on one side. By the time I have got out the anchor the tide has carried me too far in where I do not remember the depth and I row back and anchor as the rain increases. I put the tent up and sponge out and have a much needed hot meal. I am 10 minutes too late for a dry boat but it is nice to be under cover—dry and listening to the rain.

A dull overcast dark evening. Machias Bay is only 10 miles which Geoff Heath described as an excellent cruising area, then comes Cutler, and 15–20 miles of open coast to Eastport and Lubec. I'm tired—33 miles made good today.

I knew there was a main U.S. coastguard base at Jonesport so I tie up and walk into the office. I explain that I am heading for Grand Manan and my cruising guide does not cover the area so I had come in to draw on local expertise. I had heard the Bay of Fundy was a bit tidal.

"Jesus!" he says, appalled at my British understatement. "They're the biggest tides in the world!."

"What boat ya got?"

I point to *Wanderer* at the dock. He repeats the question: "Not your sailboat— what size is ya big yacht?"

"This is it—a Wayfarer."

"Jesus" is his only response.

I ask his advice: "I had planned to cross direct to the south end of Grand Manan…"

"No one goes that way. You'd best follow the coast north and round the north end of Grand Manan Island to North Head Harbour—it's where foreign yachts have to clear Canada Customs anyway." He tells me of the strong tides, rips, reefs, eddies, and whirlpools off the southeast of Grand Manan and he shows me a large scale chart of the area full of rocks and warnings.

"That's too far to sail in one day, so I'll keep close to the coast and then go through Lubec Narrows to Eastport for the night," I decide.

"There is a six-and-a-half-knot tide in the Narrows, eddies and whirlpools between the bridge and Mulholland Point, and the second biggest whirlpool in the world off Deer Island. I hope you've got a good motor."

" I don't have an engine." I don't want him to feel that I am unprepared so I add, "I do have a good strong pair of oars."

"Good Lord! You are going to need them through Lubec Narrows in a 16-foot open boat without a motor! Jesus! Well, you keep in touch by radio," he concedes.

This time, I hesitate before telling him that I don't have a VHF radio either.

"Watch for fog in the channel—it comes in real quick and the fishing boats are all using radar and they don't slow down," he says as I cast off from the dock.

It didn't seem to be the right time to mention that I don't have a radar reflector but that I plan to hang a plastic bucket full of crumpled aluminium foil in the rigging as I have heard it works quite well.

30th June, 1990

Today I intended snatching a passage as far as Eastport before the wind gets up but the forecast upped the southwesterly 15–25 knots to "small craft advisory 25–30 knots" and it pours with rain. I stay warm and dry inside the tent. I am surprised about how the temperature has dropped since I passed Schoodic.

Only 30 nautical miles to the U.S.–Canadian border!

I change the wave band on the weather radio—a Canadian forecast, loud and clear, followed by the French-Canadian translation! My first one!

1st July, 1990

A 'make and mend' day as the wind varied from nil to a faint breeze and back again all day. Not a single yacht in sight. I study my charts and the guide by Duncan and Ware. The chart finishes at Eastport, and Grand Manan is only shown on the passage chart to a very small scale. The Canadian customs for incoming yachts is on the eastern side of the Grand Manan Island, the tide runs fast in Grand Manan Channel—it may be an easier leg to cross from Eastport to the south end of the island and run up the eastern shore. The guide states there is good shelter at Haycock Harbor on the mainland in the pool but it is a difficult entrance to find.

I sort through medical boxes looking for coloured side shields for my glasses to protect from the glare of the water. I have looked everywhere else. Then I have another attempt to fit a stronger shockcord to the rudder downhaul—the standard is too light and allows the rudder to work up when running fast—an embarrassment, and even dangerous, when surging on the front face of a wave and the rudder suddenly loses grip.

2nd July, 1990. Bunker Cove, Maine

Last evening, I found my way into Bunker Cove on Roque. Only one yacht anchored under the cliff. I apologise for disturbing them as I drift past and I am invited aboard for coffee. One of the most beautiful sunsets spectacularly lighting the cliffs behind us—the prettiest sunset yet. I am told that the Cruising Club of America held their national rally in Roque Bay with 200 yachts packed in.

I row across the cove, anchor in the dark and am in bed within half-an-hour. I sleep feeling warm and wake warm for the first time…probably my wool shirt and trousers socks and pullover over my pyjamas helps. At 2:00 A.M. I suddenly realise the water is cold and I am shivering as I wake with a cold and aching back.

3rd July, 1990. Cross Island and approaching Canada

I wake to the following radio report: "A Front is coming in from Quebec. Grand Manan: South 15–25 knots, tomorrow southerly increasing to 25–30 knots. A small craft advisory has been issued." I had contemplated running for Eastport, but there will be too much wind unless I put into Haycock Harbour or possibly into Machias Bay. The anchor rope is covered in brown slime so I run my closed hand down the rope to drip it off. It's a trick I learned from a fisherman at Winter Harbor—it is efficient but messy and care is needed to prevent any fish-hook caught in the rope tearing fingers badly.

The strong tide triggers my thinking. I need to work the tides up this coast to Eastport—if I get it right I can double my speed, if I'm wrong I shall get nowhere. Today the tide ebbs south at two knots from 9:00 A.M. until 3:00 P.M., and the sea will be kicking up badly against a southerly wind. So I will delay until after lunch to make maximum use of the north-going flood. Longer term, I begin thinking about the strong tidal set when I cross the Bay of Fundy to Yarmouth—a 60 mile crossing and wind-against-tide conditions are bound to be bad and extremely dicey if I get caught out in a blow.

I turn Cross Island (American submarine communications centre) with its hundreds of masts, where it is said that no dog can live within 12 miles because of the ultra low frequencies used to talk to submerged submarines.

After so long heading 'down east,' at last the coast is heading northward again. I take a bearing on the next island and looking across the compass card I realise that I can see the island of Grand Manan 10 miles out in the Bay of Fundy. *Canada at last!* After 2,000 miles, how absolutely wonderful! Old Man Rocks ahead but I am no longer heading east but firmly on 70 degrees magnetic heading northward again and I refuse to be diverted.

I row two-and-a-half miles to the entrance of Little River watching the high clouds of the approaching Canadian weather front build high above me while awaiting the strong winds predicted. There are tide rips off the headland, wind comes in light and *Wanderer* sails into Little River fine reaching under her own power.

6th July, 1990. Haycock Harbor (just north of Cutler), Maine

A beautiful spot! I have found a delightful little cove. I was kept in Cutler because of the bad forecast enjoying the festivities of American Independence Day. The crew of a cruising yacht came in from Grand Manan and exclaimed, "It's almost gale conditions out there." By lunchtime it was blowing hard in the cove but the wind had veered into the northwest and was blowing off the land. It was really too late in the day to sail but I decided to risk it at 2:00 P.M. and I left with two reefs down and a strong flood tide under me.

There are a number of shallow bays along the coast with few distinguishing features and all are difficult to identify. "Haycock Harbor is difficult to find," says my guide, "...completely hidden until close under the cliff, only possible at half-tide but with deep water inside."

By my reckoning, at 5:00 P.M. I had been in the right bay but I failed to find the entrance so gave up and continued on for a night passage. I hove-to to re-check my navigation and returned for another look. This time I drop sails and row to within 25 yards of the swells breaking on the base of the cliff—and there was the entrance behind the rocky point, completely hidden, completely sheltered, and very pretty.

6th July, 1990. Lubec Narrows, Maine

At the lighthouse at West Quoddy Head I turn out of Grand Manan Channel and come north. Ten minutes later the wind picks up with a bang and *Wanderer* is almost planing on a broad reach, wind over the port quarter. The tide is ebbing fast and the waves are becoming short and steep wind-against-tide. This is exciting sailing, quartering downwind. A speed boat comes close and his wake, combined with the sea now running, is hazardous. A tower lighthouse marks the channel leading to the bridge and I free off into a dead run.

Now stemming a five knot current, I crawl slowly away but keep a careful eye on the tower astern—it is massive and I don't want it overtaking me if the wind drops! The narrows are clearly visible and I fit the kicking strap to prevent a spectacular gybe in the wind eddies under the high-level bridge. *Wanderer* is planing downwind at seven-and-a-half knots but approaching the bridge at less than one knot. I carefully line up and slowly creep through the exact centre of the middle span. The difficult bit is beyond the bridge for if *Wanderer* loses the wind in the shadow of the bridge she will be swept backwards at seven knots, and if she is not in line with the centre of the span she could be holed on a bridge pier, dismasted or capsized. It doesn't bear thinking about!

Beyond the bridge the passage narrows with overfalls but the wind holds and *Wanderer* crawls clear into eddies, tide rips, and overfalls that swing her violently. Eventually, clear of Mulholland Point, the narrows widens a little but tide is still fierce and I ease onto a broad reach to increase speed and get clear, then gybe across for Eastport.

I am eating my supper when a yacht comes in and I move along the dock to make room. It's a small yacht by American standards, the skipper looks competent, crewed by his wife and two small, tired children. I give him a hand to tie up then we chat about the local area. He had been cruising in the local waters of the Bay of Fundy and recommended White Head Island off the southeast side of Grand Manan: "A good harbour, no visiting yachts, completely sheltered, nice people." I ask if I would be able to purchase a folding radar reflector at White Head, as I had been unable to find one locally.

Just as I am leaving he comes across and presents me with a seven-inch folding radar reflector still packaged and priced. "I knew I had this somewhere in the boat. I've carried it as a spare for seven years and never needed it." He refuses payment and when I try to insist he suggests instead that a couple of postcards reporting on my progress would suffice. 'Richard Rockefeller' I read on his scribbled address. Fortunately, for once I manage to keep my mouth shut and didn't say: "You're not by chance related to…?" For, as I later discover, indeed he is!

7th July, 1990. Bay of Fundy

I am getting nervous about these strong tides—the guide has warnings galore! I finish writing up log at 7:25 P.M. I must cover my tent fully before the mosquitoes appear. I have no Canadian money or stamps. I assemble my new radar reflector and it comes together easily. It is an essential in the Bay of Fundy area because of fog, big ships and fishing boats.

I need some sensible, balanced information. I have been thinking about the crossing to Nova Scotia but without enough facts to work on! I need to know the dangers. I know there are bad overfalls off the far shore but how bad are they? At what at state of tide are they at their best and worst? How prevalent is fog in the centre of the Bay of Fundy and especially along the shores? How accurate are the fog and weather forecasts? What is the rate of the ebb or flood? Are there prominent landmarks on the far shore to give me my position so I can avoid the violent tide rips off Dingle Peninsular, or on this side of the bay to avoid the reefs off the southwest of Grand Manan if I have to return?

Why has no one ever built a canal at the top of Fundy across the neck of land to Northumberland Strait—it looks such an obvious short cut to the St. Lawrence and the interior of the continent? (Much later I discover that two canals had indeed been almost completed before economics and politics shut them down).

8th July, 1990. Campobello Island, New Brunswick, Canada

I arrive at a busy fishing harbour at the north end of Campobello Island for shelter from tomorrow's forecast gale. A fisherman on the quay tells me that the morning church service starts at 10:00 A.M. and the church is four miles away. Pleased, I note that I have plenty of time to walk. He laughs and tells me that I have crossed the Canadian border and I am in a different time zone (Atlantic time) and I have less than 10 minutes to cover four miles! (I make a mental note that my tide tables will need adjusting too!) The fisherman swings open the door of his pick-up and I jump in without thinking—a decision that I am to regret next day at the Canadian customs post!

I enjoy a well-attended service, and before the 'Greet Thy Neighbour' ritual, the minister requests: "All visitors please stand up, give us your name and let us know where you're from and why you're visiting."

Back at the harbour, I am introduced to the skipper of a fishing boat who brings his charts onto the wharf and I finally have the sensible, balanced information I had been looking for! "There is nothing to worry about if you go straight across from north end of Grand Manan. All the whirlpools and tide rips you have been told about are off the southwest of the island. North Head Harbour is well sheltered by a mole even from a southerly gale (which was my worry with tomorrow's forecast of heavy weather). There is an excellent harbour at White Head Island and he is surprised that I know of it. His uncle lives on the island.

My choice for crossing Fundy is either to sail straight across from North Head (Grand Manan) for the end of the long spit (Digby Neck); in this route the current is not dangerous though the seas break heavily off the end of the spit and shelter is not possible. Tide rips are not excessive: no dangerous overfalls on the line of this crossing as these are all on the south and southwestern side of Grand Manan. His alternative suggestion is that I go up to Saint John, New Brunswick and cross directly to Dingle but this is a 40 mile crossing with much stronger tides—fishermen reckon on four knots when fishing along the east shore, compared with the two knot current on the 30 mile direct deep-water crossing! "The thing to remember," he emphasizes " is if it is an afternoon tide then the southwesterly wind will come up in the afternoon and so will the sea!"

There are 'reversing falls' at Saint John, it is very pretty upriver with a friendly yacht club. There are a few deep water harbours on the western shore of Fundy but none on the eastern shore above Dingle; and there are a scattering of small harbours between Westport and Yarmouth—mostly high water only. Fog is generally accurately predicted: the traffic zone is for big ships and there are not many of them. I'm told to telephone traffic control before leaving. They will say if any ships are expected. It is a sensible appraisal and I feel much happier but with the reservation that the advice has come from one who, unlike me, has a powerful engine.

9th July, 1990. Campobello Island, New Brunswick

Wind comes in with a bang at 8:00 A.M., rain slashing down, must be a full gale outside. There are two American yachts sheltering from the gale who tell me they reported in to customs and were cleared by telephone.

When I telephone, of course, they want to see me! "Come into the customs post at the south end of the island with your boat's papers and passport." I return to *Wanderer* for my passport and small craft certificate of registry. A fisherman drives me the nine miles, and says, "Don't tell them you arrived yesterday—it will only confuse them."

The officer on duty says that they don't normally handle boat arrivals, but he can issue a three months cruising permit which can be renewed for a further period.

However, the boat cannot be left over winter except for repairs! He's about to stamp my papers when a woman officer walks in and takes over: "Have you just entered Canada?" she asks.

"Yes, through Lubec Narrows to Eastport and up to north end of island. I was heading for Grand Manan where I was told to clear customs. I came in to shelter from the gale," I answer.

She continues to question me. Eventually, I have to admit that I arrived yesterday and had even attended church.

"I know," she refers to her notes, "you arrived yesterday, your name is Frank Dye, you live in the east of England, you sailed from Florida, you are going to spend the summer sailing in Canada." She went on, "You landed and haven't reported to Immigration and Customs! This is a most serious offence!"

Shocked, I realise she is quoting word for word what I said when the minister asked me to tell the congregation why I was visiting their church. I remember seeing her too. When the minister said "Greet your neighbours" and I stood up to shake hands, I noticed a woman two rows behind me writing in a notebook—she must have been noting what I had said to the congregation—but I hadn't recognised her in uniform!

I apologise: "I didn't know there was a customs post on the island."

But she doesn't believe me and I think with exasperation: "Two thousand miles and I am about to be thrown out of Canada!" I can see them arguing in the inner office and I imagine the other officer is warning her: "If you deport him, the minister and congregation will say that you deported him for wanting to talk to God, and they'll ask you, 'who is more important: God or the Canada customs officer?'"

Instead, I get a stinging lecture, then she issues a three-day Immigration Permit and tells me to report to the area customs office in St. Andrews. I suggest North Head on Grand Manan as it is downwind. She is firm: "No. You report to St. Andrews within three days."

Meanwhile, the other officer has checked the book of regulations. I can only leave my boat in Canada over the winter for repair work in a boatyard, and Customs will want to see the repair order and they have the right to check on the work. There is definitely no way round the regulations. I inform him that I hope to carry on my cruise in Canada next spring and no repairs are needed. "The only way is to leave your boat in Eastport or somewhere else in the U.S.," he explains.

The female officer interrupts him: "You will be at St. Andrews within three days!" It is an order and I decide that this was not the right time to tell her that St Andrews is upwind, upcurrent, the tides are all wrong, and I don't think it's possible in three days! I leave feeling deflated.

The fisherman meets me outside and says: "I'm sorry about that Frank, I should have remembered she's a regular church-goer! She almost deported you though." I ask how he knew. "I was listening outside the window of course," he replies with a grin.

10th July, 1990. Deer Island, New Brunswick

Twenty-four-foot tides here and I'm tied to a fisherman's mooring post. This type of mooring is normal in this area. A telegraph pole is driven into the bottom with an inflated tire floating up and down with the tide. Boats tie to the floating ring.

11th July, 1990

8:00 A.M.: Ready to sail but there is a bank of solid grey fog at the end of the cove. Slowly, it thins from the top until it is hull deep as I row down the cove. Heading for St. Andrews, I find Little Letete Channel is shallow and blocked by a fish weir so I beat back to try another gap but sudden squalls put the gunwale under and *Wanderer* ships a dangerous lot of water, and its breezing up so I run back into the harbour behind the mole. A fisherman tells me to tie to his mooring post. It is a beautiful warm evening, white cotton-wool clouds—so attractive after more than 2,000 miles of clear, blue, hot sky.

The wooden posts in this harbour are fitted with a floating wooden raft instead of the more usual tires. When I tied up at 5:45 P.M. the top of the mooring post was level with *Wanderer*'s deck; now, just over an hour-and-a-half later the top of the post is level with my masthead at 23 feet! My home cruising ground in the North Sea has a tidal range of 12 feet but I am finding that the Bay of Fundy with the biggest tides in the world is something different. (A 30-foot rise and fall at the lower end of the Bay and 56 feet at the top end.) The other side of this island has the second largest whirlpool in the world!

"Wind in the afternoon," warns the forecast. So I decide to snatch a passage hoping that I can get across to St. Andrews before the strong wind sets in. I row across to the wharf with a note of thanks for the fisherman for my overnight mooring and two fisherman chat helpfully with me: "The ferry won't take you unless your boat is on a trailer." The second suggests going across Fundy towed behind a seiner: "Towing it will only take you a few hours—they go across all the time from north of here. Tell Young that I said he would tow you across." Two others arrive and chat about the tides in the Bay and the whirlpool off Deer Island—"the second largest in the world." One of them warns me to stay away from the tide rips and whirlpools "and especially the bridge at Lubec!" The other adds, "I heard he's sailed all the way from Florida and I saw him sail under Lubec Narrows bridge at full current."

Just short of Little Letete Passage there is lot of wind so I pull down two reefs.

Only 30 minutes after low water the tide is boiling through the passage against a strong west wind. From a distance, I can see the spume above the narrows—like the 'stromen' in North Norway. Short tacking to keep close under the land *Wanderer* is almost stopped by the breaking seas as I come about. This is no place to lose steerage way so the next tack I will go right across the bay where I can see there is a wider area of still water under the north shore. The wind begins to whistle round the mast. I already have two reefs down but the sail area is too little to keep her moving through these continuous short breaking waves, but if I hoist any more sail I risk a capsize.

This is very unpleasant indeed—there is continuous spray plus I run the danger of being stopped and losing steerage way and rolling in. I work clear into a little bay with a storm beach, shake out the second reef and back into the overfalls. Now the seas are longer but the current is running against the wind and seas are tripping over for at least a half mile. Several times water crests come solidly over the bows.

There is still a long thrash ahead: St. Andrews is four miles away, dead to windward. It would be sensible to run back. It is possible that I could get back through the narrows safely if I kept close to the side where the waves are not breaking so violently. The damned three-day temporary Immigration Permit is pressuring me into taking unacceptable risks! Ruefully, I decide that coping with the Immigration and Customs Department gives me more problems than the fearsome sailing conditions I am encountering.

Every five minutes there is a group of three waves, each bigger than the last, that come from nowhere—I luff the first, and *Wanderer* climbs it and almost stops, the second comes over the bows solid, the third stops her and I have to reverse the rudder to get her moving. Fortunately, there isn't a fourth!

Tacking becomes very fraught as the wind increases but I come round successfully and keep on the starboard tack so I can see if I am closing the land. At last, I am out of the hollow breaking seas. It is still rough but I shall be under the land in another one-and-a-half miles. I tack and sail into a patch of bad water where the wind has a longer fetch down the river against the tide. Finally, I am in the lee of the land and very thankful! Although I am in Canadian waters I am still flying my U.S. courtesy ensign as I have not yet officially cleared Canadian Customs and Immigration.

At St. Andrews at lunchtime the customs officer, Wally Jones, is friendly and helpful. He issues a 90-day cruising permit which will cover *Wanderer* for the summer. But he is customs only, and to clear immigration I must go another 18 miles upriver to St. Stephens! With great resignation, I explain that it has taken me two days to cover 10 miles from Campobello Island because of contrary wind, tide and bad weather—and I have been taking risks to do even that! Another 18 miles against the current with bad weather coming in is impossible in my one remaining day.

He laughs and picks up the telephone: "The immigration officer from St. Stephens will meet you here in St. Andrews at 3:00 P.M." I take the opportunity to ask for his help on my other major worry—I explain that the Canadian embassy in London told me there would be no difficulty in leaving *Wanderer* over winter; now I find that boats can only be left for repair not storage, and I point out that any repairs necessary I can do myself in a couple of hours. He tells me there are no exemptions but suggests that when I want to leave *Wanderer* I should contact a local customs officer and there will probably be not too much difficulty.

When I return there was an enormous black power boat alongside the dock flying a British flag, and registered in the Channel Islands. She is a beautiful boat, no expense spared—her flag is longer than my Wayfarer! The harbour master tells me she was built in Hong Kong, then shipped to the Bahamas, and British registered, and has been cruising in the U.S. for some years. Now U.S. Customs have decided they are abusing U.S. hospitality and told them to leave, so they intend moving to Canada until they are allowed back. The local customs officer (whom I found very helpful) must have thought they intended to abuse Canadian hospitality for he issued a permit for seven days only—with a warning!

12th July, 1990. St. Andrew's, New Brunswick

A beautiful, sunny morning, no wind yet and warm. For the first time this summer I do not eat my breakfast in my sleeping bag. I feel at peace with the world! I have time to see the town of St. Andrews, buy charts and change money, and still catch the tide. I pull in on the anchor rope and discover the anchor is snagged—absolutely solid—either round a boulder or foul of a mooring. I spend half-an-hour rowing round trying to free it.

The tide is rising quickly so I secure the rope to the bow mooring cleat and try to lift the anchor bodily. It pulls *Wanderer*'s bows down within three inches of the water and I hurriedly cast off before she is pulled under. There is a short nylon rope on the anchor so I heave this up to the surface to buoy it, but the tide is now rising so quickly that I am working elbow deep, my hands so cold and turning white that I fumble and lose the end, and the rope and anchor are gone. I swear viciously at the loss of my best anchor, a sliding grapnel ideal for rock and weed!

Friday the 13th July, 1990

The Magaguadavik River (pronounced 'mac-a-davy') is one of the prettiest I have seen with rocks and bluffs, vertical cliffs, meadowland, coves, and sandy beaches, granite cliffs, and fir trees. It's narrow and the tide is taking me along

---

without effort. *Wanderer* is passing buoy no. 13 in the nicest river ever, light winds, bright sun, pleasantly warm, the tide rushing me upriver—if this is 'unlucky 13' it is beautiful and I don't really want to go back to sea!

The river narrows even more and I sail under vertical cliffs—not a single yacht in sight and only a couple of houses. At St. George's Basin, I tie to the only mooring and, in the evening, walk to the bus station to collect a new anchor sent by the chandler in Saint John. There is no anchor on the bus and I walk away depressed by the thought of another day moored, but the driver calls me back.

He gives me a box addressed to 'Dye and Wanderer.' I unpack the new anchor I had ordered. I assess it and reckon it is alright. I had wondered if four pounds was heavy enough as my sliding grapnel was five pounds. This anchor is purported to have "300 pounds holding power, five-pound weight, for boats to 16 feet, up to 20 knots." The galvanising is bright but sharp where it has dripped and my first job will be to clean it off with a file before it cuts into the gel coat.

Mrs. Holmes, the baker, calls me into the shop as I walk past and asks if I would like a loaf of bread straight out of the oven? I drift off to sleep eating hot crusty bread with lashings of butter in my sleeping bag—one of the great unforgettable pleasures of cruising.

16th July, 1990. St. Croix River, New Brunswick

The fog is very dense. I can only just see the wharf! As the fog thins, I can see a vague outline of St. Croix River so I cast off quickly as the wind is easterly and ideal for sailing up river. I can pick out St. Croix Island but beyond is vague. I have no chart but I am sailing from my memory of a chart in the bookshop. The tides are strong, the buoys leaning to it, and leaving long wakes. The tide does not turn but light towers on all the bends make navigation easy.

A pleasant sail up river past a few houses on the Canadian side at the bends with boats on moorings. The light towers are distinctive pyramid structures painted white. At the end of the reach there are narrows with the tide sluicing through. I am afraid I may arrive at St. Stephens before the tide slacks off and get carried under the town bridge so I rig an anchor ready to use.

The wind drops, then dies, and I row. Last bend and the town not yet in sight, the tide has turned and the buoys are leaning the other way! I put my back into rowing helped now by a light breeze, as I don't want to be swept back downriver. Anchoring will be difficult as I am without a chart and have no idea of the position of channel in the river, depth or type of bottom. An anchor may drag in the strong tide, and hooked in the bare bottom of the channel so it is essential to anchor in the shallows on mud—but what is the range of tide?

Thunder clouds gathering quickly upriver and the wind comes from ahead at

10 knots. I beat up the U.S. shore to cheat the strong tide. The town wharf is on the Canadian side of the river with a floating dock, so I stand across looking for an eddy to help. A fierce tide is running down past the wharf and for several tacks I wonder if I'll make it but luckily, a helpful lad grabs my forestay and holds on.

19th July, 1990. Deer Island, New Brunswick

The forecast is for southwesterlies of 20–25 knots gusting to 30 knots. Westerly overnight, becoming southerly gusting to 30 knots again. High water at 10:00 A.M. I want to get through Little Letete passage not later than one hour into the ebb. Three hours after low water. *Wanderer* approaches Little Letete Passage and I heave to and view it carefully through binoculars. There is no sign of white horses, but I know the current must be running strongly. There is a haze over the water as in the maelstroms of North Norway and it makes me uneasy. I must be careful to avoid the wake of any fishing boat running against the current—it will be confused and dangerous! I put my lifeline over my shoulders and a line on the baling bucket (the two things I do not wish to lose) and head straight through.

Wanderer accelerates and leaves the wind behind, then even faster to cause a light headwind! I sweep through. A ferry is crossing the channel and causing standing breakers from her bow wave and wake. They are heavy, stationary relative to the land, breaking heavily but *Wanderer* with the speed of the current under her, bursts through them before I can think. I recover my breath and vow not to do that again.

At the point I meet the ebb running round the end of Deer Island and down-channel towards Head Point. I just hold my own against the current but the wind dies and *Wanderer* is swept back almost to the Marker Tower. The wind fills in from the east and *Wanderer* gains ground only to be swept back again. No sign of the forecast of southwesterlies gusting to 30 knots which would help. The radio repeats the forecast but adds, "Eighty percent chance of thunderstorms or heavy rain." This is too much like banging ones head against a wall! I am all too aware that tides must be worked and respected here!

I take out my oars and row towards East Quoddy lighthouse. Travelling fast at four to five knots I decide to use the great eddy off the top end of the island again. The lighthouse approaches quickly on the tide, then I am going sideways as I pull into the tide rip off the point and through the weed marking the edge of the eddy. *Wanderer* lurches sideways as she feels the current at three knots, then I am travelling round the whirlpool in a great circle with an occasional pull on my oars to avoid the worst of the rips. Opposite Head Harbour I row out of the eddy—almost like stepping off a round-a-bout at a fairground!

Sailing to the Edge of Fear

20th July, 1990

Tonight, I write in my log by lantern light to dry the boat out. There was a strong flood tide against me out in the sound but I discovered an equally strong eddy close under the cliffs, so I sailed gently within 20 feet of the cliff, letting the tide do the work. Suddenly, I came unexpectedly on the lighthouse at the north end, it's most impressive with the red cross of St. George emblazoned across it. Rain started, and has been heavy and continuous since. It has been enjoyable to work the tides successfully all day.

I am now within sight of Grand Manan Island. It's only six miles direct across the narrowest part of Grand Manan Channel, but the tides run fast so I shall need to allow a considerable tidal offset, and with the great fog bank always present in the middle of the channel, and 200-foot cliffs, I had better get it right. If I cannot find Dark Harbour and have to run down the island the south and east sides have tide rips particularly dangerous on the ebb so the whole thing needs care.

Dark Harbour, opposite Eastport, has a big sheltered lagoon with a narrow entrance only possible at slack high water. This may be the answer although the sailing guide states ominously: "Wise yachts do not linger here." My choice is from Eastport direct to Dark Harbour or I can round the north end of the Island if I miss slack water at Dark Harbour entrance.

23rd July, 1990. Passamaquoddy Bay, New Brunswick

I am now just inside the headland to the east of Eastport. The fogs of the Bay of Fundy do add a new dimension to cruising—frustration! I tried to sail down the outside of Campobello Island on Saturday but was met by great banks of fog offshore which I raced back into harbour as they came rolling in.

On Sunday, I rowed down the inside (west) of the island and tied up to a wharf near Lubec Narrows at 7:00 A.M., intending to dash across to Grand Manan. A woman from New Jersey drove me round the U.S. side of Passamoquoddy Bay where she has bought a waterside piece of land frequently visited by moose, and she says they are huge animals—like an enormous horse. I haven't seen one yet.

Leaving Passamoquoddy Bay, I aimed to pass through Lubec Narrows (the tide runs at six-and-a-half knots) at slack water but the tide was flooding early and running hard, and I had to draw on all my skill to cheat the tide, going inside the reefs and behind the rocks, using every back eddy and shallow patch, and at last using the oars as well as sail to give me enough speed to beat the current between the bridge piers. Looking back, I thought, "That was very well done; what a pity no one was watching!"

I felt my way into the shallows under Quoddy Head in dense fog and anchored on rock. After three days waiting for the fog to lift so I can slip across to Grand

---

Manan, I am still anchored. I can't believe its the same world as a few days ago when it was unbearably hot, fair winds, the sun blazing down out of clear blue skies! Yesterday was cold and foggy. Torrential rain all last night—unbelievably heavy even compared to the thunderstorms of Chesapeake Bay and New Jersey!

This morning it is grey, clammy, depressing, nil visibility. The rain washes the fog out of the air then it rolls in again. The weather radio reports that some places have reported 100 millimetres in the last 18 hours and can expect 100 millimetres in the next 24 hours. Surely, there cannot be any rain left!

Food is running low. I finished the last of the bread for breakfast; there is only a quarter of a gallon of water left and one quart of apple juice. I can do without food, but not water.

29th July, 1990. Crossing to Grand Manan (at last)

Slowly, Grand Manan shows as *Wanderer* sails through the fog that lies permanently over Grand Manan Channel. The trees and the top 20 feet of cliff materialise vaguely above the fog bank. Dark Harbour is the only break in 18 miles of cliff so I ought to be able to pick it out easily. I can already see a roadway leading down the cliff. If it is the road down to Dark Harbour there ought to be some sign of an entrance but there isn't! Is it Dark Harbour? I heave-to to check and stand up to scan the shore, then close-haul in to check.

The wind is increasing, with spray flying and I am getting soaked so I roll up the genoa. No sign of the harbour or lagoon close under the cliffs, the road has disappeared, and a dense fog bank is coming up from the south end of the island. The chart shows a channel through the stone bank at the south end and I run down to look but there is no sign of it. Fishermen are hauling a dory up the shingle bank further along so I sail in to ask, but the men have disappeared. I sail to north end of the shingle bank where there is a wood tower but still there is no entrance into the harbour. I heave-to and check the chart and guide, then completely baffled give up and set off for north end of Grand Manan.

Looking back from a quarter mile further north, I can see a narrow gulley running obliquely back behind the beach. This *is* the entrance to Dark Harbour. It is spectacular, intriguing, very narrow, less than 20-feet wide, almost dry, with a pile of rocks in the middle, with cliffs towering 200-feet above the entrance, at an impossible angle above the tower and some wood training works, and again I am struck by what is an incredibly narrow entrance.

It's a fascinating harbour—the sort I like. I am going in—it is too unusual to miss in spite of what the guide says! The coast southwards disappears into a grey fog. I heave-to, waiting for the channel to flood with the incoming tide. Two hours later, I drop sails and row in with just two feet of clearance at the end of the oar blades. "What's your name? You the Englishman we heard about?" greets a fisherman (it was another reminder that fishermen miss nothing of what is happening on the water in their area). A hard row against wind now force 4. Another fisherman comes across: "Tie to the fish farm, its not used and it will give you shelter." I ask him about 'the southern entrance' shown on my chart. "That was closed by a hurricane in the 1920s. The new channel was bulldozed at the north end and the charts were never altered. It doesn't matter—everyone here knows!"

It is a magnificent harbour, with 300-foot cliffs all round the bay, a storm beach of boulders protecting the big lagoon from the sea. There are now occasional white horses inside the harbour but *Wanderer* is well sheltered in the lee of the fish farm. I look around at the pleasant scene of small houses, used only when the islanders are harvesting dulse—an edible seaweed—and a large number of working dories all painted yellow and well maintained. I feel deeply satisfied and pleased to be in Grand Manan at last and I celebrate!

I unpack my inflatable tender, paddle across the lagoon, and walk up the steep dirt road to find a telephone. I watch two men playing 'Horseshoes.' The game looks easy and I make the mistake of saying so. Immediately, I am challenged to a game and my first three throws don't even reach the peg! One of the men offers a lift to a phone and we climb into an open jeep. "Put on your seat belt." Surprised, I ask if seat belts are compulsory on Grand Manan? "No but I sometimes lose my passengers on the sharp bends, not having any doors," he replies without a smile.

31st July, 1990. Dark Harbour, Grand Manan, New Brunswick

Marine forecast: "Grand Manan—storm force winds. Easterly 20–30 knots this afternoon, northerly 20–40 knots this evening, backing winds increasing to 40–50 knots overnight. Tropical Storm 'Bertha' has been uprated to a Hurricane again." Nasty! *Wanderer* will get a battering as Dark Harbour is exposed to winds from north round to east with minimum wind protection over the low storm beach barrier. I decide to get out and sail for the other side of the Island. Unfortunately, the ebb is running south against me but with an easterly wind I should be fine reaching and able to overcome it. Once round the headland I shall be in North Head Harbour before the afternoon Easterly 20–30 knots gets up. The harbour there is protected from the north and I can find things to do in town.

I am sluiced out of the channel at 8:45 A.M. one hour after high water. There is no wind at all under the cliffs and the tide is roaring southward. Rowing offshore for wind, I pick up a light breeze one mile out. It is a pleasant sail but one hour later I am still off Dark Harbour. It is an impossible situation—offshore there is wind but a very strong foul tide setting quickly southward: inshore the current is slacker but there is no wind.

I go further out and find a fair slant which allows me to lay the far headlands close-hauled but the tide sets me in, and under the cliffs the wind draws ahead and I am beating.

10:30 A.M.: There is a big eddy under the cliffs and I take *Wanderer* in to use it. The squalls blowing down off the 300 foot cliffs are vicious—it is too damned dangerous! I gain a lot of ground but it is not worth the risk. There is no warning sign of an approaching squall on the water as the willywars are blowing down vertically, and freeing the sheets does not relieve the boat.

11:40 A.M.: Four hours after high water and the tide begins to slacken a little and *Wanderer* is making more progress. The wind is slowly backing, gusting and gradually increasing so I put in the first reef. I am not feeling happy here. I am in the shelter of the land and I am wondering what conditions will be like beyond the headland where it is open to the Bay of Fundy. And probably with swells running in from hurricane 'Bertha' out in the Atlantic as well. The wind increases and I ought to pull down a second reef. Instead, I review my options and decide it is not sensible to carry on so I turn tail and run back, I shall be off Dark Harbour just before low water with two to three hours to wait before I can get into the channel. The forecast is for a hard northerly coming in this evening so 4:00 P.M. should give me a safe margin. Running with the first reef down and a couple of heavy gusts almost make *Wanderer* broach to.

1:30 P.M.: I am back at Dark Harbour. The net-boat has gone off the mooring—probably towed into the harbour because of the storm warning, so I tie to her buoy. I strip off my oilskins and have lunch. Wind backing into the north. I hope it is not the northerly shift for this evening coming in early! Three herring boats, one towing the net boat, head north for the other side of the island to shelter in North Head Harbour.

An hour later the wind has settled into the north and increases by 10 knots. I feel exposed with hurricane 'Bertha' in the area, the wind increasing, and a swell building along the shore—all this and nowhere to go until the channel floods. I know from my arrival that I cannot get in until the stone patch in the entrance is covered. A herring pump-out boat comes across to ask if I am alright: "There's a lot of wind coming today," they shout. " The local men will be taking their net boat in later and you should go in with them." Occasional swells are beginning to roll along the beach. This is all very worrying! Soon seas will be breaking across the entrance.

4:30 P.M.: It is two hours after low water, at last the stone bank is just covering, and I decide to feel my way into the channel as I am getting very nervous about the way the swells are building. Once in the gulley I shall be safe although I still have to wait for the level to rise before I can float out at the top end into the lagoon.

I shall have to get the sail down quickly (I cannot luff up as the current will sweep me out to sea) and I need just enough speed to take *Wanderer* slowly over the remaining ebb so I put in a second reef. The passage along the beach is no longer possible because of the swell so I wait for a smoother patch of sea and keep to the lee side of the stone patch. I am in the worst possible place, with the current setting *Wanderer* down onto the stone patch, and about to gybe into the narrow gulley, when the wind dies. I grab an oar to fend off but a sudden puff of wind slams the boom over and *Wanderer* is safely inside.

There is a risk of losing the rudder on rocks drifting astern so I stick an oar between the boulders in the bed of the channel as a stern stake and allow *Wanderer* to settle back onto it. As the water level rises I tie to the wood staging, and treat myself to instant porridge.

5:00 P.M.: The tide is flooding fast and I know it will flood over the inner bar exactly three hours after high water. Ten minutes later I scrape over the rocks into deep water. Now I must find maximum shelter if I am to survive tonight's storm of 40–50 knots. I tie to a float at the abandoned fish farm in the lee of two huts. The huts are sub-

White Head Island, Bay of Fundy. Thirty-feet tides—a long climb each morning.

stantial and will resist the storm but the rafts are only lightly tied to the main pontoons, so I collect some lengths of rope and moor them securely. Then I put out my fenders, and bow and stern ropes, springs and a long rope to the outside raft just in case I need to swing clear! I notice that there is a 20 degree compass variation so a northerly might just bring the wind over the cliff rather than over the low beach, and give more protection.

2:00 A.M.: It is a beautiful clear starlit night. There is no dew so I sit on the bows drinking tea. There is no moon but the whole lagoon is lit by the myriads of bright stars, no wharf lights or house lights either, all is completely still, and quiet, the only movement is the regular sweep of the beam of the light house beyond the cliff top.

3rd August, 1990. Grand Manan Passage

A lovely, sunny sail, beating south, past great 200-foot cliffs, 18 miles of dramatic iron-bound coast, with no possibility of shelter or a landing. I pass Ashburton Head, named after the sailing ship *Lord Ashburton*, which was wrecked here in the last century. It's a horrifying story. She safely reached Saint John, New Brunswick after two months sailing from Europe but a gale was blowing and she couldn't enter harbour. The next day hurricane force winds drove her back down the Bay of Fundy until she struck under these 200-foot cliffs. Of the whole crew and passengers only seven men survived by climbing the cliffs in snow and subzero temperature.

6th August, 1990. White Head Harbour (off Grand Manan)

The fishermen are friendly and welcoming; the harbour well-sheltered and the tides are enormous—I have a 30-foot climb to the quay. Fortunately, a fisherman told me to tie to his boat when I sailed in, otherwise I would have needed enormous lengths of rope to cope with the rise and fall. It has been continually foggy except one day when I ventured to an island nature reserve and almost got swept clear of White Head by the ferocious ebb on my return. The staff were doing a study of the Leeches Petrel which Marg and I saw on St. Kilda flying back to their burrows after dark. The warden was surprised I knew the birds and opened some burrows—the parents very small, chicks twice the size. The birds spend most of their life at sea and it always amazes me that such a frail minute bird can survive in the harsh north Atlantic.

Fog horns sounding mournfully. The fishing boats leave early but there are no wakes—everyone must be throttling back as they pass *Wanderer*. It is silent—thick fog must be blanketing every sound. Opening the tent flaps the fog rolls into the boat. It is dense indeed and I cannot see 50 yards across the harbour. Slowly, the fog thins to 200 yards by mid-morning, but by 1:00 P.M. it is dense again. It is essential to grab a passage across Fundy as soon as visibility allows. Yesterday that was possible but today it is not. I am told that it may be days before the fog clears.

The boat I am tied alongside is going out to lay a longline at 5:00 A.M. tomorrow and I ask if I may join them. Barry Russel tells me he is baiting up tonight and invites me to watch. He does one tub and his father the other. They use circular hooks which I have not seen before, which he says are better than J-type as they hold better, lose fewer fish, don't pull straight, and don't catch up in the tub. I try my hand but it is not as easy as it looks and I am very slow but I stick at it—the baited hooks are laid point down to the further side of the tub, rope laid to keep the whole surface level. They explain that the rope is taken over a steel barrel between two pegs mounted on the stern and the baited hook flicks into the air as it runs out over the drum. Hauling-in, the line is lead between the pegs which pull the hook out of the fish automatically. The catch is cod and halibut.

I am given fresh herring, and, fried in butter for supper, it is a gourmet experience. I set my alarm for 4:30 A.M.

8th August, 1990. White Head Island (Southeast of Grand Manan)

There has been continuous fog since I arrived in White Head waiting for the right conditions to cross the Bay of Fundy. I am not prepared to take any risks in this area—its dangers are well known (whirlpools, tide rips, fog, big tides, strong currents on the ebb) I am investigating the possibility of a tow by a boat fishing off 'The Soundings' halfway across the Bay of Fundy which would put me clear of the offshore reefs, or by a fishing boat seine-netting further across. Ten days in fog is too much even though I was warned that "It may never clear" when I arrived.

13th August, 1990

When I wake, I am greeted by the following: "There is a small craft warning and a wind warning for all areas; over 20 knots this afternoon and into Tuesday. southeast going southwest on Wednesday. Fog banks." Damn! I am frustrated, tired and irritable. However, despite the frustration of spending 12 days in fog, much of it has been enjoyable and the time passed quickly. The village store is the centre of island life as on all offshore islands, and there is a great deal going on, all discussed at the morning coffee session. Saturday, there was a general exodus to a festival, concert and fireworks on Grand Manan. The fog clamped down, extremely thick mid-morning, and I asked if the ferry would be running. "Of course" was the confident reply. When I asked how they could be so certain in nil visibility one of the men replied, amid general laughter: "Ah. The captain is going to the fireworks. Anything important we always find out if the captain has bought a ticket." It was an excellent concert and humorous revue of the last year on Grand Manan, written and acted by the islanders. The fireworks were cancelled.

Now I do need a tow clear of the 'Old Proprietor,' 'Bulkhead Rip,' 'Devil's Half Acre' and the other reefs as I cannot risk being set down onto them if the wind dies. Best to aim for Petit Passage through Dingle peninsular rather than Grand Passage. Brier Island at the end of the peninsular has heavy rips, and the passage much stronger tides than Petit Passage with violent eddies in mid-channel. Beyond Dingle Neck, there are plenty of small harbours in St. Mary's Bay and some small half-tide harbours. I am experiencing the worst fog yet.

14th August, 1990. Across the Bay of Fundy

I walk round to the store for groceries and the regular evening chat and to ask if anyone is fishing at 'Old Proprietor' as I would like a tow clear of the reef. A fisherman erupts into the store shouting: "Frank, there's a herring carrier going across tonight. They are leaving in 10 minutes. Do you want to go?" "Yes," I accept immediately. My groceries are abandoned: "I'll put them back on the shelves, Frank," says the storekeeper, and the fisherman drives me back to the wharf.

Fortunately, *Wanderer* is almost ready and I row out. The herring boat has already left the quay and I throw them my anchor line as they pass the harbour entrance. I slack off the rope until *Wanderer* is riding comfortably on the back of their stern wave, then tie rudder amidships, pull the centreboard up, and I am being towed at 10 knots. I huddle down on the floorboards out of the wind, suddenly realising that I do not know where we are heading.

"Come aboard and have a coffee," the skipper says leaning over his stern. "I'd like to see how she handles first," I reply. I pull on my rubber boots for warmth. I have no socks as they are in the stern locker, no pullover or warm clothing.

There is a lot of weight on the rope which is turned up on the mooring cleat. For safety I take a turn round the second cleat then realise that if one pulls out with the strain so will the other! So I ask the herring carrier to reduce power, and I take the first turn round the mast then onto the cleats, then, as security against chafe, I add my nylon lifeline onto the towrope with what I hope is a rolling hitch. Beyond this, I can do nothing more. I grab my camera and oilskins, board the herring carrier, then stand at the stern watching *Wanderer* following behind. Although I have done all I can, I still worry and feel lonely. The crew, a young lad, joins me and asks sympathetically, "You get attached to a boat, don't you?"

I watch *Wanderer* until the light goes and they switch on the deck lights. The carrier is empty and rolls heavily with the deck weight of her pumps and equipment, but *Wanderer* follows serenely on the back of her stern wave. A slight beam swell develops and the skipper moves the tow rope to her quarter and *Wanderer* follows placidly; fishermen know more about towing small boats than the amateur will ever learn! I ask where we are heading: "Three hours steaming to the weir at Sandy Cove, Dingle Neck, five miles north of Petit Passage." I can't remember it from my charts which are packed away in the stern locker so I ask to see theirs, but they don't carry charts as the skipper has sailed these waters since he was a boy and knows the waters like the back of his hand.

It's now 9:40 P.M. and an hour into the tow and I'm feeling relieved. The radar shows *Wanderer* is still following. Spectacular lightning storm ahead, continuous and vivid. Ship coming down but we shall pass ahead of her. I check my compass against ships head and the radar picture.

12:15 A.M.: I board *Wanderer* in the illumination of the deck lights and cast off into a black night. Check gear by flashlight: everything is safe and I row off. The high land is a blacker shadow in the black night. I can hear a slight swell breaking on the beach so I keep what I hope is 30 yards off as I row along. The moon rises quickly in the sky and I am 100 yards from some stakes. The cove is open to the north and northwest and it will be more open when the rocks cover. I feel cold, wind from the southwest at five knots so I cover myself with a plastic sheet. My bare feet are cold but socks are still buried in the stern locker. The penalty of a quick departure with no time to prepare anything before the tow: I hadn't even looked at the chart but at least I am safely across Fundy. Wayfarer towed well; no loss or breakage, and I know roughly where I am—somewhere about five miles north of Petit Passage.

Daylight at 6:00 A.M. and over breakfast aboard *Wanderer* I reflect how many mistakes had been made—no warm clothing, no oilskins, no charts, no food available. They were all out of reach in the stern locker.

15th August, 1990. Dingle Neck, Nova Scotia

A chilly day, light breeze. I examine the chart. Dingle Neck is a long narrow promontory separating Fundy from Nova Scotia—there is a warning that the tide reaches seven knots in the passage. I hail a lobster boat for information.

1:00 P.M.: In the narrows and the wind dies. Blast! It is going to be a long pull. The tide is already running in mid channel. I work along the shore, looking for a reverse eddy. A long pull as close as possible to the rocks, occasional gusts make *Wanderer* heel. I must ask for a tow if anyone comes along but all the boats are on the other side of the channel and too far away. I find a reverse-running eddy at last which carries me easily to a mooring. Obviously I cannot get through this passage until the ebb so I relax gratefully in the bright sun. Had I been a few minutes earlier I would have made it through the passage—the current must change direction before low water. Another lesson learned—start early and do not assume that current changes direction at the time of high water.

17th August, 1990. Meteghan, Nova Scotia

The mainland of Nova Scotia at last: Meteghan on the 'French Shore,' so named as it was settled by Acadians, French farmers known, among other things, for their great expertise for draining swamp land and successful farming in lowlaying areas. It might have been sensible to wait for favourable tides spending some days in a fascinating area and learning of the local Acadian culture, waiting for the two week lunar cycle to bring favourable tides to the early morning. It would have given me the chance to explore the area and the Acadian culture but the season was drawing on, there were great headlands to be rounded, and I had already experienced the frustration of continuous fog.

With the benefit of hindsight, I realise that I am allowing the immediate difficulty, that of crossing the Bay of Fundy to Nova Scotia—to absorb all my attention to the detriment of longer term planning for the South Shore. The guides tell me that the tides drop off very quickly once round this corner of the land and I was soon to find how dangerous these Bay of Fundy driven tides could be.

This is a vast continent and an endless shore and I was well aware that I could enjoy the rest of the season and possibly the following season as well, exploring it locally.

20th August, 1990

Beating up to the St Mary's Headland, past the great cliffs. There are dangerous overfalls off the headland and I time my arrival for slack water. The wind is uncooperative and the tide turns against me. By the time I arrive at the headland I am not gaining an inch to windward each tack because of the rapidly increasing current. There is an appalling area of broken water and I notice a fishing boat is careful to keep well clear of the race. It is just possible to clear it provided I can work sufficiently upwind another half mile. I sit out and drive to windward and gain 200 yards but no more. It is a real bad race and getting worse as I watch. Either I go through it now while I may, or I run back to Meteghan and forfeit all the ground I have gained and return tomorrow. I look at it critically—it is getting worse and in 10 minutes it will be impossible.

Wanderer will be thrown about and lose a lot of the wind in her sails but I must have the certainty of steerage way when I enter the race, so I hoist full sail before entering the overfalls. Conditions are very unpleasant indeed, waves roaring about, cresting and breaking unexpectedly in every direction.

Suddenly, *Wanderer* trips over a wave halfway across and the centreboard jumps up as she falls with a crash into a hole and I have to free off to regain speed. I can see a bad patch ahead and go to leeward. *Wanderer* is being set down onto the reef end and I close haul to windward. Several crests break over the beam (my real worry is of *Wanderer* putting her bows under). I can see the smooth water beyond with the nastiest patch of breaking pyramid waves yet in between. I free onto a reach and give *Wanderer* her head and I concentrate on each breaker, one at a time.

Suddenly, I am clear, planing down regular crests running in from the ocean. I crawl down the side of the reef, sweating from tension. I give *Wanderer* a pat and congratulate her, then bail out. The breakwater is ahead, the bay behind almost dry and the harbour behind the jetty. I land as the fog rolls in.

The fisherman from the boat I saw skirting the race comes across. With a thick French accent he says, "I saw you at the rip. I not realise or I give you a tow. I say to my crew, 'Mon Dieu, le bateau anglais, he go through centre of the rip!'" He went off into staccato French and I made out a couple more "*Mon Dieus*" then he cut off a plug of chewing tobacco and handed it across saying, "You did well; you deserve this!" We chatted later about the area and he told me that the Bay of Fundy and the offshore Georges Bank is the richest fishing area in the world but also the roughest. Winter fishing is hard and dangerous!

My only guide is a small-scale passage chart showing no detail except the main offshore shipping buoys, so navigation is basic—I count off the appropriate number of headlands and turn left into the third long estuary. The Selveges are hundreds of acres of low tide reefs, reaching out into the Atlantic, hidden at high water, waiting to rip the bottom out of a straying boat. At low water, when I pass, it is a frightening sight. All the sailing directions recommend a long passage offshore from buoy to buoy but the pleasure of coastal cruising is 'exploring.' I am fortunate in the weather, calm seas, light winds but this is the stuff that dreams are made of—or rather nightmares for the sailing man—and for many nights I dream of hundreds of acres of reefs rising suddenly from a deep bottom to rip the bottom out of an unsuspecting vessel, unmarked except for a lonely light tower hidden in the fog.

23rd August, 1990. Woods Harbour (northwest of Cape Sable Island)

9:24 A.M.: A late morning in bed. There is a foul tide of four-and-a-half knots. The last few days have the most interesting of the cruise so far. Fog horns booming off-shore all night.

I left Wedgeport yesterday to cross the bay in light wind and sun and got completely lost. I had

Dried out in Hell's Gate, a passage cut through the reef inside Great Tusket Island, used by fishing boats to avoid the strong tides, rips, and occasional "square" waves of Schooner Passage.

sailed off the north edge of my chart and then got confused by a lighthouse which I didn't think ought to be there! I should have gone into Pubnico Harbour as the wind was dying and the chart warns of difficult tide in the channel.

A long, hard beat against a foul tide just beginning to run and rapidly increasing. I push into a lovely anchorage behind Woods Harbour rather than tie up to a fishing boat.

27th August, 1990. Little Harbour Cove, Nova Scotia

According to the chart, there are four rocks in line along the coast, and then I am to turn into a cove. I clear the last rock, turn left and locate the green buoy. It is a fine sheltered cove with a government wharf at the far end. I decide to stay as the forecast is poor, with wind and fog. I could get to Jones Harbour which has a wharf but it appears from the chart that the wharf faces south so I may not be too sheltered and the fog in already coming inshore.

29th August, 1990

7:30 A.M.: I wake and enjoy the boat as I always used to do. Wind is 10–15 knots.

11:00 A.M.: The wind gets up quickly and the fog is rolling in from the sea in great banks.

11:30 A.M.: The wind is 'whistling' through the rigging of the fishing boats.

The wind goes round twenty degrees and is a steady moan all evening as it continues blowing. Fog, with visibility less than 50 yards, prevails even with this strong wind. "The northwest wind tomorrow should clear the fog," remarks a fisherman, and we chat about the old wooden 'double-ender' hauled up and rotting on the bank. "The old boats always were double enders. The old men say they were superb sea boats—best there was for their length." He had recently had his 40-foot boat *Karl and Jackie* sheathed over the wood hull. "This is a hard coast—there's times you need a good boat." "Weather was bad last winter," he explains. He recounted that after one trip a gale was blowing 35 knots when he finished hauling his trawl; 65 knots by the time he got in. He thought every sea was his last and it took him three hours. "A good sea boat but she's wood and 17-years-old, and it made me decide it was time to have her sheathed."

In my experience, it is rare that fishermen talks like this to a yachtsman about the conditions they sometimes work in and I am flattered. I could so easily visualise the weather, and the fight to survive—every comber likely to be the last—the loneliness, the violence of the storm, the fear and the cold. I think how hard a life fishing is miles away from the experience of the rest of us, and how tough and skilled are the men who practice it.

1st September, 1990. Towards Liverpool and the River Mersey, Nova Scotia

Swells are breaking on Rocky Isle off Wreck Point and I beat outside. A slow passage even with the ebb under me, into Sandy Bay on the next tack and a long tack out. Swells are breaking on Port Joli Head and on Little Hope Shoal just over a mile offshore but there is a deep passage between. Light easterly makes for a dreadfully slow passage, beating past the rollers on the reef. The swells increase to eight feet, probably caused by Hurricane Gustav, 400 miles southeast of Cape Race, Newfoundland. I see Little Hope lighthouse on rocks halfway to the horizon but distances are vast and it's difficult to tell if I am gaining.

The swells are now big. I tack and tack until the lighthouse is abeam and I stand up to look at the rollers crashing onto the rocks of Port Joli Head. The mist banks have cleared, and looking back, I see two enormous swells crash onto Little Hope Shoal and continue breaking with enormous violence all the way across the one mile-wide, deep water channel to the headland, like the great Hawaiian rollers shown on TV. I estimate them to be 14–16 feet. The swells return to normal size. But I am horrified for what might have been. The light easterly couldn't have been worse and there was nothing I could have done because I had no speed to get out of the way or even to luff.

I check my chart: two-and-a-quarter hours for the last four miles headland to headland. I am not going back—not after seeing those two great, unpredictable rollers. It is a memory that will be with me for the rest of my life.

At the next headland, Black Point, the reef extends a long way and occasionally a big swell crests way out and roars in. I keep clear and round the reef end with relief, then it crests half a dozen times; great rollers crashing along the reef only 100 yards away but *Wanderer* is safe on the leeward side and only the white water and the noise reach us, and *Wanderer* slowly crawls into the bay leaving the 'crash' astern.

Gales are forecast and I need shelter. The guide mentions that in bad weather swells work into the river Mersey and in such conditions Liverpool is uncomfortable; there is a hidden haven at Moose Harbour with an entrance difficult to identify; the name 'Coffin' Island' just off-shore intrigued me and the island appears to offer a sheltered cove.

6th September, 1990. Coffin Island (five miles east of Liverpool on the River Mersey), Nova Scotia

A nice sail yesterday, sun shining, light stern winds, small swells moving lazily. Coffin Island has a fine sheltered harbour at the north end of the island where a storm beach of big pebbles almost completely encloses a lagoon, except for a narrow gap over an underwater reef. It's a lobster fishing community occupied in winter only, half a dozen wood shacks each with four bunks and a big wood burning stove. All are now deserted but it feels like a quiet, nice, friendly spot and I tie to a wharf while I explore, then anchor in five feet.

Only last night I was thinking that it's September and soon the autumn gales must arrive and from now on I must pick my anchorages with care. This morning I switched on the weatherbox radio: "Today light winds, Friday southwesterlies strong, increasing to a southerly gale overnight, then becoming a northerly gale on Saturday." I have been planning to reach Le Have River Yacht Club by the weekend but now I have to make a different choice.

I can:

a) *sail towards Port Medway and look for a sheltered harbour (but my map is not detailed enough to show the government wharfs and a 180 degree wind shift in a crowded fishing harbour could lead to my light boat being crushed);*

b) *stay at Coffin Island—a good harbour with trees giving shelter from the south gale but the storm beach giving minimal wind protection from the northerly;*

c) *sail across the bay to Moose Harbour which I passed yesterday. I could not see the way in but the RNSYS/Boston section of CCA Guide has a sketch plan and says the inner basin is small, completely sheltered, and with a straight-forward entrance—sail straight for the great boulder on shore and you can see the entrance before you hit.*

I sit on deck. There is no dew, a brilliant moon, almost full. There are more stars than I have ever seen before, and there is a perfect mirror image of the harbour and shore with the huts and the trees upside down in the water.

3rd September, 1990. Moose Harbour near Liverpool, Nova Scotia

It's 3:00 A.M and there's vivid, violent lightning and thunder. It is continuous and brilliant, the thunder cracks overhead immediately after the flash. Rolling thunder in the distance, rain torrential on the tent, but I am warm in my sleeping bag, and dry. After half-an-hour all the lights throughout the harbour go out which wakes me again. Suddenly, there is complete blackness, shouting, noise and confusion everywhere. Tremendous thunder, vivid lightning continues until 5:00 A.M. I need to select my harbours with great care with the approach of autumn gales! I read my guide and find there are several small coves for shelter.

Sailing to the Edge of Fear

4th September, 1990. Moose Harbour, Nova Scotia

My chart finished at Liverpool (on the river Mersey) where I was hoping to buy the next set of charts but I was unsuccessful. Eventually, I visit the fisheries office hoping they might let me have a worn or outdated chart but they had recently destroyed them. However, they were helpful. From an up-to-date chart they photocopied the coast on letter-sized paper, then taped the strips together, and I had a usable long chart four inches wide and four feet long. I mentioned that it needed bearings so they grinned and photocopied the compass rose and stuck it on the end! It will take me to LaHave River where I can buy more.

The weather is breaking, there have been four gales in the last 10 days, the trees are changing colour and there is brilliant phosphorescence at night.

15th September, 1990. The Ovens, Nova Scotia

"Hurricane Isodore is 650 miles south of St. John's, Newfoundland travelling northeast at 10 knots but should not affect winds in our area." I accept the wind prediction but I make a mental note about the big ground swell already breaking heavily on the coast and which will build quickly. The sky is typical hurricane-beyond-the-horizon weather.

I turn at Ovens Point Headland towards Lunenburg; I will need a stroke of luck to find an anchorage before sunset but the wind looks like holding. The cliff is undermined with a row of caverns looking for all the world like a row of Dutch wall ovens—each one 'booms' in turn as the swells roll along the cliff compressing the air. I creep into the cove at the far end of the island when it is too dark to see, anchor under the shadow of the land and listen to the waves. A good passage today, the forecast is 25–30 knots for tomorrow, but I am safely in shelter.

A day spent reading and listening to the wind climbing up the scale. Mid-morning I lay out a second anchor. The rain is slashing down and the forecast 25–30 knot wind has proved to be an underestimate. I tighten the skirt line and the tent quietens enormously. The wind becomes vicious with shrill squalls whistling across the water—much more than 30 knots—a whole gale, at least!

Waves are building. *Wanderer* begins to pitch and heel. There are battering squalls, violent movement, and an overwhelming din. I am too far from the shore for these conditions, anchored on weed, and the anchors are too close together. Fog rolls in as well so I cannot see if/when my anchors drag. I consider letting out more scope but at low water I had noticed a patch of weed only 20 yards astern which may be a rock! I decide to sleep fully dressed and pull on oilskins just in case!

At 8:30 P.M. the wind drops to 30 knots and I can see the lighthouse on the mainland now as the fog dissipates. That was rough. One of the few times I got myself in a corner with no way out if things went wrong!

23rd September, 1990. Peggy's Cove, Nova Scotia

The coast now rolls ahead. Newfoundland/Labrador type tundra—barren rock, no trees, a few patches of heather. Houses scattered amongst the boulders built on rock, colourful and outstanding but a bleak and desolate coast. It is difficult to see even the big navigation buoys in these huge swells until one is very close.

This is probably the last day of barefoot sailing. In this area there is a whole mass of new island and easy to see the way ahead. I beat along the coast, the colours changing to autumn browns, shading to brilliant reds. There are no trees, only bare rock at the waterside and no vegetation—not even lichen. I suddenly realise the rocks are planed smooth by the winter sea ice.

The autumn mornings are now lovely; no mosquitoes, mist on the water, trees turning gold in the first rays of the morning sun, brilliant orange and red of the weeds below the high water line on the rocks as the sun's rays rests on it. I can see why this place is so popular. I am already planning ahead for another year.

25th September, 1990. Southwest Cove, Nova Scotia

One of the great pleasures of small boat cruising is in visiting all the lonely coves and suddenly coming across the unexpected. Today in Southwest Harbour I anchor under the ramparts of a Rhineland castle. It is magnificent with two towers, turrets, balconies and pinnacles, set on the waters edge, pebble inlay in the main courses and flint above; the main hall is on the second floor, a walkway along the battlements, and even a watergate. The owner is Swiss and shows me round. He emigrated from Switzerland to Canada and has spent 19 years building this castle as a reminder of home.

The crypt (basement) is high and arched and built over the wooden house that he and his wife still live in. The main hall is superb with big arched windows from floor to roof with wonderful views but I notice, as a concession to the North American climate, they are double-glazed! The watergate leads right into the living quarters and in the crypt he has a live raven—the traditional 'tame castle raven'—- and an Old English guard dog. He is presently roofing the highest turrets. With great enthusiasm, I climb the ladders to the uppermost point of the roof to see a panoramic view of the cove. Only when I look down to photograph *Wanderer* under the castle walls 100 feet below do I remember that I am scared of heights and I "freeze" unable to move without falling! Eventually, the owner/builder has to climb and guide my feet down the rungs of the ladders, and by the time I reached terra firma my legs are shaking, my knuckles white with the effort of hanging on.

I sail for Owl's Head and Peggy's Cove, feeling deeply impressed.

Sailing to the Edge of Fear

29th September, 1990. Halifax, Nova Scotia

The Maritime Museum of the Atlantic is excellent, friendly and hospitable. They offered me use of a shower, docking as long as I liked to stay, and told me to tie *Wanderer* in the same dock as the *Sackville*—the only World War Two corvette still in existence. Now I open the tent flap first thing and the corvette is silhouetted by the morning sun.

Yesterday, I was shown round the corvette. She is immaculate, restored to her war-time camouflage and fitted with her war-time armament but imagine her in her historical role—far less immaculate on duty in the North Atlantic, smelling of unwashed bodies, sea-sickness, bilge water, with weeping rivets and her crew trying to load 300 pound depth charges while she rolled like a pig in a cross sea.

An American replica of a British frigate came in under sail just after me—she's the largest wooden sailing ship afloat. She blockaded the U.S. during the War of Independence and the Americans became so used to seeing her off Boston that they felt lonely when the war ended, so they built a replica. She sounded a gun, luffed, backed sails and blew back very competently into the dock.

I walked into a photographic shop for two rolls of slide film and the owner offered to take me for a driving tour of the city. We passed by some of the city's highlights, including the Citadel and Dalhousie University—he knows the city's history so it was most enjoyable.

8th October, 1990. Atlantic Agricultural Show of Nova Scotia

The provincial show was well worth the struggle to get there by foot. I walked into the Pumpkin Hall and stood in amazement. It was unbelievable. The Grand Champion Squash weighed 464 pounds (210 kg); the Grand Champion Pumpkin 658 pounds (298 kg) and there were dozens over 400 pounds!

The staff at the Maritime Museum have booked me into a conference at the museum during the weekend. The subject is small boat exhumation and preservation with expert speakers from all over North America. I accepted but I am not sure if I might be out of my depth being the only engineer in the antiquarian environment.

10th October, 1990. Halifax, Nova Scotia

The forecast is for an east-northeasterly gale so I shall have to move for shelter. This wind will make the Maritime Museum dock rather bumpy so I shall sail to Bedford Basin (Bedford Basin is the deep water inland lake above Halifax Harbour and the assembly point for so many of the convoys of World War Two).

When I return from the Agricultural Show I sail, and well after dark, I tie up in Dartmouth Yacht Club in Wrights Cove.

11th October, 1990. Bedford Basin, Halifax, Nova Scotia

This morning I pay my dues before I assemble and hoist the radar reflector in Bedford Basin while waiting for the beginning of the ebb to take me back to my berth at the Maritime Museum of the Atlantic. There is dense fog in the narrows and I can hear fog horns in Halifax Harbour. I am tense because I have to go past shipyards, naval docks, commercial traffic and cross-harbour ferries. I get out my fog horn.

Approaching the narrows, I enter a thick grey blanket that smothers visibility and sound. It seems sensible to cross the harbour and close-tack along the south shore letting the tide do the work. The high-level bridge is out of sight above me, and visibility must be less than 10 yards. Suddenly, the overhanging bows of a frigate travelling slowly loom above *Wanderer*'s masthead and I throw round onto the other tack to avoid being run down, and the frigate slides silently past. She is a dead ship: no engine noise, no bell, no fog horn no one aboard and I realise that she must be tied to an invisible dockyard quay.

It is early October and autumn is now here. For three days there has been fog all round Halifax Harbour; now a gale is forecast for Saturday evening and a small craft warning has been issued; Hurricane Willie off Cape Cod is expected at Cape Sable Island on Saturday. Storm warnings are in effect for offshore Georges Bank and LaHave Bank just to the south. The docks I'm tied to will be exposed to the weather. I wonder if I can snatch a passage early tomorrow morning and slip into shelter in the other arm of Halifax Harbour before the gales and fog defeat me?

15th October, 1990. Back Passage, Heckman's Harbour, Nova Scotia

It is a calm night, flat water, no wind, a dark black night with no lights on the shore. The days of autumn have a magnificence and splendour missing from other seasons. There is a softness too. The occasional balmy day between the rush of late summer and the bleak gales of winter. It is some three weeks since I was last in Bayswater and I notice that the trees have changed colour and suddenly the fall is here in all its magnificence.

There is a narrow cleft through slate rock between Heckman's Island and Lunenburg Peninsular almost two miles long, and the passage leads from the "inland sailing waters" between First and Second Peninsular out to the sea. It must be the most impressively colourful passage anywhere in the late fall. Starting from the eel-grass covered shallows of Heckman's Back Passage, there is an elbow bend behind the spit and narrow lagoons reducing in width to the narrows at the bridge.

Beyond the bridge comes Tanners Pass, lichen-covered rock slopes, patches of white and pale green on barren rock. At water level are low bushes and ground cover of brilliant reds, purples, scarlets, blues, and a mirror reflection repeated upside-down in the still water, and the almost vertical fissures in the slate cutting an impossible angle with their reflection as they touch the surface.

It's 4:30 A.M. and a sudden heavy gust reminding me that there is another side to the beautiful days of autumn—the equinoctial gales!

late October. LaHave River, Nova Scotia

The weather has broken now. Real autumn gales, one after the other. The easterly gale (which had a long fetch across the river) was upgraded to a storm with gusts to 70 knots with only half an hour warning before it hit! Fishing boats are dragging their moorings, and a sailing dinghy at the dock has a broken mast and is being pounded against the wharf by force 10 winds, and getting knocked to pieces.

Already there is snow and biting cold. There is another full gale this evening. Fishing boats are getting damaged alongside the wharfs. It is a disturbed night trying to help hold them off and keeping fenders in place.

Red tape in Halifax: I pack my ship's papers, my cruising permit, immigration document, passport and a list of possible repairs needing attention, and visit the Customs at Halifax for a winter permit. It is sensible to go to headquarters where they know all the regulations and be able to sort out any difficulties.

I play it by ear and it went surprisingly well until the officer said, "You do understand that this permit must be stuck inside the bridge window so it can be seen by our officer?" I explain that my boat is an open 16-footer and it doesn't have a bridge deck. "That's okay, stick it to a cabin window."

"It's an open boat—it doesn't have a window," I point out.

But she insists. I explain again that there are no windows (bridge, cabin, or hull) as it is an open boat. I offer to attach it somewhere else. But the officer's resolve does not weaken: "The regulations say it must be stuck on the inside of a window so a customs officer can see it from outside the boat." She is getting irritable, and still holding the permit firmly.

I decide to take a risk and tell a lie (being fairly certain that she doesn't know what a transom is). "I have just remembered—there is a very small glass inspection window in the transom. Will that be alright?"

She agrees, and hands over the piece of official paper and I flee.

Now I understand why Wally in St. Andrews had recommended contacting a *local* customs officer!

20th November, 1990. Dartmouth, Nova Scotia

I am staying with the family of Jim Fraser, the Wayfarer owner in Dartmouth who I met last year. He insisted on trailing *Wanderer* the last 15 miles to LaHave. Fortunately, he over-ruled my objections for there has been only two days of good weather in the last two weeks. Jim tells me he and his young family spent a few days cruising on a canal from Kingston to Ottawa called the Rideau Waterway. It sounds fascinating for the small boat enthusiast—it is the sort of information that I store for possible reference but I don't suppose it will be of use as I am not travelling that way.

After a few days with his very pleasant young sailing family, Jim drove me to the airport to catch the night flight to England. I left *Wanderer* at the bakery in La Have, under cover.

There were letters awaiting me from the two Members of Parliament. They enclosed replies from the minister to their representations on my behalf. The legal position is that a foreign registered boat cannot be left overwinter for storage only. If it requires repairs in a boatyard it can be stored for the winter while the repairs are carried out; there are no exceptions. It was a long letter but stripped of the bureaucratic jargon I condensed it to "go to the local officer 'who knows the score' and will be more sympathetic."

I have written to the MPs to thank them but it remains an unnecessary end-of-season worry for the future.

1991. Prince Edward Island
And Hurricane Bob

6th June, 1991

My return ticket (Air Canada) from last November was unusual. It was open ended, available for twelve months, weekdays only, issued only to the "over 60s," non-transferable and non-refundable. I was intrigued by the thinking behind the scheme: presumably, if the airline sell enough tickets to the elderly, a statistical proportion will die during the 12 months—and the vacant seats can be sold for a second time. Undoubtedly, if morbidly, profitable.

It is a delight to be back at LaHave Bakery. Michael and Gale Watson run an efficient, friendly business with a marine department where the visiting yacht always gets a congenial welcome. They run a small hostel and their large bakery with the reputation for the "finest bread and cookies in Nova Scotia." I first heard of their well-deserved reputation far down the New England coast. Since I've arrived, I make a point to rise early as I am allowed to select two cookies each morning as they come out of the oven!

We got *Wanderer* out of the marine warehouse where she had been covered up and kept warm over the winter. Now there remains the problem of where to launch. The public slipway was a long way away at the ferry terminal—too far without a trailer. Next door was a small beach which looks impossible at first sight, with a vertical drop from the road over a four foot stone wall. I ask the neighbour's permission—they had already invited me to accompany them to church—then launched *Wanderer* early in the morning before anyone is about to watch in case it went wrong. We rehearsed and *Wanderer* was in the water in half-an-hour.

I have not used the big frame for a long time and now that I am single-handed, the boom tent is adequate, so I post the large one home. Kevin, the local boat builder warned me of the predicted "40 knots gusts tomorrow" so I helped him to fibreglass the edges of my centreboard and rudder which were chipped and worn after 3,000 miles of shallow water sailing.

Michael Watson has promised to build a wharf to berth a new schooner in what I think is a impossibly short time, and I am interested to see how he does it, but I have been thinking in English terms. Here, they use a traditional Canadian method of 'crib' construction of which I had seen many examples but not realised its advantages.

First, they built several square (crib) towers on rollers on the beach—the wood is rough squared so there is little squaring up needed; the first is pushed into the water filled with enough boulders until it has only slight buoyancy, held in position and filled with stone until it settles onto the river bed. The first deck is constructed from the shore and used by tipper trucks to fill the crib with boulders; the second pier is sunk further out, and filled by trucks across the extended deck, and the following stages are completed as far as required. It is a very quick form of construction, it uses local material, assembled on any neighbouring beach, requires the minimum period of good weather, rock is available from the roadside, and the surface of the timber deck can be finished at leisure.

14th June, 1991. LaHave, Nova Scotia

I am sleeping in one of the rooms in the LaHave hostel in the warehouse. At 3:00 A.M., I am awoken by the wind, roaring and hammering at the sides of the building. I don't want to leave my warm sleeping bag, but I shall have to be up at low water when the tide turns and runs into the wind.

Ten minutes later, I get up and dress and add an oilskin jacket. The wind has gone round further and almost blowing directly down the river, short hollow waves now breaking right across the river.

Michael Watson's boat *Teal* is rolling her gunwales under and I am glad that I didn't tie alongside her. *Wanderer* is alongside a half-deflated inflatable and although she is rolling heavily it makes a perfect fender. The yacht *Storm 5* is hanging on her mooring ropes, her bow out of the water, and I give her another two feet on both bow and stern ropes.

18th June, 1991. Herring Cove, Nova Scotia

Chebucto Head is an impressive entrance to Halifax where the wind dies and leaves me with a seven mile row along a rocky coast. In these conditions, Herring Cove is a convenient staging post. This harbour is the centre of championship dory rowing in Nova Scotia. The team selected to compete in the Dory Championships in Gloucester, U.S. this weekend, are two local girls with a good prospect of winning and the fishermen are ever so proud of them. They were practising by rowing up and down the harbour at high speed, so I waved them across, we chatted, and we agreed that they would tow *Wanderer* half-a-mile out of harbour for additional exercise.

It was cold last night; cold head winds and raining today—my fingers are tingling.

It is two days since I left LaHave River and I am missing my early morning tour of the bakery to sample the day's bake.

Since I had visited last autumn I did not intend to linger but the kindness of the staff at the Maritime Museum of the Atlantic tempted me and I had time to explore and learn something of the history of this city. I had heard about the Halifax Explosion, a disaster occurring when a munitions ship in the harbour caught fire after colliding with another ship. The ensuing explosion killed 1,600 and injured thousands more.

The museum gave me photocopies of the large scale topographical maps of the coast and also of the Bras d'Or Lakes as I left. These show the land contours and are going to be very useful when sailing offshore in an area where the forested foreshore always blends into the forested background, and the charts give no hint of the land silhouette.

19th June, 1991. Cole Harbour, Nova Scotia

Twenty-four hours ago I was in Halifax but now the fleshpots of the city—ice cream parlours, restaurants, and cookie shops—are already fading into a hazy memory. I sailed past the headland and through the gunnery range to Cole Harbour which looks interesting on the chart, a pleasant half day sail north of Halifax. It is a lovely marsh estuary, several channels, sloping forested shores all round.

The channel at the bar is narrow and I feel my way across in 18 inches, with seas breaking on both sides as I come in even though there was little wind. This must be the reason no one visits and why there was no local information available in Halifax. I feel my way up the channel and turn behind the spit.

The sun comes out. It's a beautiful place. I anchor on sand, and check the anchor has dug in as the ebb currents will be strong. I put up the front half of the tent for shelter from the keen southerly wind. A sunny spring evening with no insects—too late for blackflies; too early yet for mosquitoes—and I enjoy my peaches and cream porridge, apart from the sound of continuous shooting from onshore.

One hour later the fog is rolling in—great banks of wet grey. June is said to be bad for fog but I've become complacent about it, for there was only two days of fog last week. It is rolling in across the marshes in great curtains as I drop anchor and hurry the tent up before everything gets damp and heat a hot meal.

I must sail as soon as possible as I could get bottled up with an onshore wind. The banging stops at 8:00 P.M. It must have been a 'clay' shoot for I heard the shout 'pull.' I study the *Chart and Guide for the Eastern Shore*. Several coves have bars which will break in winds from the south, several have no shelter from the east. I need to be careful.

A lone mosquito wakes me several times. It doesn't attempt to bite but its whine is enough to prevent sleep. The fog has completely cleared by 2:00 A.M. and I can see the lights on the causeway. It is a lovely, still night, silent marsh all round. I aim to be across the bar at 9:00 A.M. at low water. Wind is light westerly but goes southerly at breakfast time. I take a leisurely breakfast with two cups of tea as I was up at 6:00 A.M. I lay the oars in the rowlocks ready for a quick pull across, or back from, the bar. The current still ebbing at one-and-a-half knots.

The five-pound danforth anchor is on its side but the blade has not dug in. It must have turned on its side when the tide turned. It is amazing that it held

Sailing to the Edge of Fear

Wanderer and we did not drag out to sea overnight! As I sail down the estuary and start to beat out, wisps of fog blow across the headland and rapidly thicken. The channel through the sand is deep, but the bar is rock, only 15 inches below the surface. There are breakers with the ebb still running out but not dangerous although I don't need a wet boat at the beginning of the day.

I put on my oilskins mainly for warmth and within 100 yards I enter the great bank of fog. A steep-to stone beach enables me to sail close in without risk and follow it easily. Then comes a sandy bar, small breakers further out.

The fog clamps down. It's now very unpleasant sailing with visibility down to 30 yards. An additional difficulty is that I have sailed off the edge of my Halifax chart with a gap of three miles to the edge of my next, so I really am sailing blind. The beach is shelving, the swells top up and break further out and I am forced out into the fog. Working in fog so dense, I sail into the breakers before seeing them. The coast is out of sight but I keep edging in. A wooden frame appears in the fog 50 yards ahead—massive timbers set on rocks are towering above my masthead. As I sail closer, I find it is only eight-feet high, but is distorted by the fog.

I have no idea where I am and I feel completely disoriented. My estimated time of arrival at the next headland, three-and-a half miles away at three knots, is 10:30 A.M. Over a reef—only 18 inches and I tack out then edge back in. The swells are now topping up, no sign of the shore and I tack out for safety.

I have no idea where I am—and I dare not go closer in. If I go further out I may sail past the next headland without seeing it. Suddenly, a massive headland appears above the masthead—it is Terminal Beach and Half Island. I scrape over the reef, keeping the top of the cliffs in sight, then at the point I head on a compass bearing for the buoy off Shut-in Island. Finding it, I set off along the shore, very relieved to know where I am. The fog is clearing to one mile and an island appears. The next buoy is not the usual type—this is round with a round topmark, lettered 'HX2' very small indeed. I can see back to Cole Harbour headland now, and down the length of Three Fathom Harbour.

With a fresh breeze from the southwest visibility has increased to two miles, so I decide to risk the eight-and-a-half mile crossing direct to Jeddore Cape, hoping that the fog will not return. If it clamps down, I can run off to Chezzetcook Inlet or to Petpeswick Inlet both of which are identified by bell buoys. I set the genoa. I'm probably doing five-and-a-half knots.

Out of the greyness, the outline of hills appear ahead then halfway across the bay I am able to pick out the end of Jeddore Cape. This is wonderful downwind sailing, broad-reaching, the swells urging *Wanderer* along. Offshore, I can hear a whistle buoy but it is invisible in a great bank of fog. Then the cape becomes a vague shadow and almost disappears. I take a quick bearing on Naufft Point in case I have to run for Musquodoboit Harbour but the buoy appears. The swells are now topping up but there is no sign of them becoming hollow and breaking.

Jeddore Cape comes abeam and surges astern. There are 30–40 big dolphins playing all round *Wanderer*, some are less than 30 feet away. I enjoy their company.

21st June, 1991. The Eastern Shore of Nova Scotia

"Summer begins officially at 6:15 P.M. today," said the forecaster this morning. I hope this bodes well for smooth sailing. I walk to the bend of the road. Jeddore Rocks and lighthouse are easily visible. I drift down the channel marked with branches, and gybe round Marsh Point. A fishing boat throttles back and I wonder if she will offer me a tow but they have only slowed to wash out their fish hold.

Wind slowly fills in from the southwest and fog thickens until only the end of Jeddore Rock and the tip of the lighthouse can be seen. The whole morning spent in intricate navigation through islands and rocks sometimes going outside, sometimes inside…

Tangier Reef—swell suddenly eight feet—abeam at 2:47 P.M. I ought to go into 'The Bawleen,' a ring of islands with two entrances, completely sheltered,

Fog banks rolling in north of Halifax.

or on to Popes Harbour also sheltered, but I want to round Taylors Head today to get into the more sheltered islands and inner passages. The islands astern have disappeared into fog, the buoy is sharp and clear but fog wraps the warm cliffs as I watch. Black clouds astern: is this wind or rain? The boom is skying and *Wanderer* is rolling on a dead run, so I tighten it down with the kicking strap. I keep a careful eye on the clouds astern and put on oilskins. The black clouds cut off the sun and it turns cold, then they pass out to sea.

The dark clouds bring with them a cloud front and the wind slowly veers 20 degrees and I gybe over. I pass Mad Molly Reef with the seas roaring and swilling

Sailing to the Edge of Fear

over it, and harden in behind Taylors Head. I almost decide to run on another six-and-a-half miles to Sheet Harbour Passage as the wind is still fresh but it tends to die suddenly in the afternoon. So I lay inside Pyches Island then through Little Gates and Malahash Island to Mushaboom. This area is very attractive, small tree covered islands that reminds me of Scandinavia.

I drop anchor at the west end of the pool at 5:25 P.M. It's a bigger pool than I expected with a rock in the centre, a few houses at the west end, one fishing boat, and a slipway of poles with several dories pulled up. I make a mug of tea and a sandwich of 'Heavenly Jam' from LaHave Bakery.

Cold and overcast so I put up the front half of the tent. The wind veers from west to northwest, to north, then northeast and builds a chop before dropping as the sun comes out at 8:10 P.M. and it turns into a warm, pleasant evening and I settle down to read the next section of the *Cruising Guide to Nova Scotia Coast*. I have travelled 26 miles today, rounded exposed Taylors Head, and moved onto a new chart. Inside passages tomorrow.

22nd June, 1991

Away as soon as the morning breeze fills in. A sparkling sea as *Wanderer* close-hauls towards the islands and along the shore to the headland.

My surroundings would make a lovely photograph although getting the exposure correct with the great contrast would be difficult, but I have to come onto a new heading before I can get the camera out. Round the end of Sober Island is the stark remains of a rusting ship on the rocks. A light northeast wind right on the nose, and I beat and beat and seem to get nowhere in this vast cruising area. My stores are getting low and I am beginning to realise the Eastern Shore, Halifax to Canso, is much less inhabited than the Western Shore.

When I eventually land, a motorist drives me to Sheet Harbour grocery store. I have one $50 bill and another dollar in cash so I rely on my Visa card, which seems to be honoured everywhere in Canada. The bill comes to $48+ and the staff direct my attention to the notice "No credit cards." It's Murphy's Law. I buy a cheap exercise book to continue my log book and postcards and I have $1.25 left.

25th June, 1991. Factory Cove, Nova Scotia

At one time there used to be a lobster factory here hence the name. It is a beautiful, sheltered cove. All day I close-hauled through the prettiest islands imaginable—the Bay of Islands. I put into a little cove between Goose Island and Slate Island. It is a lovely spot protected by a crescent shingle bank on both sides.

I anchor on mud in eight feet with lovely little wooded islands as far as the eye can see: a wonderful cruising ground. I ought to explore and stay a few days but I am conscious that the fog may be back with a southwesterly and if so, then without radar I am stuck. The inland passages are marked with small buoys—no swell in here even with onshore gales.

26th June, 1991

2:30 A.M. and it is very cold. I am wearing a light vest, shirt and cotton pyjamas, socks and a balaclava hat inside my sleeping bag. I should have got out more clothes. Instead, I make a hot chocolate drink and pull my balaclava down over my shoulders and tighten the drawstring of my sleeping bag hood. Too cold to sleep and at 6:00 A.M. I make a hot breakfast. There is no wind, the waves slapping across the bar as it floods and I row out past Hog Island.

The swell is three to four feet to Rober Rock buoy where the swells top up to double size and the odd one becomes hollow. Tobacco Island has a long reef but I cut it close, moving very slowly. I see a ship's mast behind the island. As I clear the tip of the island I realise she is very high in the water with the rudder half exposed. She is hard on the end of the reef of Cape Gegogan—the ship must have caught the very tip of the reef as she is a wreck; masts still standing, an old ship, centre bridge, sides rusted through. I hove-to, photographing her when I realise that the tide has carried *Wanderer* onto the reef and I am in broken water.

I hurriedly put the camera away and beat clear. Wine Harbour, which looked so attractive on the chart this morning, now looks considerably less appealing with six foot swells running into the bay. I keep a careful check on the coves in case I have to row for shelter if the wind dies. The reefs off Nixons Mate and Fiddlers Head don't seem to be breaking but as I get nearer, the swells double in height with an occasional one even bigger with hollow faces. Another patch of even larger swells from the southeast building as they run onto Fiddlers Head reef but they are not hollowing so I carry on and *Wanderer* climbs each in turn, but I am still relieved when she is clear.

The wind goes southwest and *Wanderer* is broad reaching for Cape Mocodome reef and I lay a course to take me inside the Calf Rock although it is breaking heavily further out. I gybe over to skirt the broken water and run down the far side of the reef where the swells builds up in the shallows and I work out into deeper water. The wind comes with a bang and I roll up the genoa and plane all the way to Neverfail Cove, along the long stone beach to an almost new government wharf in a big area of sheltered water. I tie off the stern of a fishing boat with a line astern to the wharf. There is a lot of wind in the trees.

29th June, 1991. Towards Coddles Harbour, Nova Scotia

This morning I listen to the wind and storm warnings issued for Cabot Strait and a gale warning for all northern areas. There is fog so dense now that I can't even see the light shining at the harbour entrance, only a very light breeze and fog. Do I sail? If I do will the fog lift in time to find my way into Drum, Marsh or Coddles harbours? Dead reckoning will be difficult with strong tides and low boat speed, even worse if the wind gets up before the fog lifts. Maybe the fog will not thin until the wind goes northwest and blows hard?

I am up at 6:15 A.M. and walk along the wharf. There is no wind at all and the fog is even thicker. I wait to decide. It is only three miles to Drum Head but visibility is less than 100 yards—the light tower on the shingle bank is not even a shadow and I walk round to ask the fishermen for their advice. The forecast is "25–30 knots" but the wind won't get up until the afternoon; and anyway 'they' (the weather people) always add 10 knots to covered themselves!" he counsels.

It's now 9:45 A.M. and the breeze is becoming northwesterly and the fog clearing immediately. It should be a pleasant broad reach across to Country Harbour Head, and a continuing reach for Harbour Island and for Drum Head beyond. By the time *Wanderer* is stowed and sails hoisted the wind is fresh outside and waves are building from the long fetch across the bay. The seas running into the ocean swells from the Atlantic create an uncomfortable sea.

The wind is now much stronger, and producing general white horses. I pull on my oilskins as a lot of spray is coming aboard as *Wanderer* shoulders her way through the crests, rolling in the hollow breaking beam seas. Beyond Harbour Isle the waves are bigger, breaking more heavily and I hove-to to look at the chart which shows this as "the Sound." The seas ahead are very heavy indeed, breaking, and too dangerous to run through. So I come onto a broad reach and quickly find that is too dangerous as well—the waves lift *Wanderer's* stern and she planes down into the trough, digging her bow in to the back of the preceding wave and it is almost impossible to prevent a broach-to.

It would be sensible to drop the mainsail and reach through under genoa only. I am thrown about heavily while reducing sail but the patch is only 200 yards to calmer water, so I decide to hold onto sail, fine reaching to bring the waves on the beam to increase speed and manoeuvrability, and get it over as quick as possible. I get a lot of water aboard and I am very glad indeed to get clear and into calmer water and run off to Drum Head.

This was an instinctive decision and it was a mistake that I was lucky to get away with! I can look into the entrance of Drum Head. It looks attractive with two breakwaters of boulders, a narrow entrance, a big pool with a Government Wharf on the far side, excellent protection from this hard northerly and I am tempted to

---

go in, but *Wanderer* is planing fast on a beam reach, two reefs down, the weather is settled, visibility is excellent and I can see the whole length of the coast ahead.

The wind off the land is becoming vicious in the gusts, and I am beginning to doubt my ability to work to windward against the squalls. I carry on as it is a pity not to make ground eastward while I have a fair wind and no fog. By the time I reach the next low rocky point the wind is stronger, and the squalls even heavier and I decide it is time to come onto the wind and beat into Coddles Harbour for shelter. *Wanderer* is overpowered (two reefs down), and I am not sure if I may not be losing ground and being driven offshore and out into the Atlantic.

Almost imperceptibly, I gain ground close-hauled but I am unable to beat round the end of a shallow reef as I lose ground every time I tack and I have to take a calculated risk to skate over the rocks to gain shelter under the land. Even so the squalls are overpowering. I am playing the main sheet continuously, and making a lot of leeway. The wind must be 25 knots, the gusts 30 knots. I heave-to to look at the chart of Coddles Harbour but a squall lays *Wanderer* on her ear and water pours over the lee gunwale and I give up chart work and free off for a little bay behind an island.

From here, I can see up the cove to the village, and I beat in, staggering and overpowered. I tack close under the eastern shore to get a lee, close-haul across the cove and have to wait for a lull before I dare attempt to come about. I drop a line over a pile of the inner wharf, and pull the sail down with relief. I meet a friendly face: "I saw you sailing along the coast past my house, so I drove along to see who was out sailing in this weather. Come for a mug of tea. My name is Brent and I own a Drascombe." I accept and when we return, the wind is roaring in the trees and whining round the buildings and rigging.

The squalls are cutting the top off the water lower down the cove. A fisherman is waiting for me. He came down specially to tell me to use a hold off anchor to keep *Wanderer* clear of the remains of the old wharf at low water. He throws me his hold-off rope from the shore which he uses for his fishing boat and I tie off to it.

30th June, 1991. Coddles Harbour, Nova Scotia

Some excellent sailing the last ten days. This is a beautiful cruising area. Mushaboom Islands, Bay of Islands and dozens of Scandinavian-type tree-covered islands and sheltered coves. It is sparsely populated, and I haven't seen a single yacht sailing except in Halifax Harbour since I left LaHave River!

I've been reading about the Bras d'Or Lakes in the centre of Cape Breton Island—it really is a cruising paradise—a big inland sea, fog-free and sheltered with a rich Gaelic culture.

1st July, 1991 (Canada Day)

After the experience of almost being driven offshore at Coddles Harbour, I am reluctant to go out into open water again unless it is necessary. The chart shows a dotted line across the neck of the peninsular labelled imprecisely as 'canal.' This is worth investigating. I row across to the canal and tie to the timber at the entrance while I walk the bank to inspect. It is very narrow, dry-stone rock walls, eight feet in width, dried out, a quarter mile long with a low road bridge one third along. It is too narrow to row through so I shall have to lower the mast into the short crutch and pole with an oar. I use the short crutch and I shall have to wait for the tide to rise.

The tide is flooding through, there is enough depth, the bridge has a clearance of less than four feet and this reduces as I watch; I could so a lot of damage to *Wanderer's* hull if she scrapes the rock sides. I lower the mast onto the stern deck, kneel on the floorboards, and pole through. The far end of the canal is a surprise with a fishing village, a big government wharf with a Pilot boat alongside, numerous fishing boat wharves and houses round the bay.

A man on the Pilot boat waves me across to inquire where I am from and I tie alongside to swing up the mast, tension the forestay and keep one reef tied down as the forecast is 15–25 knots. I ask the mechanic on the Pilot boat if the canal is much used. "It was only ever used for dories from one side of the peninsular to the other," he explains. "So I expect that I am the first British yacht to go through it for some time?" I inquire. "You certainly are—the canal was closed in the 1960s!"

He loans me Robert Leggatt's *Canals of Canada* dealing with plans for building canals from the head of the Bay of Fundy to Northumberland Strait and from Fundy to Dartmouth and Halifax. There has been so much successful canal construction in Canada that I have always wondered why this obvious connection has not been made although the enormous tidal range must pose great difficulties.

3rd July, 1991. Bras d'Or Lakes, Cape Breton, Nova Scotia

Once through the canal entrance to the Bras d'Or Lakes, the fog disappears completely—just as the guide promised. A lovely long inlet like a Scottish sea loch. It's quite beautiful. Forested, going miles into the hills, islands everywhere. I enjoy a two mile reach down the loch to Spry Point and White Head Island clear beyond. Half way through, White Head wraps in mist, then disappears, so does Spry Point—fog again. I look back—it's clear up the fjord. I run into the fog bank. Visibility is less than a half mile. This should be enough, provided it gets no worse. The chart is already marked with courses and distances.

Spry Point appears ahead and once I'm around it, I anchor, I'm invited aboard a moored yacht named *Salamander* for a look round. She is an 'Oyster' yacht built by Landamores of Wroxham near my home in England, and is a beautiful yacht fitted for serious cruising, with immaculate wood work, every modern navigation aid imaginable including radar, satellite navigation, full set of Brooks and Gatehouse instruments. Her owner remarks that his ambition is to fit an interface between his navigation equipment and radar and autohelm so he will be able to fill in the waypoints and leave the yacht to sail itself across the Atlantic while he meets it the other end, thus avoiding all seasickness and bad weather.

(I suddenly realise that the last time I saw *Salamander* she was exhibited at the London Boat Show some years ago and I told a man, not realising he was her owner, when he was looking round *Wanderer* that: "I will get more enjoyment and sailing out of my Wayfarer than ever that chap will out of his great big Oyster!" It was tactless and wrong for he is an experienced cruising man—it is fortunate that he doesn't remember me.)

10th July, 1991. Bras d'Or Lakes (heading north), Cape Breton

A spectacular and wild view back to Straits of Barra and Iona. The wind is a little south of southwest and slightly off the Boisdale shore so I stand across to get a lee. The wind increases, seas heavy and breaking in the centre of the channel. It's getting very hairy, with *Wanderer* planing continuously and white horses everywhere. A big white maintenance ship is well down channel. I luff up, pull down my reefed mainsail, unroll a quarter of the genoa and run. *Wanderer* is much eased and safer. I head for the starboard shore hoping to obtain a lee from these heavy seas, quartering down the hollow faces, there is no shelter until I can get behind Long Island—and that is a very long way to go in these conditions. I have no chart and am working from the sketches in the *Guide to Cape Breton* (labelled "not to be used for navigation").

The wind increases—it must be 25 knots, and more in the gusts. Then it veers into the west, so I gybe the genoa to cross back as the wind is now off the other shore. Very heavy seas, planing continuously. A slight cross sea building, breaking heavily and I have to watch every sea astern carefully to avoid rolling in. There is a marker on the shore which confuses me. The white repair ship is moving ahead slowly so I run down her lee side to get some shelter, then cross her bows, and resume my course across the seas.

Gradually, the seas become less as *Wanderer* gets a slight lee and I run along the coast looking for shelter. I suddenly remember that there is virtually no tide in the Bras d'Or Lakes and I have been forgetting the great advantages of the Wayfarer: the ability to pull ashore. I can beach anywhere. There is a slight lee so that I can get ashore without being swamped. No identifying features, although there might be a bay behind the next little headland.

The wind increases viciously as I get out another film for the camera. It must be blowing 30 knots but *Wanderer* is already crossing the bar and luffs behind the point safely. It's a big bay going back a long way. It must be Island Point Harbour. I roll up the genoa, hoist the two-reef mainsail and beat. The cove is enormous; it must be one-and-a-half miles long and the wind blowing down the length of it. Wind roaring, whining in the rigging and I don't think I can get up to windward. I short tack up the shore keeping very close in. Several times water pours over the lee gunwale on both tacks. A little bay opens out behind the brilliant white gypsum cliffs and I drop an anchor close in, taking a line to a tree to pull *Wanderer* close to the shore. The wind is roaring in the trees, waves and white horses are running across the mouth of the cove but I'm just within shelter by a few feet. If the wind goes round tonight I shall have to get out in a hurry.

I photograph *Wanderer* from the shore amongst masses of blue iris but there is also a pool of stagnant water so there will be mosquitoes aplenty tonight. Forecast southwesterly dropping to 15 knots overnight. Strong westerlies are predicted for tomorrow.

11th July, 1991. Northern Bras d'Or Lakes, Cape Breton

Astern, I can see all the way back up the Straits of Barra and Iona, mountains stretching into the distance on both shores. It is beautiful and incredibly clear. Long Island has a bar from shore halfway across the entrance with anchorage behind. The seas top up as I run down-channel and the bottom shallows; wind increasing rapidly. Approaching the bar there is a sudden drop in wind strength as *Wanderer* loses speed in a trough, at the same time as her stern rises to a wave, a crest breaks against her transom and the rudder blade loses grip, and with no wind in the genoa to hold her bows off the wind, she broaches! Only savage use of the rudder brings her back on course but it was a very close call.

The wind is now whistling, I clear the end of the bar and roll up the genoa, gybe and ask if I may tie up alongside a fishing boat at a dock for breakfast. It is a wonderful view astern, hills and mountains, lochs, and kyles. Suddenly, I realise how this island has grown on me and I don't want to leave it. It is beautiful this side of Barra Strait.

At the north entrance of the Bras d'Or Lakes, there is a tremendous current so fast that the big navigation buoys are fitted with planing hulls. I just managed to sidle across the tide into a fishing harbour before the tide carried *Wanderer* backwards. A fishing boat skipper is fitting a steering position at his masthead and a harpoon platform in the bows. "Net fishing season has finished and we are fitting out for sports fishing in the Gulf Stream," he explains when I ask. "Tie alongside if you are staying and come aboard for a cup of real tea. I'm Nelson MacNeil." He offers me a large mug and we sit on the deck drinking. "It's 'King Cole,' a New Brunswick blend. What do you think of that? Isn't it far better than your Red Rose?" he asks. I think it no better than my Red Rose and tactlessly say so. An argument quickly develops as Nelson maintains his opinion. I am wondering how to get out with honour intact when the fishing boat's automatic bilge pump starts and the argument breaks off—I have tied *Wanderer* under the bilge pump outlet and she is rapidly filling with bilge water, oil, fish scales and other good things. We both grab buckets and bail but *Wanderer* stinks for days after.

Afterwards, I think to myself, "How stupid to get in an argument over tea."

14th July, 1991. Sydney, Cape Breton

Sonny, the steward of the Sydney Yacht Club, allows me the use of the top floor for writing, studying charts, and to do a TV interview. I spread out the charts of Newfoundland and examine them in detail for the first time. It is a rugged inhospitable coast on the southwest, a number of small harbours from Port au Basque to Ramco Island but virtually no shelter the following stage without running deep into fjords. I am becoming nervous about the great depths of the anchorages and the 'williwars' blowing down from clifftops (called 'knock-me-downs' by Newfoundlanders). The southwest is high and rugged (and Valley Cove, Mount Desert, was an illustration of what can happen in strong winds). Even taking a departure from the north end of Cape Breton Island it is a long haul across Cabot Strait to Newfoundland, and the Strait is notorious for unsettled weather, the strong tides will made accurate dead reckoning impossible, and the prevalent fog will prevent coastal identification.

Before leaving England, I heard rumours of a small battery-operated Decca set being developed for use on unpowered boats, which might be the answer, but no one seems to know much about it except it is not waterproof, nor how long the batteries last without charging or when it will be available.

I am wondering if I've bitten off more than I can chew. The alternative is to put *Wanderer* on a ferry and to explore once there. I settle down with *Sailing Directions for South Newfoundland*, marking dangers and warnings with a yellow highlighting pen. Supper with Sonny and his wife, then I return to my studies. Yellow illuminations from my pen are now prevalent throughout, and on some pages there is more yellow than white and I reluctantly conclude that this is not a small boat cruising area, particularly for one without an engine.

It is a decision I make with regret as I have been looking forward to Newfoundland sailing for many months and I have heard so much about the spectacular coast and the delightful people. Additionally, I have been reading the book *The Saga of Direction* by Charles Vilas. It contains fine descriptions of cruising the area in a Colin Archer.

I can always go back to my original plan—the St. Lawrence river—or return through the beautiful Bras d'Or Lakes and head for Prince Edward Island. I pull the yacht club door closed behind me at 9:20 P.M. and to bed. The rain starts at 10:30 P.M., steady and continuous. I look round *Wanderer* with great pleasure before drifting off to sleep—the rain pouring down outside but I'm warm and dry inside with no drips.

25th July, 1991. Iona, Cape Breton

I head across the bay for Benacadie Pond which looks an interesting harbour on the chart, with a narrow entrance (probably shallow) running a long way inland, steep sided on the west side and the best shelter under the shingle spit. "You'll never get in there, I wouldn't even attempt it with my boat," warned a man aboard a yacht who kindly towed me against the current through the bridge at Iona.

The wind comes in from the southwest at 4:00 P.M. at 15 knots and soon there are white horses running from the long fetch across the bay. I ought to reef but I am fine reaching past the headland and I don't have far to go.

The harbour opens out with a very narrow entrance between shingle spits and I run down removing my ensign in case *Wanderer* needs to gybe. In the entrance, I can see the bottom clearly but we do not touch. I run down the harbour half a mile. There are few houses, no wharves or boats except for one sailing dinghy and one small lobster boat in a little brook below a farmhouse. I reef and beat back to anchor under the spit below the farm land. It is a lovely evening anchorage for my last night on the lakes and a delight to be on my own. Two boys chase down from the farm and enthusiastically wave me ashore. "We've been sent to invite you for supper. Remember—we met you at Baddeck?" The boys pull *Wanderer* up a little channel in the turf invisible from out on the water, and I have a very pleasant evening with a Gaelic-speaking family.

29th July, 1991. Approaching the Strait of Canso, Cape Breton

Head winds again. The sailing guide states that "A westerly becomes northwest in the strait and usually gusty." Once out of Inner Haddock Harbour the wind becomes a full mainsail beat up to Lennox Passage to begin the six-and-a-half mile beat to Bear Head at the entrance to the Strait of Canso. This is a commercial waterway but fortunately there are no ships in the approaches. I can see the wind-blown waves running in the straits—short seas, occasional white horses. In the centre of the straits it is rough and I come round to get back under the slight lee of the Cape Breton shore. Hard work, gusts increasing and *Wanderer* is overpowered, so under the land to pull down the second reef. Big waves now. I heave-to to look at the chart and the navigation light on Ship Point gives my position. Squalls are vicious and great care is needed to meet them, even with two reefs down.

Continually playing the mainsheet, I am tired with the concentration and sitting out. There is a ship-loading wharf beyond Ship Point and I intend to tie up for a rest. I am exhausted and don't intend to leave until the wind drops even if the shipping company doesn't like it. At the wharf, only a quarter mile short of the ship terminal, the wind drops and I am able to shake out one reef and press on past the power plant which lets off a blast of steam which startles me and I jump. The roar lasts five minutes then stops. The Straits of Canso are closed by a massive causeway from shore to shore, so I tie up at Hawkesbury's public wharf for the night.

30th July, 1991

Now there is no way through the Strait of Canso except by going through the Canso ship lock, 80 feet wide by 900 feet long. I am wondering if they will allow a sailing dinghy through rowed by oars. I walked up to the office to give my details.

"Size of boat?" the lock master asks.

When I respond with "16 feet," he counters: "No, I didn't want length. What's her tonnage...thirty ton?" he suggests.

"Oh no, she is only 16-feet long."

"Ten tons?" he asks. I shake my head.

"Ten tons?...five tons?...one ton?" I continue shaking my head.

"You'll have to give me some figure for the record before I can let you through!"

"How about a quarter ton?" I propose.

"OK," and he writes it down.

I can't resist asking: "Long or short tons?" He receives this with a long, expressionless stare. Then ignores it.

"There is a ship coming through shortly, so you'd better come in straight away," he advises.

I row in and tie up in the 80-foot wide lock. I feel dwarfed! The lock master walks across and watches me tie up. "I'm raising the crash cables across the far end of the lock so there is no chance of you hitting and damaging the gates." I look at the far gates still some 800 feet away and at the steel hawsers capable of stopping a 60, 000 ton ship and slowly realise I am being teased!

Cape George is the beginning of Northumberland Strait—a landmark between the hard coast of Nova Scotia and the more gentle sailing of Prince Edward Island. I am within striking distance of Cape George and beyond the coast turns southwest, 20 miles to Merigomish Harbour. If the wind turns southwesterly it will be a long beat into the prevailing winds—in that case it may be better to go straight across to Murray Harbour at the end of Prince Edward Island; the crossing is virtually the same distance, 20 miles, but *Wanderer* would be reaching. In either case a very early start is needed.

31st July, 1991. Havre Boucher to Bailie Brook Wharf, Nova Scotia

Awake at 4:45 A.M. There is a light air from the southeast but not enough to move a sailboat. I listen to the weather forecast from my sleeping bag: "Southeast 10–15 knots overnight increasing to southeast 15–20 knots by mid-day, then becoming light in the afternoon; and southwest 10–15 knots by Thursday morning." The prevailing wind is southwesterly so it is essential that I use every bit of the present south-

easterly.

I get out the next chart to plot my course to Prince Edward Island, the oldest province of Canada. Cape George is 19 miles. Then I can head for Pictou Island or follow the coast, depending on

Strait of Canso ship lock. Wanderer *is rowed through this enormous 900-foot lock, capable of passing a 60, 000 ton ore carrier.*

whether the wind changes direction and strength. The passage chart indicates an open coast with no harbours but the large-scale one shows a wharf at Livingstone Cape just beyond Cape George; an inset shows a harbour at Arisaig 12 miles further that is well sheltered; another at Baillie Brook Wharf another seven miles; and numerous coves after another nine miles; and Pictou Harbour another nine miles.

I ignore breakfast to get under way early. The wind is still light and *Wanderer* does little more than drift through the cove entrance. Outside there is nothing except the greyness of the fog!

I look round for a last sight of Cape Breton Island where I have spent such a

---

pleasant two-and-a-half weeks but it has disappeared. How I am looking forward to Northumberland Strait! "We never get fog in Northumberland Strait," the locals tell me. Two-and-a-half knots increasing to three knots as the wind freshens. Cloudy, unsettled sky, now doing four knots on a dead run and *Wanderer* is in the centre of a grey world. As always with fog, I feel that I am sailing but not seeming to move. Disorientating. I hope that Cape George is still there. Anyway, two mile visibility is fine. Need to consciously avoid steering higher in order to make sure that *Wanderer* doesn't sail past the end of the cape. Now beginning to plane on the front faces and *Wanderer* takes a long time to drop back into the trough. It would be wonderful sailing if not dead downwind with the continual risk of a gybe.

The wind is 15 knots but reduced by *Wanderer*'s speed to 10 knots. I gybe occasionally as the wind varies direction. The kicking strap is pulled down very tight so there is no rolling. I push down the self-bailers as I didn't sponge out yesterday, and the dinghy is soon dry. Numerous fishing boats appear at the limit of visibility, now three miles, and then a vague shadow appear slightly darker than the cloud. Five minutes later I can follow it along to where it drops into the sea— the high promontory of Cape George. Several fishing boats are pushing upwind, looking spectacular, throwing spray over their bows each time they hit a sea in a fan of sparkling foam. I gybe over to bring the wind over the port quarter. *Wanderer* is planing fast but the sea is smoother so I don't bother to reef. The wind is now 20 knots. Excellent sailing crossing St. Georges Bay, and I round the headland just as it starts to really blow. Twelve miles beyond Livingstone Point is Arisaig Harbour—the inset on the chart shows a big quarry with breakwater labelled 'Ru' (probably an old loading wharf now derelict and offering no shelter). The wind has been light and off-the-land for sometime, and I am now averaging two to three knots. The curve of the land ahead to Merigomish disappears in the murk, but Cape George behind is still clear.

Suddenly, a half mile short of Merigomish harbour wall the rain falls down by the bucketful. A few last puffs of wind carry *Wanderer* another 200 yards then expires and I row. Visibility is 200 yards in the heavy rain, decreasing to less than 100 yards as I row round the end of the rocks. A dredger in the channel stops his grab until I am safely past, and I row past timber-lined wharves, a fish factory, up a narrow channel with boats breasted up at the bend, then it opens out into a basin completely filled by fishing boats moored sterns to the jetty. They are smart, tidy boats. There is a slight easing of the torrential rain and a fisherman on one of the boats hails me and tells me to tie alongside the Fisheries Patrol boat on the floating dock: "He won't mind. He may be going out early, but it's the only place as there are still six boats to come in."

I tie alongside the patrol boat in pouring rain, remembering to check for any bilge pump outlet. (I did not wish to repeat my experience of a few weeks ago, when I tied up beneath the automatic bilge pump outlet of a fishing boat.) Tent up, everything is sodden and I light the stove for warmth, sponge out, and make a mug of tea. I have covered the last 15 miles in four-and-a-half hours. Excellent going in light winds—there must have been a strong favourable tide with me. Heavy rain until mid-evening then I walk to the harbour entrance. There is a strong northeasterly blowing, visibility is excellent and the whole coast ahead can be seen in great detail. The basin is so sheltered that I had no idea there was any wind at all. The fishermen tell me the dredging is necessary to lower the sandbar across the entrance—the bigger fishing boats draw four feet and touch coming in.

A friendly, busy, fishing harbour, attractive too, with the brook running down the valley and situated close under the high shoulder of the hill protecting it from the sea. Forty-one nautical miles today, and I used every scrap of the fair easterly. It's nice to be in shelter for tonight's gale.

9th August, 1991

Once in Northumberland Strait I'd been aware of the increasing tidal currents, but it took time to learn that I was back in another world where tides rule. I do not have tidal diagrams, my tide tables are based on Sydney now a long way astern, and I am working on my ob-servation of local high water and probably not very accu-rate.

Crossing the Northumberland Strait. Wanderer is sailing herself—when I woke up two hours later, she was still on course and the camera still aboard.

Over the next few days, the re-alisation dawns on me that the strong tides will sweep *Wanderer* far down the coast while she is beating across to Prince Edward Island.

12th August, 1991. Pictou Island, Nova Scotia

Halfway across Northumberland Strait I realise that with the ebb already setting down the coast I cannot gain ground into shelter against wind and tide, patches of heavier seas are well above head height, hollow, breaking, and each wave needs careful judgement, and I run off for my bolt hole of Pictou Island. The tide is running hard across the narrow entrance, too fast to row in safely, instead I sail in fast, hoping I have room to luff and drop sail before I hit anything.

It is a sizeable basin, holding a pontoon barge and four fishing boats. It is only 9:27 A.M. The hay on the barge has been uncovered and everyone is unloading bales before it rains, so knowing how urgent it is to keep good hay dry, I tie up quickly and help to load the truck, help unload into a barn and return to make one of the gang throwing bales up onto the quay. The barge is being loaded with clapped-out trucks—with broken chassis, axles hanging off, detached bodies—stacked three layers high and tied down.

Tomorrow a morning crossing to Prince Edward Island is impossible if the wind remains west/northwesterly. It is a 15 mile beat, and with the tide ebbing when I have done beating across, *Wanderer* will have been set at least six miles downtide; and if I come about I shall lose more ground trying to stem wind and tide; and if I wait for the afternoon flood tide to help me, the wind will have increased and 'strong-wind-against-strong-tide' conditions will be rough indeed. I shall have to stay until the wind alters. Anyway this is a sheltered harbour, nice people, nice island, and a pleasant break halfway across the Strait.

I must remember that I shall be in a different world in these flat salt-marsh estuaries of P.E.I. where the tides scour the channels so that an anchor will not hold in the hard clay bottom.

18th August, 1991. Summerside, P.E.I.

A gale roaring across the marina in the early hours. At breakfast, the weather radio announces that, "The present gale winds are forecast to drop in the afternoon...Hurricane Bob, 100 miles south-southeast of Cape Hatteras, will pass up the Bay of Fundy, cross New Brunswick, and bring hurricane force winds to Northumberland Strait." I mention this in the yacht club to several people but they smile without concern and obviously think that I have imagined it. "We don't have hurricanes here; they always pass up the Nova Scotia coast to Newfoundland," they scoff. Someone goes back to his yacht to listen and returns to confirm the forecast. There is general consternation.

Wind roaring all day, a full gale from the southwest, breakers heavy on the seawall. My neighbours, on a big yacht named *Maia* which I had first seen in Baddek, tell me they are leaving for the Bahamas. He tells me that once you own a yacht of

Maia's size and strength, wind speed and sea state doesn't make much difference, be it 10 knots or 50 knots, apart from a reduction in sail area. He refuses to believe that a hurricane is expected on Tuesday: "They always change direction at Hatteras or Cape Cod," he states emphatically. Most people are also unconcerned about an approaching hurricane. One man, who has only just started sailing, intends to cross to Pictou as soon as the present strong wind drops this evening. Talking to the commodore, I mention that a hurricane will be a new experience for me, and he says dryly, "And for most of our members too!"

There is a continual roar from the wind all day; it doesn't let up until 4:00 P.M. when it drops a notch, then resumes, and continues without ceasing until 2:40 A.M.

19th August, 1991. Summerside, P.E.I.

6:00 A.M.: Hurricane Bob is still predicted to arrive this evening or early Tuesday and the forecast includes a warning of an 'abnormally high tide.' This is what concerns me: a hurricane hitting at high water and when one jetty collapses they all go. Some people are more concerned than they were yesterday but most are not. I decide to borrow a trailer if possible and put *Wanderer* in the lee of the strongest building that I can find. I mention this to a man on the dock and immediately his friend volunteers to go home, unload his own boat, and brings his trailer back for *Wanderer*.

Spenser, the club boatman, suggests we move her into the curling rink as it is the most substantial building in the area, and by 10:00 A.M. she is inside with all her gear. I am wet through, and even my rubber boots are full of rainwater. The owner of my neighbour yacht comes down. "I am taking off the canopy and all gear, putting dinghy and motor in the curling hall and I'm staying on board tonight in case the docks collapse. They now say that 'Bob' will hit in the early hours—well after high water."

4:08 P.M.: Waiting for 'Bob' which must be the second tropical storm of the season as they are numbered alphabetically from A–Z. Steady rain, visibility one mile, no wind. A still afternoon with slight drizzle, a dark cloud mass far beyond the horizon, but with no sign of the violence to come.

A small yacht leaves at 4:00 P.M. heading for the ferry terminal on the New Brunswick side of Northumberland Strait. The owner tells me that he works there, they have a safe boat shelter from hurricanes, and he estimates that he should have time to get across…unless his motor fails! Thirteen fishing boats come in during the evening from Borden where there is no adequate shelter from hurricane winds; all the boats at Victoria were hauled out this morning as were all the small boats at Charlottetown too. *Wanderer* is safe in the curling rink and I am sleeping on a fishing boat in the marina.

I have done all I can. The next yacht has three lines out to the seawall to hold her off the floating docks. *Maia* has three lines aft to the dock, four lines from her bow. She is the boat with the greatest windage and has moved inside the floats where she can tie direct to steel piles with additional ropes across to the sea wall. Several small yachts and power boats pull out at the slipway during the evening.

I go over in my mind the warnings I remember from the U.S.:

1. Hurricanes are especially dangerous if they hit at high water.

2. High water is much higher than predicted because of storm surge. (In Charleston there was an ocean swell on top of a 13-foot surge as well.)

3. The damage caused by even one boat breaking loose is enormous—she goes onto her neighbour, causing more damage, the next breaks away and next thing the whole dock system goes!

4. The only certain way of preventing loss and damage is to deliberately sink boat and equipment.

Perhaps I'm exaggerating the danger? Possibly had I lowered the mast and turned *Wanderer* head-to-wind there would be nothing for the wind to get hold of, but I know in my heart that this is untrue: a hurricane is capable of lifting her clear out of the water.

I examine the dock system. It is strong, the heavy 'H' section piles rise almost to the same level as the quayside, and are driven deep, the pontoons are substantial but there are several big yachts with a lot of windage. Anxiously, I wonder what will happen if one of their lines go or a cleat pulls out? I go for a walk in search of a burger, and a full stomach, in anticipation of a disturbed night. As I return, the wind is rising and it is beginning to rain.

Gerard MacPhee the owner of the big double ender *Arjuna* is aboard as are several other crews "...in case the docks collapse," they tell me. Midnight forecast: "'Bob' has lost some power—now degraded to a 'tropical storm.' Winds expected to be 55–65 knots." Much better than the hurricane force 65–75 knots we have been expecting, but nasty enough and there is always a risk of regained strength as it crosses water.

I tune in again to the weather report which warns of "tides in excess of one to two metres above normal....Small craft are warned that winds in excess of 20 knots may be expected." I smile at the last item—rather unnecessary! I sleep badly although comfortable through a still night waiting for a hurricane to hit. The sky is completely overcast. No wind. It will be difficult when power fails and the dock lights go out.

20th August, 1991 (Hurricane Bob day). Summerside, P.E.I.

3:40 A.M.: A steady build up in wind strength. It is dawn. Heads appearing through hatches to check mooring lines, bodies testing mooring lines, especially on neighbouring boats, as soon as it is light enough to see. Wind roaring across the harbour, spray driving across the sea wall. Wind is storm force southerly. Big waves crashing on the breakwater even though it is only a one mile fetch across the estuary.

The owner of the fishing boat that I had slept on puts a line across to the sea wall as she has compressed her two foot diameter fenders flat under the beam wind. Other yachts are doing the same further along. Clouds are low, black and travelling across at enormous speed. Tide is already at high water level on the breakwater even though there is still four hours to go to high water. I take a walk round the marina; securing lines all seem fine. One fishing boat's tire fenders have worked between the piles and she is rubbing badly—three men push her off while I give her another six inches.

Continuous storm-force winds all day. The constant unvarying 'roar' hour after hour, is wearing mentally and physically. I walk to Tim Horton's Donut Shop for coffee, and I have to lean 25 degrees into the wind to stay vertical. The big yacht *Maia* is waving and three men go to help. She has her anchor chains direct to the steel piles and she is hanging on the chains as the tide drops. The wind between the yachts is almost enough to blow us off the docks as we return.

4:30 P.M.: The wind drops, clouds are an almost solid grey wall gradually decreasing in height as they travel north beyond the horizon. What relief. Everyone walks round checking boats but there is no damage. We were lucky indeed.

5:15 P.M.: Wind down to 15 knots and I decide to get *Wanderer* afloat before dark. A couple of men help me prevent the trolley from running away down the slipway. I row round and under four 'hold-off' lines not yet removed and I am back where I started yesterday.

A French-speaking lad from the yacht from Quebec takes my lines. His English is as bad as my French. I mention that I am nervous of cruising in French-speaking Quebec and he tells me that his family are just as nervous of cruising in the English-speaking maritime provinces. Conversation is difficult and we soon give up. Not until the following spring did I realise that he had unknowingly given me the key to cruising the great St. Lawrence River.

It is amazing how a hurricane (even downgraded to a severe tropical storm) enhances everything: food tastes better, the air is clearer, and I enjoy a hot chocolate drink more than usual before turning in.

22nd August, 1991. Summerside, P.E.I.

Two interviews with newspapers and radio. Today the wind is roaring. The forecast is for 15–20 knots but the wind meter on the neighbouring yacht already shows 25–35 knots, so I'll be staying another day. I have been invited onto a neighbouring yacht for banana pancakes with maple syrup, then my neighbours the MacPhees have invited me to a 'Scottish' concert at the College of Piping. It turns out to be a lovely concert: Scottish dancing, pipes and drums, songs and ballads, virtuoso playing by International Champion Piper 'Scot' Macauley holding the audience spellbound, and finishing with 'The Sheiling Song' and another song in the Gaelic which Marg and I last heard in the Hebrides.

Since the reporters called there have been a continuous stream of visitors wanting to inspect *Wanderer* and some anonymous person has put a large blueberry cake aboard. Wylie Barrett introduces himself as a Canadian who hired a car from me years ago when I was building up my Ford dealership in Norfolk. He was so pleased with our service that he wants to return the favour by showing me Prince Edward Island. First we visited Green Gables (the home made famous by L.M. Montgomery's fictional book, *Anne of Green Gables*) which, on P.E.I., is obligatory. Then to North Rustico to see a typical 'north shore' harbour, and return via Woodleigh Miniature Gardens. This is a park of famous buildings, many of them familiar to British eyes: St Martin-in-the-Fields, the Tower of London, the Olde Curiosity Shoppe, the Church at Stoke Poges, Stoke Poges Manor House, St. Paul's Cathedral, Dunvegan Castle, all to 1/20th scale and accurate in every detail, and each with a comprehensive history alongside. I expected to be disappointed—but no! It was enthralling to see the construction of the roofs and towers that are never visible to the visitor to the full scale buildings in Britain. A wheelbarrow was standing alongside York Minster which was having its little roof re-built. I mentioned to my host that the full size cathedral in York had recently also lost it's roof after being struck by lightning.

31st August, 1991. Festival Acadien

The Festival Acadien was an education for British eyes—a two-day celebration of Acadian customs interests and tradition, a celebration, a music festival, and an agricultural show. I was a privileged visitor too as I knew so many people from my stay in the harbour, and I was staying with locals Jerry and Sally Arsenault and family, who insisted that I sleep in the house after hitch-hiking to the festival rather than roll out my sleeping bag in their barn.

Acadians were originally French settlers, thousands of whom the British deported in 1755 when they refused to disavow their French heritage and pledge allegiance to the English. Acadian villages are still found throughout the

Maritimes and the Acadians I've met have had lively senses of humour and I have liked them instinctively.

The competitions were based on the province's traditional industries of timber, agriculture, and stock, and many were outside my experience. I buy tickets for two one-metre plots for 'Bingo de la Vache' (cow bingo) which is the finale of the festival, after the Heavy Horse Pulling Contest, and the 'Blessing of the Boats.'

'Bingo de la Vache' is also the highlight of the festival and enormously entertaining. The squares on a field had been marked out, and a cow was let in while the men, women, and even young children yell to the back end of the cow about "where to do it" while the front end was offered handfuls of fresh grass soaked in molasses and castor oil, hoping that the square they bet on will soon have fresh manure. I left before it was over and the next day, a lady at the fish processing factory mentions they waited three-and-a-half hours but "the cow did nothing, so the judges had to send for another one."

I made a memorable departure from the harbour. I had met many of the fishermen, and had been giving a local man, Benny Huot, some sailing lessons, and several had helped me pull *Wanderer* to the top of the wooden slipway, and chatted while I repaired the tent and sewed on new velcro. The slipway is built of fir and the resin sticky, so it seemed a good idea to sluice several buckets of water down the ramp and under *Wanderer* for lubrication. The next moment I am sliding down the planks on my back followed closely by *Wanderer*, and I swim back towing my boat to applause and laughter from the fishermen. "What did that chap say in French that caused the laughter," I ask. He said "I've heard they always launch their boats like that in England.'"

4th September, 1991. Cap Lumier, New Brunswick

The fishing boats leave and wake me. There is no wind and I breakfast at 6:30 A.M. The tent is dry except for a little condensation. No rain last night in spite of the 30 per cent probability forecasted. High water is at 6:00 A.M. so I shall have the ebb tide under me until noon. The Northumberland Strait opens out once round the next corner so the current will decrease from the two-and-a-half knots shown on the chart. I am tired of harbours and I need some time on my own so I will find a deserted creek tonight if possible. The chart shows there are plenty in the next section of coast.

I row out of the inner and outer basins two hours after breakfast to use the first of the breeze, but it is northeasterly and I can only just lay my course along the coast.

An enjoyable day spent sailing along a coast of long sandy beaches backed by sand-dunes covered with maram grass, with occasional gaps where the channels run through into the large inland Baie de St. Louis.

6th September, 1991. Baie St Anne to Douglastown, New Brunswick

The latest forecast predicts, "Northeast 10–20 knots today. Strong northwest tomorrow and areas to the north will have gales." So I need to find shelter for Saturday and Sunday. Head winds for crossing the 15 miles to the northern shore of Miramichi Bay. It's a long beat but more sensible instead to run up Miramichi Bay and River to Newcastle, where I can find George Washburn the boatbuilder who has offered to store/maintain *Wanderer* over the winter. A light breeze which was from the north when I breakfasted has veered to east as I spread out the tent by the mast to dry rather than in the stern locker to dampen other items. I skate over the shallows following a local skiff whom I assume knows where the deeper water is, then down the buoyed channel to slightly less shallow water. There is a dredged and buoyed channel leading into a little cove at French River and I examine it through binoculars. It looks nice with only two boats.

There are no navigation buoys and the shore is featureless so I lay a course on the chart to cross the seaward end of a long submerged spit running out from the land. I shall know my position when the centreboard touches, then steer a compass course out to deeper water.

It does not work out as planned. *Wanderer* is in shallower water than I expected when the centreboard touches and the rudder blade is kicked up and, lacking grip, she tries to broach towards the shoal. I glance back: it looks spectacular behind me with seas breaking as they run into the shallows, sparkling and azure blue in the sun, but I have no hands to spare to take a photograph. Heavy use of the tiller brings her round and she gybes out to deeper water. Hundreds of cormorants flap off from Baie de Vin Island in a great black cloud as I pass. Another four miles to Point au Carre and *Wanderer* is planing on the front faces, full mainsail and genoa.

Wonderful sailing, a planing breeze from the quarter, the islands across the mouth of the Baie breaking the swells and I run on into the rapidly narrowing Miramichi Inner Bay. At Chatham, I stop for supplies, tying alongside a fishing boat whose two man crew are deep in a game of chess. They wave me aboard and then towards the coffee pot without glancing up from their game, and I pour them each a cup too. I have travelled 23 miles in six hours, including light winds for the first one-and-a-half hours. Across the river in the new Douglastown Yacht marina I tie up after a total day' sail of 26 miles with the tide under me and a stern wind. It was worth changing plans.

11 September, 1991. Neguac (north shore Miramichi Bay), New Brunswick

Four very pleasant days in Douglastown near Newcastle. Met another small boat enthusiast Dave Tweedie, who builds his own boats, organises sail and power boat courses and knows the creeks and harbours of the Miramichi like the back of his hand. He saw *Wanderer* in Pictou when he was on a motorcycle holiday so immediately recognised her in his local yacht club. I asked if I might stay overnight as I needed to work on my boat and rigging but I did not realise he is a skilled amateur boatbuilder until next morning when he turned up before I was awake with a friend who was a professional rigger, and they set to work while I ate my breakfast dressed in pyjamas. Dave produced my article "Northern Harbour" which he had liked so much that he kept it. It was published many years ago in an American magazine. I had almost forgotten it.

Dave sailed with me to Neguac yesterday. The temperature is dropping quickly; trees changing colour; and the big freeze-up starts in October, and soon local fishermen will drive onto the sea-ice to set nets under the ice for smelt.

19th September, 1991. Anse Bleue to Stonehaven, New Brunswick

Rain all last night starting at 11:00 P.M., heavy and continuous until dawn. Very little wind overnight, certainly not the predicted strong southerly of 25–30 knots which made me anchor last night in the shallows close under the shore in Anse Bleue Harbour. This morning's forecast for the marine areas: "Northumberland Strait and Baie des Chaleurs: southerly 25–30 knots this morning becoming northwesterly 20–25 knots this afternoon." This is followed by the forecast for the land areas: "Upper St. John and Chaleur: light winds." It's difficult to reconcile two such different forecasts for the same area! In any case, I have no intention of going anywhere with a marine forecast of 25–30 knots, even of it is off-the-land. Even the predicted onshore north-northwesterly is only acceptable for a short time. Not even the four mile passage to the next harbour, Grande Anse, is worth the risk!

21st September, 1991

Midnight: On the point of being sea-sick in my sleeping bag all night long because of movement. I move *Wanderer* back alongside a fishing boat where I find more stillness but now there is an occasional snatch. Glad to be laying flat again, and I move the bailer within reach.

22nd September, 1991. To Stonehaven, New Brunswick

I roll back the tent. It's a lovely morning. A leisurely breakfast. I have run out of my usual grapefruit but I finish the last of the apple juice instead, then porridge, a marmalade sandwich, and a mug of tea. I consider the problem of getting ashore without *Wanderer* drying out all day (the wind is now northwest; depth two feet and much shallower than when I anchored last night, but for some reason, morning tides are much smaller than evening tides here). A calm, sunny day with the faintest breeze from the west.

Idly, I estimate the speed of the clouds to be 40 knots; then I realise that the clouds on the other side of *Wanderer* are not moving! The storm clouds have a clearly defined edge just two miles to the eastward. *Wanderer* and Anse Bleue Harbour is on the sheltered side of the weather front which the synopsis said had stalled over the Maritimes until the vigorous front pushes in from Quebec tonight. I can snatch the passage to Grande Anse (possibly even to Stonehaven where I may be able to leave my boat over the winter) before the next front rolls in.

I scramble the tent down; its very wet so I fold it loosely behind the mast to dry. It's a big harbour, no boats moving, and a light wind so I sail out but with oars ready. I'm hailed by some fishermen on the end of the wharf. "Au Grande Anse?" they ask. "Oui," I reply. "Bon voyage!" they shout with doubt written all over their faces.

9:30 A.M.: Wind light westerly, dead on the nose. Unroll genoa and start beating. Wind very light close to land so I put in a long tack out to the wind ripples a half mile offshore. Low cliffs, scattered houses, and a road along the crest. Soon beating past the small headland Cap Pete and in the long shallow bay running round to Grande Anse.

11:30 A.M.: Off the harbour at Grande Anse, four hours for last four miles. Eight-and-a-half miles to Stonehaven equals four hours although the tide may help a little later on. I estimate my time of arrival to be 4:00 P.M. (I may be able to get in at Pokeshaw halfway where the chart shows a stream running into the bay under a bridge). A long tack out, and the whole coast opens out, and I can see far headland, probably Grindstone Point and Stonehaven. A flash of a harbour light confirms it. Eight miles of unbroken cliff and no shelter—a long row if the wind dies, or a long run back if it blows up!

1:00 P.M.: A shallow indentation in the cliffs. Maybe it's Pokeshaw? But there is no sign of a stream or bridge. The chart shows an island off Pokeshaw about the size of a pinhead but there is certainly no island here! Wait, there it is! A two acre island 100 feet above my head—a great mass rock just detached from the shore by a narrow channel. But where is the stream and the bridge? Suddenly, I spot the stream; it has been hidden under the road embankment. There is no shelter here.

Stonehaven on a low spit just beyond Grindstone Point is now clearly visible at four miles. High cliffs, occasional stacs, big caves cut into the cliff face by gales, and heavily undercut by rafting winter sea-ice (sedimentary shale, brown shading to green in places). I sail close under cliffs to take photographs. The wind dies. I roll up the genoa, raise boom, start rowing—only two miles to go. Four hundred strokes later and the last headland and stacs slowly recede astern. Seven hundred strokes and I'm in New Bandon Bay, opposite the village. Only one mile to go. I'm eagerly anticipating getting in after a pleasant day's sail. A light wind from ahead fills in. Excellent! I unroll the genoa and start beating. I can pick out the wharf and details of buildings now.

Immediately, the wind picks up and I roll up genoa just in time. *Wanderer* is sailing but I have to jump to pull down the first reef. The second reef is already needed and I don't have time even to tie reef points. Then it hits from the northwest.

The wind is screaming and I am surrounded by white water, spray and breaking seas. I half raise the centreboard and try to get *Wanderer* sailing, but am overpowered even with two reefs down. I must reduce sail but I don't want to lose ground so I pull the boom off gooseneck and roll two turns of sail round boom as well, forgetting the centre mainsheet. I have to unroll the sail again to remove it. Next time, the mainsheet blocks wind up round the boom end! Done at last. Mainsail head now two feet below the hound fittings on mast. I can just keep *Wanderer* moving providing I don't pin her in and play the mainsheet but its dicey!

I wait for my chance then tack to try for a little shelter close under the headland, but seas are breaking erratically in the shallows, so I tack again and head out. This is no temporary squall—everything points to a blow from the northwest—it must be the front which was forecast, certainly it is far above 25 knots! I stagger on, as close to the wind as I dare, until I'm sure *Wanderer* is losing ground. Seas are breaking heavily and increasing. I shall have to run back. I'm so near; even now the harbour is only one-and-a-half miles but I have no hope of getting there. Instead, I have now a long run back of seven miles to Grande Anse with the seas building. Probably, I'll have to run under the genoa only, but I'll try with reefed mainsail first.

I broad reach under the minute mainsail and we are planing, though under control. The wind reduces but it's as strong as ever when I come round and *Wanderer* is overpowered and staggering as she meets each sea. I run off again. Another quarter of a mile and I try again and I can just lay close-hauled although knocked about by each breaking sea. I hold her at it for another hour—hard, wet work, intense concentration, but the wind has definitely eased and five minutes later I need to unroll the two turns of sail round the boom to keep her moving though the crests. It looks as if there is more to come: grey, heavy, overcast from horizon to horizon from the northwest. It's taken 55 minutes and I've lost at least one-and-a-half miles. Now with two reefs in, I try again—a 'long-and-short'—but I have to free off from close-hauled because of the weight of water in the breaking seas.

Slowly, I gain ground past the village of New Bandon again, watching the weather carefully for more wind, and think "thank goodness no one was watching." A tack out to weather the headland. I'm close enough to pick out the individual boulders in the harbour wall. The seas are still nasty but the wind is dropping, so I shake out the second reef and *Wanderer* points and handles better. The rain starts. Another tack out to clear a long reef. I put up the full mainsail again as wind drops. Two more tacks, then heave-to to photograph the harbour entrance. The wind suddenly increases and I have difficulty to get *Wanderer* to pay off under the mainsail only. We plane the 20 yards into the lee of a harbour wall, row in and tie alongside a fishing boat at far end of harbour. Already it's blowing hard out there again: very glad to be safely in.

A fisherman comes down to check his boat: "Move into the cabin of my boat tonight," he offers. "It's clean, warm, and comfortable." But it's nice in my own boat, warm in the tent now I've lit the lantern. I strip off my oilskin, and am soon warm and dry, and tucking into a hot 'beef ragout' while outside the rain pours down, the wind roars, and the seas break loudly on the outer wall.

When I wake the next morning, I climb the wharf to find three fishermen: "It came in quick yesterday—a northwesterly is always bad here!" We live in New Bandon—we were all watching you!

5th October, 1991. Bathurst, New Brunswick

Dave Tweedie from the Miramichi has passed me onto his sailing friends, Ken Gammon and Don Furlotte along the coast who have taken me under their wing. Ken arranged docking for me at the Bathurst Yacht Club next to his English-built yacht, then drove me to the falls on Nepisiguit River to see the autumn run of salmon. The rapids through the rock narrows are spectacular, with wonderful fall colours, and salmon jumping from one level to the next. I find it exciting—much more so than I'd expected. Then came a visit to the provincial championship ploughing match of a standard as high as I have seen anywhere, and to see the inspection of animals killed in the moose hunt. It is wonderful to have friends with transport—especially in a country so vast that a car is essential.

I'm feeling very tired now that *Wanderer* is ashore. I try to work out why. I had believed my distance this year was less than last, but it is virtually the same when I work it out. Now, I realise that once I had rounded the top corner of

Nova Scotia and turned east, the fair southwesterlies had become head winds and there was a much higher proportion of westerlies and northwesterlies.

This was hard work but at least I had left the infamous Nova Scotia fogs behind. The temperature had been dropping quickly recently and the local fishermen had been telling for some time that I had only seven to ten days more sailing before it becomes too cold. They say in a few weeks they will be driving out onto the ice in their pick-ups, cutting holes in the sea ice with chain saws to net smelt. So snatching passages and using every breath of the infrequent easterlies had become my normal practice. No wonder I was tired!

I am happy that Bathurst Yacht Club are keeping *Wanderer*. They have found a place for her inside the sail store where she is warm and dry.

6th October, 1991 (Canadian Thanksgiving)

The delightful extended group of small boat enthusiasts along this coast with shoal draft yachts—Drascombes, Wayfarers, and dories—have befriended me. Along with their families they have come together to give me a Thanksgiving Supper of turkey, cranberry, and pumpkin pie. The Thanksgiving celebration has been advanced from next weekend for my benefit.

I decide to travel to Halifax by train. This will give me two days to see friends, and to rehearse my talk for the Maritime Museum of the Atlantic before I fly home.

9th October, 1991. En route to England.

I spend the flight home in a more sober mood than usual, thinking of how I had survived Hurricane Bob, the frightening sail in Somes Sound, and the grounding in Hell's Gate, and the nightmare view of the Selveges which had almost drained my enthusiasm. Only the lonely stay on Coffin Island, and the days in secure friendly Moose Harbour with its ever-present smell of honeysuckle and wild roses, the wonderful concert in Liverpool and the fun I had washing-up the dirty dishes with the kitchen volunteers afterwards re-established my sense of perspective.

The last few months have reminded me more than ever that the Wayfarer is a tough dinghy, ideal for my type of sailing, but the wind and the sea are ultimately the master!

10th October, 1991. Well-next-the-Sea, England

When I return, I notice in one of our quality British newspapers reports that the Canadian Department responsible for 'Gaming' has studied 'Bingo de la Vache' and has concluded that "it is not entirely a game of chance as the result can be influenced by the spectators," and has recommended that it be banned!

For some reason it cheered me to no end to imagine this man in his government office dedicated to preventing a man and a spectator with a handful of grass dipped in molasses and castor oil from loading the odds in a game of Bingo de la Vache in Prince Edward Island.

It is a wonderful world after all.

CHAPTER FIVE

1992. The Lower St. Lawrence:
The Impossible Equation

26th May, 1992

Nineteen ninety-two was the cruise we dubbed the "St. Lawrence River Marathon." Luckily, when I set out for Canada on May 26th I had no hint of the sailing conditions ahead of me. Had I known, I might have thought twice about attempting it at all.

Ryerson and Ann Clarke, friends from the previous year, collected me from the airport at Halifax, showed me the sights for a couple of days, and delivered me to the railroad station to travel in one of the new trans-Canada passenger trains fitted with sleeping cabins and an observation car just like the ones in old Hollywood films. I spent almost a full day bringing up a mass of gear from Dave and Gerry's cellar where it had been stored since last winter and checking it. I am always amazed how much gear the Wayfarer will carry without affecting her sailing ability.

2nd June, 1992. Bathurst, New Brunswick

Wanderer emerges from the Bathurst Yacht Club with the Canadian maintenance permit still taped to her foredeck as the regulations specify. Dave gives me a hand to scrub the hull, then we settled down to the hard boring work of removing stains and dirt from the gel coat. A quick coat of anti-foul and a visit to Canada Customs to exchange my maintenance permit for a cruising permit completed *Wanderer*'s refit. I settle down to check the chart and tide tables in detail for the first leg as far as Gaspé Bay.

I am worried about receiving marine weather forecasts as *Reed's Almanac* lists different wavebands to those available on my pre-set weatherbox radio. Maybe I need a hand-held VHF radio and I have been checking types and price but I find that I must pass an operator's examination. Another worry is that Gaspé and the Lower St. Lawrence are province of Quebec where, in the less populated areas, few people speak English and, since I do not speak French, communication will be difficult.

The tent needs some work, the clam cleats inside the transom that tighten the skirt line are worn and need replacing, the boom crutch must be reduced by an inch to allow for canvas shrinkage, and the velcro tapes at the quarters need extending to avoid pulling the tent out of shape when it shrinks in the rain.

My thinking has become negative—a sure sign that I have been ashore too long! I attend the local church where Gerry, who is a bilingual Acadian, guides me through the Catholic service.

7th June, 1992

Ashore I sleep badly—it is time to get afloat. I rig *Wanderer* for sleeping, erect the tent and I'll move aboard this evening after my 'thank you' talk to the Bathurst Yacht Club.

9th June, 1992. Across the Baie de Chaleur

Surfing on the front faces of the waves and *Wanderer* takes a long time to drop back into the troughs. Visibility is wonderful and Pointe de l'Ouest is visible from many miles away. An occasional wave breaks at the quarter and the sound makes me jump. There are heavy breakers off the point which looks like a deep water 'race' caused by the current from the bay running into the ebb tide and against the wind, rather than the distinctive 'rip' of a current running over a shallow reef. It seems better under the point and I work close in. It is the right decision as there is an inshore passage, as I half expected.

At Pointe au Loups Marins the seas build and start cresting. I'm approaching a shallow reef. I stand for a better view; it doesn't look too bad and soon I'm through it. The wind has increased and is breezing up even under the land. I can go no further today. The next harbour is 10 miles away which means another two hours and the afternoon wind is increasing. There is a strong ebb from under the bridges so I luff and row in and tie alongside a boat in the lee of the 'L' at the end of the breakwater. The guide says the wharf is exposed to strong south or easterly winds. I expect a surge sets round the end and with a strong southwesterly of 25–30 knots. Tomorrow I will have to move under the bridges for shelter. An English speaking fisherman tells me to "tie close under the end of the wharf and you will be completely sheltered." My first sight of the Quebec flag, a white cross on a blue background with a fleur-de-lys in each quadrant.

Crossing the bay, I am at shivering temperature after the heat of the last few days. A wonderful days sailing. A good passage across the bay on a very fine reach but it was cold storming along the coast cliffs even on a dead run in bright sunshine, surfing before dropping back into the trough. The sort of day's sailing that is remembered all of one's life!

13th June, 1992. Anse aux Gascons, Quebec

The tent is in good condition. I put back into Anse aux Gascons with an ominous black front coming in from the south, and a forecast of 20–30 knots. It's a sheltered fishing harbour with inner basin. A thunderstorm warning is now issued for afternoon and evening. I decided to go to the 'Claire de Lune' overture at 8:00 P.M. Just as I am walking into the hall the wind switches 180 degrees, unbelievable lightning sizzles down, in addition to thunder, gale force winds, and hail for half-an-hour.

When it slacks a little I run back to *Wanderer* (I had already decided that 'Claire de Lune' was probably the name of a pop group and not the rather attractive music of the same name), getting soaked, and expecting to find the tent torn off by the wind, but *Wanderer*'s tent is still in place, I undo the front flap and slide into the boat and strip off, then towel down and look round -—there is not a drop of water inside—the boat is completely dry. Hurrah for canvas and a good tent maker!

As I write up my log, lightning is sizzling down all around, illuminating the inside of the tent, thunder banging deafeningly and rain bucketing down again. I consider making a mug of hot cocoa but I am warm from changing out of my wet clothes and towelling down, and the stove would make the inside stuffy. There is no trace of damp on the underside of the canvas anywhere, and I notice that ventile cloth doesn't absorb water and dries quicker than ordinary canvas. I cut off two pieces of candied peel as a reward. I'm not sure whether the reward is for *Wanderer*, the tent, or me but it is well-deserved anyway.

9:20 P.M.: The rain stops, thunder receding into the distance to the north. I am warm and snuggle down into my sleeping bag, The forecasters got their 20–25 knots wind wrong, but the thunderstorm forecast was dead right.

10:15 P.M.: Heavy rain and tremendous thunder returns for ten minutes. I retire well satisfied with five miles made good today.

3:15 A.M.: The fishing boats leave so I have to move *Wanderer* along to a vacant section of quay. On this coast, boats are moving out of harbour all the time so I am usually sailing by 6:00 A.M.

16th June, 1992. Grande Rivière, Peninsular de Gaspé, Quebec

A long day yesterday. Light winds (part rowing) but sailed 23 miles to here. It is still very cold on the water. I have visited two of the prettiest coves I have ever seen. One had no boats or houses but a pool with a narrow entrance; and here the old river harbour is lovely—up the river is a pool between the modern road bridge and the old railroad bridge—originally industrial, but now deserted. I came into the new fishing harbour for the convenience of being alongside a pontoon, which is comfortable but not pretty. There are many acres of fish racks loaded with drying cod, an unusual sight these days. I have my fleur-de-lys Quebec courtesy flag now.

18th June, 1992. Gaspé, Quebec

A day fitting out. I took care of all the little jobs: extra hole drilled in the radar reflector so it hangs in the 'rain-catching' position; clips to the washboard on the bows for the front tent flap elastic; got out the waterpump pliers and screwdriver for ready use; opened the end of the split pin holding the clew of the mainsail; checked the forestay end for any signs of fatigue, fitted a new line to retainer for genoa reef drum; adjusted the tent skirt line which has chafed under the clips in various places, and checked the rudder fittings.

I put all my tools away at 5:00 p.m. and then have a meal in the local café.

22nd June, 1992. Grande Grave to Rivière Reynard into the St. Lawrence River, Quebec

1:30 a.m.: So far there's been heavy rain all night. But it was an enjoyable night listening to its noise while I stayed warm and dry in my sleeping bag. *Wanderer* was laying comfortably. I'm feeling glad of my extra clothes.

4:10 a.m.: Several trucks arrive—I don't hear anyone going out of harbour but I thought I had heard breakers. I make porridge then go back to sleep.

7:10 a.m.: Slept late. Still raining. Inside the tent still dry. Radio reception is poor because of interference. Twice the newsreader fades as he gets to the local forecast. I think he said "15–20 knots" but I'm unsure. My bedding is wet although the underside of the tent has not been leaking. The water has run down the halliard onto the toe-straps which wick it down to the foot of my sleeping bag.

I walk across to fishing boat that came in earlier and ask about the forecast which I'm told is "Easterly 10-15 knots all day, rain. The same tomorrow." I question the wind force but the fishermen are certain: "No more than 10–15 knots was forecast." I decide to look around to investigate and as it turns out, the breakers I heard last night was actually the waterfall at the head of harbour.

Wind now south along the shore. It is really a one-reef breeze but I might just carry a full mainsail off the wind. Sailing out, I have to shout "Ahoy" to get the fishermen on the pier head to pull in their lines enough to get past. A long tack out, the far shore hidden in the mist. Waves are approximately three feet and *Wanderer* shoulders her way through like the superb sea boat she is. I'm enjoying myself in spite of the rain; one reef down and nothing ahead but endless waves to the horizon and far beyond—and a good boat under me!

Suddenly, I realise that I can lay Cap Gaspé on the other tack; I must have been musing and sailed on the offshore tack far longer than I realised! Ten minutes later I have to unroll the genoa to pull *Wanderer* through the seas instead of lolloping in the same place. Now I am beating into the race; the seas are confused, standing up on end—ugly but not breaking so I tack and work out. Several big boats are fishing in the calmer water just clear of the race. Inshore, the overfalls are possible so I free off for a little extra speed and maneuverability, and pick my way carefully. The seas ease and I am safely through, but it is a frightening place, and I decide it is not an area that I would chance in anything more than ideal conditions.

The sheer size of the peninsular end makes it spectacular and I get out the camera to record it. Blast! *Wanderer* is in the race again—ugly, short, vertical, big and breaking. There's a race on the north side of the point as well! I'm scrambling the camera back into the underdeck bag, leaning forward, head down, when a breaker comes over the bows six inches deep, down my neck and inside my oilskins! I had been broad-reaching down the north side of Peninsular, now I sheet in quickly and close-haul to get the hell out of it. I can feel the current pouring out over the bottom, waves six to seven feet steep and dangerous. At last, I'm clear and seas become smaller and less ugly, and I am able to run off for the lighthouse.

Suddenly, under *Wanderer*'s bows there is a four foot drop, a vertical-sided hole. Paralysed with shock, I am unable to move. *Wanderer* teeters on the edge for ages, bows overhanging the hole, then slowly drops back into the trough behind. That was truly frightening! Now I have run right into another race! The waves are steep and breaking dangerously. I close-haul offshore. Even now the wind is only 10 knots and it takes a long time to get clear. Good God! I run off for the light-house when the seas reduce.

I can feel the current pouring out of the St. Lawrence and half-a-mile astern there is a great crescent of tide rips, overfalls, and cresting seas and it is getting worse as the tide increases; and the wind is only 10 knots, dead astern, the slowest point of sailing. I'm afraid that I may be slowly losing ground so I take continuous careful bearings on the cliff. I feel my fear building. What happens if the wind drops? *Wanderer* will be carried stern first into that frightening long line of great breakers and there is no way of surviving that maelstrom.

An hour later the wind increases marginally and *Wanderer* eases forward. I am safe and have time to relax and absorb the atmosphere of this treacherous place. Cape Gaspé is even more impressive on the north side with vertical cliffs, mountain heads disappearing in cloud, vast, impersonal, dangerous. Entertainment is provided by hundreds of gannets looking for their lunch and diving into the waves, wings closed, from 100 feet.

The lighthouse is some six miles away and the enormous cliffs dwarf the two-and-a-half knot speed that *Wanderer* is doing. After a long slow goose-winged run I am relieved to crawl into the bay at the base of the Gaspé peninsular out of the tide and, after hours of tense concentration, let the tension drain out of me. The wind is southerly and increasing, and now *Wanderer* is reaching and covering the ground faster. A pity to go into the harbour in the next bay so I carry on. The chart shows L'Anse au Griffon harbour only five miles beyond the point and another harbour five miles beyond that.

Writing in my log, I realise only 15 days have passed since leaving Bathurst and I have covered a quite respectable distance, considering the weather. But since I crossed the Baie des Chaleurs into Quebec, language has been a problem. There has been almost no communication with the French-speaking fishermen.

Thinking about the difficulty, I visualise the lad on the Quebec yacht in Summerside P.E.I. last year saying, "We are worried about entering English-speaking areas—just as you are of visiting French-speaking Quebec." He gave me the key to St. Lawrence cruising: it is up to me to 'break the ice,' and, bad though my French is, I must risk making a fool of myself if I want to meet local people, and as a matter of courtesy I must always ask permission to tie up in a fishing harbour. Confirmation comes from remembering my first French village, Port Daniel, after crossing Baie des Chaleurs: at the store I asked for "Marmalad, du pain, le eau, si vous please?" and added as an afterthought, "Et un drapeau de Quebec avec les fleur-de-lys." There was a great roar of laughter and customers and staff flocked round to help.

24th June, 1992. Rivière au Reynard, Quebec

Very cold. The foot of my sleeping bag is wet again from water running down the halliard, via toe strap as at Grande Grave. The hollofill lining is said to retain 85 per cent of its insulation when wet, and certainly I was not conscious of wetness overnight although I did wake several times with cold knees and feet although the rest of my body was warm. An outboard boat ties alongside wharf just ahead at 4:30 A.M.

5:30 A.M.: Up and quick breakfast, wind northerly light, fog at the headland, approximately one mile visibility. I expect that it will improve as the day warms. I stow the wet tent in the cockpit to dry.

6:50 A.M.: I close-haul out of the harbour, followed by a trawler which turns, and immediately disappears! It's fog, and visibility is only 200 yards. I start short tacking along the harbour wall, light northeasterly wind, and I am disorientated as soon as out of sight of shore. Off headland I can see the tops of the cliffs before I'm in the breakers (better than the other way round!) but I need a quarter mile visibility for safety. It's not a happy situation and I realise that I could easily miss the narrow entrance to Anse au Valleau on the outward tack if visibility doesn't improve. The fog clamps down. A vessel appears vaguely at the limit of my vision. Is it a small boat close in? Or an ocean going ship further out? It is impossible to tell. I reluctantly turn back.

Breakers appear ahead, the headland has disappeared, and I have to head out before coming back to 160 degrees magnitude hoping to find the harbour wall. Another open outboard from the small boat harbour comes across and offers me a tow. "Merci, oui" I accept happily. The two men, one wearing a white yachting cap, have been fishing for 'moreau' (cod) but caught nothing. I drop sail and throw them a line and two chocolate bars as a 'thank you,' and we are away into a pall of fog, nothing to be seen or heard, then they turn to starboard. Twenty minutes later the harbour entrance materialises, grey and ghostly on both sides and we make our way out of the fog into bright sun for the last 200 yards to the small boat basin. By the time I have tied alongside, put out fenders, rolled the sail onto the boom, and put up the tent again, the fog has rolled over the headland and crept down the hills into the town. I got nowhere but had one-and-a-half hours of interesting, invisible sailing!

24th June, 1992. Rivière au Reynard, Quebec

I am deeply depressed by 'le brume.' There are enough difficulties in the St. Lawrence without the complication of fog. I have had my fill of fog the last two years: Cape Cod to Maine, the Bay of Fundy, southern and eastern shores of Nova Scotia and now the St. Lawrence. The further north, the thicker it gets!

25th June, 1992. Rivière au Reynard to Cloridorme, Quebec

Cold and fog over background hills and *Wanderer* is drifting across the harbour. The headland at the west end of the mole is only occasionally visible so I row out. It is a long pull against the east wind and I am glad when I am round the end of the wall and can hoist sail.

10:20 A.M.: I am through the entrance and can free off. The harbour wall is just visible at 100 yards but along the coast only the top of the headland is visible. The tops of the cliffs come and go as fog banks come in. A spectacular bank of fog climbs up the cliff and I photograph it. I begin to wonder if I have misjudged but the fog thins a little so I can pick out houses in the next little cove vaguely white at 200 yards. It is eight miles to the next harbour—Anse au Valleau—which looks attractive in the photo in the guide.

Fog in the St. Lawrence

My speed increases from three-and-a-half knots to four knots when I goose wing the genoa. The coast is now big hills with mountain ranges behind. It's a spectacular site for the church at St.

Sailing to the Edge of Fear

Maurice de l'Echouerie. It's right on the headland looking up and down the St. Lawrence with a great cross at the cliff edge (the passage chart does not show churches but only the villages). Visibility is improving; it's now four miles but the fog is still dense.

1:30 P.M.: Off Pointe a la Renommee and I can see the whole coast—an unending line of enormous cliffs as far as the eye can see—tremendously impressive, but impossible to identify. So enormous that *Wanderer* does not seem to be moving but I give her a pat to tell her she is doing well. A valley going back into the mountains is marked on the chart only as a road coming down to the coast—but it is the only road I have seen; at least it gives me a positive position line.

The wind jumps round off the land, I roll up the genoa smartly and pull down the first reef and *Wanderer* jumps into a broad-reaching plane at six to seven knots. I sail a one third of a mile out, almost in the edge of the down river Gaspé current, as I don't want to be underneath the squalls coming down off the mountains The wind blows hard down the last valley and I hoist full sail as the wind drops away and then I can see the buoy off the harbour. The cliffs drop away but still there are spectacular mountain ranges behind. There is an enormous seawall of concrete fabrications but it is difficult to see the entrance so I follow the range markers. It is a big 'L'-shaped, long commercial quay but there are small boats on mooring so go further and pick up a spare mooring and a spectator shouts "OK."

It is now raining heavily, so I quickly fold the sail on the boom and tent up. I realise I have made a mistake as the cove is open to the sea and the boat is rolling. I should have tied alongside the commercial wharf close under the 'L' as it is unlikely any boats will come in tonight. It's too late now to move as it's pouring with rain and the prospect of a long row upwind is unattractive. A cold, wet, raw evening, the sail rolled on the boom is dripping, the boat is wet even after towelling down, and life is miserable. I light the lantern to dry the boat, and it is cheerful inside immediately. What a difference a lantern makes.

There is no reception on the weather radio with heavy interference on all channels. The chart shows almost 12 miles to Grande Vallee which appears to be open to a northeasterly, although there seems to be a river bridge; then another seven-and-a-quarter miles to Rivière le Madeleine, a good harbour.

8:45 P.M.: The boat is cheerful, warm and dry but I shall need to wear extra clothing inside my sleeping bag tonight.

26th June, 1992. Cloridorme and back again

Who could tell what a nice day this was going to be after such a bad start! I slept well indeed. A quick breakfast; fog thinning quickly; light easterly and I drop the mooring buoy at 6:15 A.M. Fog comes in quickly as I sail round the end

---

of the breakwater, made of enormous three-legged concrete blocks, and I sail out to the outer buoy before coming onto a course of 300 degrees to avoid a reef just awash and breaking. The land is invisible—just a blanket of grey all round, visibility approximately 100 yards. Above me, a cross appears on the top of a few feet of headland and the rest hidden in fog. It is eerie and I feel this may even be a sign and a warning, so I turn back and tie up; it's exactly one hour since I dropped the mooring.

Cold, drizzling and unpleasant. A boy with a bicycle walks halfway into town with me and asks: "Vous êtes froid?" "Oui," I reply. Walking back through the village, I am called across the road by the lady in the café and the group of boys I met on the dock: "I've had several telephone calls about you. The fishermen are worried about you. They say, "an Englishman, very cold, no heating on his boat, probably looking for a hot drink, probably walking this way. So please come in." The boys had pointed me out.

"Chocolat chaud, tres chaud, s'il vous plaît," I request. The drink is free—

Coridorme, St. Lawrence. A much needed hot chocolate drink. Outside it is cold and raining. For warmth I relied on the Coleman stove on the stern, a closed tent, and my oilskins.

compliments of the fishermen. The woman who called me over is the only person in the village who speaks English, and she comes to the village from London, Ontario to work in the restaurant as her summer holiday. "The people in the village are nice," she tells me.

Crossing at a road junction, I step off the pavement looking the wrong way and there is the scream of tires as a driver brakes hard to avoid me. We are both shaken and I try to explain that in England we drive on the other side of the road and I was looking the wrong way, but it is beyond me, and he insists that I climb into the car in spite of my wet clothes and drives me back to the docks.

Half-an-hour later he returns with wife and family, and a meat pie for my supper, and they invite me home for a coffee and shower. An English/French dictionary is produced and we try to talk by looking up words. It is an impossible system, and we get extremely frustrated until we descend into mime.

27th June, 1992. Cloridorme and return

11:00 A.M.: Two hours out from Cloridorme; probably three-and-a-half miles away and the fog is moving into the coast in great white banks, creeping over the village, and only the top of the headland is visible. Fog is drifting in behind me but slower and I decide to return. The wind dies as *Wanderer* turns back. The fog is filling in quickly but thank goodness I can see one-and-a-half miles towards Cloridorme. I have a long row ahead of me. Fortunately, the seas are rolling up astern to help the rowing.

A fishing boat comes across to see if I am alright and they pass with friendly waves. Some waves are cresting over submerged rock patches but I ignore them. The cliff strata passes surprisingly quickly and soon the white house set high that I noted a little way back, is abeam. The current must be running at one-and-a-half knots, rowing adds one knot, and the seas cresting astern add another half knot totalling three knots over the bottom. The seas flatten as I pass beyond the rock patches. Fog is making the coast vague and ahead is invisibility, but it is a pleasant downhill row and I am thoroughly enjoying myself. There are heavy breaking seas a half mile out where there must be a very strong current running offshore: the notorious Gaspé current!

The cross on the headland, the reef, and the harbour tower are vague shadows as I row back round the breakwater and tie up again at 12:30 P.M., two hours out, one-and-a-half hours rowing back. Fog is climbing the inland hills, along the coast it is dense but the harbour is clear and bathed in bright sunshine.

I spend the afternoon reading the *Yachting Guide to Fleuve de Saint Laurent* and combining it with local knowledge from the yacht *Tanagra*. From Quebec down to Rimousky, the tides run hard and there is a scarcity of harbours and a long way apart: the north shore is worse, Sorel is the northern limit of comfortable cruising. Surprisingly, Montreal has strong currents too, there is a lot of traffic above Quebec and little protection from wakes at night.

I am beginning to think it may be sensible to trail from Matane or Rimouski to

Quebec (or maybe as far as Montreal or even Sorel) to avoid the dangers. I spend a pleasant evening with the Fontin family. I suggest that we all go to church in the morning but papa will be up early fishing. He offers to knock on my boat at 3:00 A.M. to make sure I am awake. I mime that I will ignore him and go on snoring! A nice family.

29th June, 1992

A warm day, no wind at all, no fog. Not a breathe of wind, very hot already, clear skies and sun blazing down and I need sun glasses. An excellent, enjoyable day's sail today, 18 nautical miles made good through using the strong flood tide close inshore. The tidal effect would have been cancelled out had I gone further out to search for wind as I would have been into the Gaspé current, the permanent downstream current running close to the southern shore at four knots.

My mileage along the coast is now 175 miles in three weeks of difficult sailing.

30th June, 1992. At Cap Madeleine New Harbour, Quebec

A rough night. Heavy gusts make *Wanderer* shear about violently on her mooring, and I almost get up to remove the rudder to let her swing into the wind more quickly. Southerly wind roars down off the small cliffs overlooking the harbour—most of them must pass above the harbour and breakwater, but enough reach down to water level to keep me awake. Heavy rain all night. An unpleasant, difficult night.

I feel fortunate to be safe in a small well-protected harbour with no swell or fetch and comfortable swinging to an anchor in the shallows. Yesterday, I almost went into the river at Cap Madeleleine, but walking along the river bank I realised I would have been uncomfortable tied alongside a wharf or another boat. I doze but get no real sleep until 7:20 A.M. when the gusts decrease and rain slackens.

The wind varies between south and west but that may be the effect of cliffs. Looking through the stern flap I see a great weather front of gale clouds across the whole horizon above the St. Lawrence. I peep through the front flaps to see more dark, forbidding ranges of black clouds stacked above and behind each other. It looks ominous. Maybe the front has passed but perhaps it hasn't. There is a lot of wind in those clouds so I think to myself I'll stay in harbour until the weather settles. If the recent spell of easterlies is replaced by southwesterlies there is bound to be unsettled weather, and strong southerlies gusting down from the mountains further up river could be hazardous!

Sailing to the Edge of Fear

1st July, 1992

A whale crosses *Wanderer's* bows, but too far away to make it worth getting out the camera. Suddenly it 'blows' again only 30 yards ahead, and heading straight for *Wanderer*. A collision is inevitable and I push the tiller hard over, it's far too late but 10 feet away, the whale is diving and *Wanderer* rolls heavily in the disturbance. That was so sudden and too damned close for comfort! It couldn't have missed the rudder by more than a few millimetres as it dived (fortunately, the centreboard was up). I understood whales could pick out solid objects by echolocation but maybe it was hungry and thought that the noise of the bow wave was a shoal of fish? That was frightening and a danger I had not anticipated.

Approaching Mont Louis, there is something in the water ahead and I just avoid hitting a full-sized tree floating below the surface. I consider going on but it is now 1:00 P.M., with three hours of favourable tide left, 12 miles to Marsoui. If the wind dies, I cannot row against the combined ebb and Gaspé current and it will be a long row back. It is not worth the gamble (as it turns out, the wind dies at 4:00 P.M. so this time I got it right).

Mont Louis Bay is big and I turn left, drop sails, and have a hard row up into the northeast corner where I am out of the wind. A fisherman motors over to warn that there is a reef extending from the shore and recommends I anchor amongst the local row boats or come alongside the little wharf which dries at out at half tide. It is sheltered and warm in the lee of the quay and we walk across to the shore. He tells me that his main catch is whelk as in my part of the North Sea, and if there's anything I need I am to call at his house which he points out just yards away.

I anchor with the local boats as it start to rain and in half an hour it is pouring down and bitterly cold again. I am sheltered in this corner of the bay from all winds except from the northwest and I am relieved that the forecast is southwesterly. At 2:00 A.M. *Wanderer* is rolling abominably and a swell is running into the bay from the St. Lawrence. I am almost sea-sick but in half-an-hour *Wanderer* settles to an acceptable roll.

At 7:00 A.M. the motion is awful. The wind has veered into the northwest. Now I have no choice but to get out and cross the bay for shelter and tie up alongside the fishing boats. I estimate that I can safely row across the wind but I have underestimated surface drift and the size of the waves where the centre of the bay is open to St. Lawrence. The waves crest and I cannot keep both oars in the water when pulling; and the reefs to leeward get closer and closer no matter how hard I pull. I realise I am going to be wrecked unless I can set sail.

Fortunately, as usual, I had put in both reefs last night and the double reefed mainsail goes up without a hitch or snagging. Now I am desperately short of sea

---

room with the reefs close to leeward, with no room to tack. Thankfully, *Wanderer* pays off without 'getting in irons.' The fear drains out of me and I enjoy the easy sailing even against the six foot swells and I close haul into the lee of the fishing boat harbour, tie up alongside, pleased with the way *Wanderer* got me out of trouble.

Supper is rice made in my thermos, mixed with ravioli from the saucepan. This is the first time that I have used Marg's method of putting rice in the boiling water already in the thermos to cook at leisure. I must tell her it works well. I get out a down-filled sleeping bag and put it inside my mummy bag.

I feel that I am coming to terms with the St. Lawrence at last. Sitting in *Wanderer* and just looking and absorbing the country is most enjoyable. The province of Quebec is vast and a majestic but hard land. For the first time I am warm with two sleeping bags, woollen pyjamas and a wool hat. I wake next morning warm and happy.

3rd July, 1992. Mont St. Pierre, Quebec

Mont St. Pierre is an absolutely spectacular site and for once the St. Lawrence is bathed in sparkling sunlight. The highway skirts the bay in a great curve round to the village, the government wharf is at the western end of the bay alongside the coast road, the cliff rises above the wharf spanning a thousand feet of sheer vertical rock; the road is sombre in shadow but the wharf is still sunlit and very hot.

I strip off my sweater during the long walk into the village of Mont St. Pierre along the beach. A car gives me a lift and the driver speaks no English and we mime our conversation. He tells me that the hang-gliding championship take place later this month from the top of the mountain. The village sign is a great pterodactyl made of welded sheet steel: "It was the ancient Pterodactyl which inspired man to invent the hang glider," the sign says. The mountain rises 3,000 feet above the village, vertical above the water, the houses below are minute, and there is a great cross on the ridge behind.

I invite Claude, my driver, to join me at Les Joyeuse Naufrages Restaurant for a 'thank you' coffee, and while we watch a hang-glider jumps into space above us and glides down. I look through the menu and ask Claude and several girls he knows for a recommendation. There is a lot of laughter and they point to "Cod's tongues," a local delicacy. I cautiously ask if I would like it? "Oui, oui, c'est trés bon" and they nod enthusiastically but I notice that a girl at the back is shaking her head, and I wonder if they are playing a joke on me; I ask the waitress who encourages me to try them.

4th July, 1992. Mont St. Pierre to Marsoui, Quebec

Waves slapping under *Wanderer*'s bilges and movement wake me. The wind is across the bay southeasterly at 10 knots. At 5:40 A.M. I have a quick, cold breakfast and I thoroughly enjoy my fresh pamplemousse (grapefruit).

7:00 A.M.: I turn along the coast and head for Pointe de Chasse where the white church makes an excellent landmark. I have a foul tide but the wind is pushing *Wanderer* over it well. I set the genoa, then goosewing it and speed increases to four knots.

8:00 A.M.: The wind is freshening but 25 minutes later we are planing in the front faces of waves for far too long and I roll up the genoa but leave the jibstick rigged in case I need it later. The wind increases steadily, we are planing almost continuously. Within sight of Marsoui breakwater I decide to put off reefing until in the lee of the wharf. The seas build very quickly as they run into the bay—are they shallows? *Wanderer* is trying to broach-to and putting her bows down into the back of the wave as she overtakes each trough.

The wind is now far too heavy for a full mainsail and I ought to round up and reef but it will be easier to do in shelter and there is only 200 yards to go. I run to the end of the breakwater and round up. There is a line of young fishermen with lines out and no one moves. I shout to indicate that I'm coming into harbour and ask if they could please haul in their lines. Still no one moves and I have to keep off, and the wind catches me. I am surprised at the strength of the wind and quickly pull down a reef—I ought to pull down the second reef but I have already lost 50 yards and I fight back into the lee of the wall. I grab at the ladder but the current has already sluiced me out of the river again, so I drop sails and row back, then row even harder, and row desperately to avoid being swept out to open water. I secure a line, trembling and exhausted. I am only 10 feet into the river but I am sheltered.

9:30 A.M.: I walk across to the windward side of the government wharf. It is blowing hard, and the foul tide running into the wind now 20–30 knots is kicking up a heavy sea now in the open. I am fed up. I thought, when I left with an easterly wind today, I'd be 20 to 30 miles further up the St. Lawrence River by this evening. Instead only 10 miles made good! There is a general air of dereliction: there are no fishing boats; a break through the centre of the breakwater; the top capping is overhanging; and further along the concrete face is broken and jagged. The river is small and turns 90 degrees into a pool and slipway in the village but the current is so strong that I cannot move *Wanderer* upstream until the tide floods.

I am tired after the early start and a restless, broken night and drift into a troubled doze. A trout fisherman tells me tomorrow's forecast is for very rough conditions. He suggests that I ask one of the local fishermen about moving *Wanderer* into the river. "Fishermen do like to be asked first," he points out. This is understandable and courteous, I think. Later, one of the locals agrees and I move *Wanderer* up to the end of the wood facing where she is sheltered. No sign of the wind dropping so I go for a walk. It is a nice village, a main road halt with two small food stores, and lots of trout fishermen everywhere. Three people in a small double ended Shetland-type boat are going out so I take my weather radio and ask them to translate the forecast "pour la demaine pour moi, sil vous plaît." They tell me to expect northeasterlies of 20–25 knots. I return to the hotel to telephone Dave in New Brunswick who is following my progress, then treat myself to a most enjoyable 'house' meal for $5.95. I almost ask for a shower but decide that I would rather enjoy a leisurely evening in *Wanderer* and an early night.

5th July, 1992

The northwest horizon is dark with high cloud coming in too. A new weather front? I keep a wary eye on it and feel nervous. A long run back if it brings wind. The forecast didn't say anything about a front from the northwest but it did predict northeasterlies of 25–40 kilometres per hour. Instead it has been calm. I have an uneasy feeling that I might get 'pasted' today before I get in!

It's noon and the black clouds have passed over but there is a low black mass in the northwest still looking ominous. If I go further out for wind I shall be in the Gaspé current running down to the sea, if I stay inshore I have no wind close to the land and still a weak foul tide. The wind goes northwest, then west 10 knots and I am close-hauled. I hope that I shall get in before it blows because it's looking nasty, then the wind dies completely. Rowing a quarter mile from shore seems to take for ever along this enormous coast with no landmarks or net markers by which I can judge my progress. A breeze returns from ahead, then veers to northeast for 10 minutes. It gives me a nice lift towards the harbour now clear in my field glasses.

The wind pipes up northeast and I roll up the genoa as a precaution and it backs to northwest and dies, and I return to rowing. A fishing boat going east comes close and hoots 'hello' as all the family wave. I have passed the last headland, two miles to row and the horizon is even blacker. For the last mile, the wind pipes up from astern and *Wanderer* is planing, almost out of control and trying to broach. I drop sail and row in through the very narrow entrance. There are two basins, with big fishing boats tied stern to the wharves, small outboard boats in a jumble which I join when a fisherman permits me. The fishing boat family return and there is a lot of good humoured laughter at their description

Sailing to the Edge of Fear

of my rowing. I walk round the wharves to the shore—the wind is still blowing but erratic, and there is as yet no wind from the intensely black northwest.

I settle down to hot porridge, a mug of tea, and two slices of raisin bread. I mop the boat dry, and have my log written up by 5:45 P.M. The sailing directions indicates another five miles to Sainte Anne des Monts and the photograph shows a long wharf and I notice the owner of the guide has pencilled in extension break-waters, so it should be an excellent sheltered place. Cap Chat is a further eight miles, a total of 13 miles from here.

6th July, 1992. St. Joachim de Tourelle to St. Anne des Monts, Quebec

The tide is running across an underwater reef causing an unpleasant jumbled sea. *Wanderer* is only just gaining ground, even with me rowing hard with one hand while steering with the other until I am able to tuck in close behind the reef out of the tide. I enjoy this rowing one-handed with the whole bay laid out be-fore me. There is a magnificent church halfway round the bay, and I can see a harbour through my binoculars still over two miles ahead.

I am now well into the bay, out of the worst of the tide, the wind has not blown up yet and if it does it is only two miles to shelter, the swells are big but not crest-ing, rain has stopped and I am enjoying being afloat.

An outboard motors across from a group of fishing boats moored behind a line of rocks—one man and a boy, probably his son. They head straight for me waving and I look back to check if I have run over their net. Once alongside they grab hold of *Wanderer* and look at me inscrutably. Alarmed, I make apologetic noises, and then without expression, they tow me towards the far harbour. It is kind of them and I don't feel that I can refuse without being churlish, so I roll up my genoa, throw the younger man my heavier anchor rope and run out some extra length—and we are off at a fast plane with *Wanderer* on the back of their second stern wave, riding bows up, stern down.

They look back a couple of times to check if their tow is following comfortably and then ignore me. They are warmly dressed with thick wool shirts, trousers, heavy insulated boots, but no oilskins and it is beginning with rain, and it is a long way to go and they came out at least another half mile to meet me.

Fog is coming in; the far side of the bay has disappeared; the swells are big now that we are clear of the lee of the headland, probably seven to eight feet; sometimes, I am looking down into their boat from a crest, other times they are six feet above me. They don't look round. *Wanderer* is towing well with the centre-board up and rudder on shock cord so I go forward to get my camera to take a photograph as they tow between the harbour breakwaters at full speed.

It is raining steadily and they must be getting soaked. We plane past the pontoons until they find an empty berth, cut the engine, point out the berth and cast me off. I only have time to shake hands and say "merci" before they are off at the same speed. The last I see of them is planing through the breakwaters. They do not look back and they do not wave! They came some five miles especially to give me a tow. How can one say 'thank you'?

I tie alongside with bows facing the harbour entrance in case a swell works in overnight, fenders out, two springs to hold *Wanderer* steady, and the tent up as quickly as possible. Already it is raining hard, and the tent, sails and boat are soaking, and the sails dripping steadily. I walk to the end of the breakwater. There is no wind, and it looks a nice town presided over by a prominent church over-looking the harbour and bay. I pay my harbour dues to a friendly harbour master who says: "Any problems you come and see me."

It is a cold, wet, foggy day outside the tent, only slightly less miserable inside a wet boat being dripped on by a wet sail. I doze, using my lifejacket as a pillow wearing oilskins.

7th July, 1992. St. Anne des Monts to Cap Chat, Quebec

Wanderer has been snatching all night. It is not her fault—our neighbour is rolling and snatching at the docks, then pulls *Wanderer* onto her. I try various remedies—increasing the length of lines to allow *Wanderer* to float further off down wind makes the snatch more violent but less frequent; lowering the centreboard reduces the amount of sideways movement, but does not prevent an occasional violent surge followed by a sudden stop as the fenders squash against the gunwales; tying tight causes more frequent but less violent movement. It wakes me every time.

As I lie awake, I go through my conclusions about this type of sailing: an eight mile passage is pleasant; a 25 mile leg is less so with the worry of the wind holding or increasing; working the strong tides is a pleasure; the strong Gaspé Current just offshore prohibits going out to find wind and complicates dead reckoning; the fog is a nagging worry with the consequent problem of finding or overshooting the fishing harbours in 100 yard visibility; and the impossibil-ity of anchoring in deep water on a rock bottom to wait for fog to clear, or the tide to turn, is another constant worry; and it is always cold as the water from the ice-bearing Labrador Current runs behind Belle Île up the St. Lawrence be-fore crossing and running east as the Gaspé current.

Flat land at last: I follow the shore round to keep out of the tide, visibility 200 yards. Cold, foggy, fine reaching, occasionally close-hauled, but really en-joyable sailing. The fog clears and I can see inland. Amazingly, there is not a cliff in sight. I was believing that there were 1,000–3,000 foot cliffs all the way to

Quebec City. What a pleasure to see sandy flat foreshore even if there is an occasional rocky outcrop. There are a few small boats moored inshore and my binoculars show a small wharf but without any real shelter, so I close-haul for the far point—Pointe de Cap Chat. The fog clamps down immediately to 200 yards, the northwesterly wind is still light and the shore disappears. I keep *Wanderer* close-hauled until a cottage and large building appears vaguely beyond the bow and I am in breakers on the beach, and I throw round.

Bitingly cold, my fingers tingling, body shivering in spite of wearing long underwear, a heavy wool shirt, two sweaters, oilskins and boots and I am still cold. I make a hot chocolate drink from the thermos and glad of it. The chart indicates a long bay with Cap Chat harbour halfway so I cut across directly through the fog and the shore appears 20 minutes later and I catch a glimpse of the next headland with a lighthouse at the far end of the bay at three-and-a-half miles but it turns out to be the end of the harbour breakwater at 200 yards—a distortion by the fog. The wind drops and backs. This is the last of the breeze and it has served me well today.

Yvon Lemieux comes aboard for a chat. He has seen *Wanderer* sailing along the coast, and it is great to meet a small boat enthusiast again. Later he drives me along the shore to see the small boat harbours I have missed, like Anse au Capucins which is all rock at low water with boats pulled up on the beach, and the river at Cap Reynard (where he keeps his Mirror dinghy), which is a pool at high water and a trickle across the beach at low tide. Spectacular scenery along the coast road, a great

Rowing the St. Lawrence. Note the boom is lifted on the aft reef line to give extra headroom.

bank of fog out in the St. Lawrence, the ranges of the Chic Choc mountains inland and ahead.

His family insists on letting me use their shower, giving me supper and washing and repairing my clothes. It was a most enjoyable evening at the heart of a kind family.

The Lower St. Lawrence: The Impossible Equation (1992)

8th July, 1992. Cap Chat, Quebec

Cold again last night. Maybe the St. Lawrence never warms up!

By the time I have breakfast, the day is warm, rapidly becoming hot. A French speaker listens to the forecast for me (too fast for my limited vocabulary) and repeats it slowly. I get out the chart for the next section—St. Anne des Mont, Cap Chat, to Matane to Rimouski. It is to a much bigger scale than the passage chart I have been using and gives much more detail. It is a long leg of 26 miles from Les Mechin to Matane. I decide to stay another day rather than beat 13 miles against a head wind and foul tide to Les Mechins. I take the opportunity to air my sleeping bags, dry the tent, service my stove and other routine maintenance.

By noon, it is so hot that I strip to an open neck shirt and light trousers to walk along the coast road. The views along the coast are spectacular; the visibility so clear that it is impossible to judge distance and the lighthouse on the next headland looks to be close enough to touch. It is difficult to appreciate that here is a river some 60 miles wide and the far bank is way beyond the horizon. On the way back to the harbour, I explore the village just above and inland of the coast road, and walk round the Catholic church. It is beautiful inside, all white plaster with gilt ornamentation, immaculate and breath- takingly beautiful but I wonder how it can be afforded by a small community. Back at *Wanderer*, my drinking water is down to one-and-a-half pints including the contents of the vacuum flask. The harbour water pipe is turned off—"a breakage" an elderly man explains and takes my water containers home to refill.

In the evening, families walk down to the harbour to enjoy the evening sunlight including the chap who filled my water jugs with his family and friends and two young schoolgirls. It is my first warm evening in the St. Lawrence, and several people tell me it is the first hot day of the summer. The two schoolgirls (eight and ten years-old) overcome their shyness and come aboard to examine my boat and equipment but really to practice the English words they are learning at school. It is hard work and we relapse into my French which causes them great amusement. Pointing to the glorious half-moon high in the evening sky, I tell the schoolgirls: "Mon papa et mama tell me when je suis un enfant 'la lune et fabrique de fromage vert," and this causes general laughter.

A jolly crowd and a pleasant evening learning about the people and the area. I am putting my boat to bed when Pierre, a local small boat sailor, comes aboard to look round and tell me of the coast upriver. There are no rivers useable as a stopover between Les Mechins and Matane, although there is a small wharf at Gross Roches made of boulders—acceptable maybe for a night but offering no real protection. There is a great wind electricity generator on the headland, the highest in the world. He tells me tomorrow I must go on a bus ride to see it as it is very impressive, the biggest in the world, controlled from Montreal. It's said to generate enough power to supply a whole town. However, I decide on an early start to take advantage of the flooding tide and the early land breeze before the southwesterly sets in.

I am woken at 4:15 A.M. by a man sliding fish boxes down the gangway and already a light land breeze is filling in. Another group of fishermen cause me to put my head out of the tent to say "bonjour" and one man imitates a dawn cockerel as my head appears and we all join in the laughter. A light wind takes me out of harbour into the tide and I have a pleasant sailing breeze on a very broad reach but I notice the wind generator on the far headland is stationary, it is enormous dwarfing the lighthouse to the size of a pinhead. Several boats are already fishing and pulling in cod and almost all wave and shout, "bon voyage."

9th July, 1992

A long stretch, five miles of rock and stony beach, to Anse au Capacins. The coast is low but there are hills inland, all very pleasant after the sheer cliffs rising straight from the water of the last few weeks. A dead run, wind astern and I have averaged four knots from harbour to the last headland but now speed has dropped to two-and-a-half knots. I have been looking in vain for the point that the chart shows masking Capacins, expecting high land, but it is just a low reef with the cove behind!

Beyond, I can see a number of boats going in and they appear to land just round into the bay. The wind drops more and I row to assist the sails. An uncomfortable swell is running in from the north and it throws *Wanderer* about and empties the mainsail of wind, and makes rowing difficult as she sometimes almost rolls her gunwales under in the wave troughs. According to the tables, I should have lost the benefit of the tide by now but I mark various transits on the shore as I row— a boulder and a house behind; a telephone pole and a house; a shed and electricity pylon and *Wanderer* is still covering the ground at one-and-a-half knots. I begin to work in towards the shore to cheat the tide when it turns.

I've rounded Cap des Mechins and am onto the last leg of one mile. There is no sign of the harbour entrance although I can see a bridge spanning the river beyond. The chart shows that a line drawn from the last point (Cap des Mechins) to the church passes through the harbour entrance. So I follow this bearing and it all becomes clear.

A clap of thunder surprises me from overhead and the rain becomes a really solid downpour. I stretch out and listen to the rain with pleasure. This leg of the journey worked out very well—much better than I had any right to expect—with fair easterly winds, a fair tide for most of the passage, within 100 yards of the harbour as the wind shifted to northwest and died, there was someone to tell me where to tie up and the rain held off just long enough to cover my boat. I drop off to sleep feeling pleased. The rain slackens, then stops and I walk round the village now bypassed by the road. A stone-built church catches my eye; and I take a closer look at it; the interior is magnificent and once again I wonder how such small villages manage to finance their fine churches. It is spotting with rain so I hurry back. It increases to heavy rain as soon as I get back on board. Luckily, I manage to stay dry.

The next leg will be difficult—twice as far as yesterday with no harbours or landings, and I cannot beat 25 miles. I shall need a fair wind and a reliable forecast. I switch on the weather radio and I catch the English translation coming through loud and clear.

10th July, 1992. Les Mechins to Matane, Quebec

9:53 A.M.: Opposite Grosse Roches wharf: eight-and-a-half miles made good out of the 23 that I had planned for today. The wind is now from the northeast and freshening, and travelling four-and-a-half knots through the water on a very broad reach with another knot from the flood tide makes a total of five-and-a-half knots over the ground. I keep a careful check on distance to go as I am very conscious of the approaching weather front and wind shift to the west, and the distance I shall then have to beat. It is five miles to Cap a la Baleine, four miles to cross the next bay (by noon), then onto the last leg of seven miles which I can beat to windward if necessary.

Wanderer is storming along. Grosse Roches wharf is quickly two miles astern and Cap Baleine coming up fast, when the wind backs to north. Blast! The wind is changing direction early. I sheet in and *Wanderer* is reaching at four-and-a-half knots under full sail.

10:36 A.M.: Halfway and it is still only mid-morning. Cap a la Baleine is abeam and I have to work off the shore to clear the off-lying rocks. Anse au Croix bears away with the great church of Sainte Felicite at the far side. The next point is low with a prominent hut at the end and I head on a straight line across the bay hoping the wind will hold until I close the land! The wind freshens a little, still from the north. The swell which was originally three feet has now built to above eye height.

11:05 A.M.: A church is abeam so there must be a village but it is invisible and there is no shelter. The seas are steepening but not breaking except for an occasional crest breaking noisily but not dangerously. The prominent hut on the end of Le Longue Pointe is only a quarter of a mile away when a wave comes aboard unexpectedly over the quarter, shoulder-blade deep. *Wanderer* is planing away from it so there was no danger, but I am shocked by the impact and the sudden cold I feel even through my oilskins!

Approaching the point, the seas steepen rapidly. The tide is now running against me and swirling fast round the end of the reef and into the eye of the strong northerly wind, resulting in very confused broken seas. I ought to have gone further out but I'm committed now. I should work away from the shore but it looks even more dicey further out with heavy breakers. If I hold course it is only 100 yards until *Wanderer* will be clear, so I keep straight on through the overfalls. At least the seas are coming up dead astern and urging *Wanderer* on. But I'm forgetting the foul tide and the next 100 yards of standing waves take for ever! One wave comes aboard over the quarter but fortunately *Wanderer* was at the bottom of a trough and it fell down into her or she'd have broached; another one foot of solid water comes across the sidedeck (plus froth), and suddenly water is swilling above the floorboards. I look behind to heavy breaking seas. A few moments later another breaks with a roar, comes aboard and *Wanderer* almost broaches! Dear God, this is getting dangerous!

For safety, I should drop mainsail and run under jib, but this will reduce *Wanderer*'s speed through the water, and the current will carry her astern through the race again. Anyway, I don't dare to go forward for fear of losing control—already I am as far aft as possible. I concentrate on keeping true with the waves and slowly, ever so slowly, the hut on the point crawls aft, and the size of the waves reduce, although occasionally one still breaks heavily alongside. One comes aboard over the beam and washes solidly over the tent, food, and gear stowed by the mast. *Wanderer* is wallowing heavily with the amount of water aboard and I put down the self-balers and resume my course across the bay towards the far church, and *Wanderer* picks up speed as the water empties.

The swells are still big but we are now buoyant and she slides quickly out of the way of the odd breaking crest. The church is Petite Matane according to the chart, and I have to work a long way out to avoid a shallow reef. Fog is coming in, and soon the shore is just a vague shadow. At long last, the harbour breakwaters appear and I fine reach to get to windward of the entrance, and I am surprised to find how large the waves have become. I consider rowing in but the swells are too big with too much risk of *Wanderer* being set onto the steel piling, so I work upwind then free off and run in. Luckily, there is still a fresh breeze to give speed and manoeuvrability.

Between the breakwaters the swells are big and erratic, reflected from the vertical face of the steel piling back into the middle of the channel to meet the reflected waves from the other side. The waves running along the pilings are eight feet, the humps in the middle far higher; there is a wind shadow between the breakwaters and only the top of the mainsail is pulling, but *Wanderer* slowly works her way through the confusion, surging dangerously and rolling abominably.

The yacht club harbour before the bridge is completely protected, a big haven with few boats against the floating docks. Only one yacht *Blue Heron* flying an American flag, has a crew aboard. "Must be cold out today," they remark. "No I kept warm rowing," I reply but they don't believe me for it is raining steadily and bitingly cold again.

I book into the club for two nights "Combien s'il vous plaît.?" I ask. The dock master writes down '12.07' and I pull out my wallet thinking 'this is cheap' but he takes $29.00 and I am about to query the amount when I realise he was writing the date.

11th July, 1992. Matane, Quebec

The swell has died and there is only two feet running between the breakwaters. The fog disperses quickly with the warm dry westerly wind and the temperature rises to 69°F in town but it is colder near the water. The north shore of the St. Laurent is visible for the first time 30 miles away!

A yacht *Fleur d' Ecume* comes into harbour sailed by a big man with a beard. He kindly offers to give me tips on sailing the river to Montreal tomorrow before he leaves, and I examine the charts from Matane to Quebec in detail—there are lots of shallows in this section, currents varying from half to three knots, predominating winds are southwest headwinds so I shall have to make maximum use of the flood tide but all the while taking great care to avoid the worst of wind-against-tide conditions. It is possible without an engine given plenty of time to select weather/wind and tides but the warnings in the guide make me worry a great deal about the lack of shelter and possible friction with rod fishermen. Currents are very strong at the Montreal rapids, the sea locks have a minimum length and *Wanderer* is below the minimum so somehow I have to bypass the locks.

I'm beginning to wonder if it may be more sensible to truck to Montreal but I lack any knowledge of the river. A group of sailors in the clubhouse invite me to join them. One couple from Grosse Roches saw me sail past, the man opposite built his own 28-foot wood yacht and sailed it across the Atlantic to Europe and back. He is obviously very capable, a good seaman and I notice his eyes are always on the horizon. He tells me he dreamed of building his boat because he loved the lines and the photographs, and gave up his job to sail.

I am impressed and tell of some wise comments I once heard from the sailor David Lewis which seems to fit this man. He said that "Most people dream their dreams in the night and forget them at daylight, but just a few live out their dreams during the day. "Such individuals are 'Dreamers of the Day' and they are dangerous!" There is friendly laughter. I say my 'au revoirs' at 9:30 P.M. and retire to bed very tired from several early starts at four in the morning. My light sleeping bag is too hot for the first time this season.

12th July, 1992

Having coffee in the clubhouse, a local man named Clermont Gaudin joins me. He suggest that there is a haulage firm in Matane which truck frequently to Montreal and may have space available, or an alternative is to buy an outboard with the freight money saved and motor along the St. Lawrence. He tells me that the ship locks have a minimum length but this will be no problem—just join a big yacht downstream as it's 'tender.' The yacht club manager joins us and we talk of how to load *Wanderer* if I freight to Montreal as weight is close to the maximum that the crane can lift.

14th July, 1992. Matane, and Quebec City to Montreal, Quebec

It is a warm night but all things are relative. Anyway, it is warmer than the last three weeks but colder than the previous night. I was just warm enough with one sleeping bag and long underwear and a wool hat.

At Matane, the St. Lawrence narrows from 63 miles to 35 miles. It has been the most difficult sailing ever: the fog; the four knot Gaspé Current just offshore constantly running seaward; very cold water; air temperature never above 10 degrees celsius. I have been fortunate to have a high proportion of easterlies to drive me upriver, but easterlies also bring fog, rain and even colder weather!

Sailing becomes even more difficult upriver from Matane and Rimouski—longer distances between harbours, stronger downriver currents, and less favourable weaker tides running upriver for a shorter period, and dense fog ("Fog is a reality which is impossible to avoid below Quebec," says the sailing directions). There is an additional hazard warns my *Yachtman's Guide to the Saint Laurent* which is that many of the public wharves are not safe and sometimes you are better off to drop anchor off the wharf on the side best protected and where water is deep enough at low tide. Even worse there is friction with rod fishermen.

I book *Wanderer* on a truck to Montreal for two days from now. Thinking that I had two more days to explore the truck arrives today—two days early undoubtedly due to my bad French. My boat finally arrives and is lifted aboard by numerous helpers. No time to build a cradle as intended, bilges supported with timber blocks and roped down by the driver who obviously was experienced with unusual loads—and we were off. Fifteen minutes later I notice in the rear view mirror that the mainsail is blowing about. In the hurry *Wanderer* was loaded stern first and although I had lashed the mainsail to the boom the 60 miles per hour wind (the truck travelling at 63 miles an hour) has got under the leach of the sail and flogged it apart. There appears to be a lot of damage and a whole panel missing.

The road runs along the coast—the whole foreshore is a shallow area of isolated rocks—a nasty shore to anchor off at night with no possibility of moving without hitting a rock if the wind gets up. Numerous small rivers flow down from the hills but fan out shallowly over rock—strewn beaches.

Isles de Bic is spectacular as we approach with the sunset behind it. There are a lot of possible anchorages but care is needed not to settle or swing onto a rock with a falling tide. It is completely dark by 9:30 P.M. and we have now been travelling for three hours at a high speed and a sign says Quebec City is another 124 miles. It is a vast country. Montreal is 150 miles further—and still in the province of Quebec!

16th July, 1992

While the mainsail was being re-sewn by a very competent sailmaker, named Laurie Anne, I went on a waterbus tour of Montreal's harbour to see what I had by-passed on my truck ride.

The Lachine Rapids are horrifying, and extremely dangerous for a small boat with currents running at 12 knots and steep-sided standing waves. The rapids were bypassed last century by the Lachine Canal but the canal fell into disuse with the opening of the St. Lawrence Seaway and has since been filled in.

It is time to plan: The St. Lawrence Sea Locks have a minimum permitted boat length and having a 'motor' is mandatory, so *Wanderer* would not be allowed through (other waterways the regulations specify merely 'power' so I can always argue that *Wanderer* 'rowing' is under power). This proves to be a problem until I remember Jim Fraser, the Wayfarer sailor in Nova Scotia, mentioning an inland waterway from Ottawa to Lake Ontario. So I detour 125 miles up the river to Ottawa, then through Canal Rideau to Kingston. The river leg is bound to be hard work bucking both current and head wind (the river runs northeast-southwest and the prevailing wind is west-southwest so the wind will follow the valley).

19th July, 1992

After several happy days at Point Claire Yacht Club my sails are delivered personally, and, after writing my thanks to the staff and officers of the club, it is time to move on. The chart doesn't start until some miles from Pointe Claire but I had been told: "It's easy. Sail due west until you are between the mainland

and Pointe Dowker (on Île Dowker)—then it is obvious." The temperature was 69°F and rising quickly as the sun climbs and I remove the oilskins, boots and sweater which I had automatically put on after weeks sailing the St. Lawrence. I had forgotten how pleasant it is to sail in sun with the warm temperatures and water, blue skies, no tides, plenty of small bays to anchor, and numerous beaches to haul out on easily.

I was expecting difficulty at my first river lock in Montreal—Saint Anne's—a large, commercial lock with a mere three foot lift. Everyone agreed they enforced the regulations strictly being the first lock on the river system but no one was sure of the paperwork required of a yacht 'not Canadian registered and licensed,' but they doubted if a sailboat would be allowed to pass through *sans un moteur.*

I prepare carefully. I stick my small ships registration number to the bows in letters large enough to be read across the lock, tactfully flying the Quebec flag alongside the Canadian.

At the lock, I walk to the office with my papers. One of the lock keepers grins at my appalling version of the French language: "Speak English if it is easier for you" he suggests with a laugh. Avoiding the problem of 'no moteur,' I ask him to take a photograph of *Wanderer* entering his lock so it can be seen in England. I ask where he wants me to tie up, and I hand over my camera, avoid looking at the lock keepers, so there is time for the friendly lock master to say, "I told him it is no problem." They shout across, "How many photographs?" and ask if they may stand in the foreground "to be seen in England." No mention of my lack of a *moteur* thank goodness.

There are 19 boats packed into the lock and the big power boats wave me out first. Half a dozen strokes and *Wanderer* is moving well. There is applause from the Sunday afternoon spectators standing above which increases to a cheer, with handclaps and laughter and cries of "*Bravo, Bravo pour le bateau Anglais. Bon voyage!*" as I clear the gates. It suddenly hits me how much I shall miss the spontaneous warmth of the French-speaking Quebecois.

20th July, 1992. Lac des Deux Montagnes, Quebec

I lay off a course on the chart to clear the reefs of Île Hay. Clouds fill in from the southwest and the sky is soon overcast. The wind drops, then increases, drops and increases again—the cycle takes seven minutes and each time the wind is a little stronger. I decide to cut across the Île Hay shoals (the chart shows a four foot swatchway) and slip into the cove between Îles Pelees and Île Paquin through the back door (one to two feet). I use a back transit of the northeast end of Île Hay in line with Hudson Yacht Club—a transit is always easier, quicker, and more accurate than using a compass bearing. Rain is pattering down.

At 3:00 P.M. the radio forecast reports that "severe thunderstorms have formed in the Ottawa River and the north shore of the St. Lawrence, travelling north east, winds gusting up to 56 miles per hour with heavy rain and severe lightning." While supper is heating, I work out distances: it is nine miles to Carillon lock, where it looks from the chart that I may get shelter behind the lock wall except from the north. The current is one knot down river so I need a fair wind.

21st July, 1992

Saint Anne's lock had a mere three foot lift. Carrillion Lock yesterday was another matter lifting boats 63 feet up the power station dam. The bottom gate is an unbelievable 100-feet high, unimaginably massive. It rises slowly and I row in and tie to the floating pontoons which lift with the water level, and I have time to look round as the guillotine gate closes behind. The lock is enormous and claustrophobic; the walls of the chamber tower over *Wanderer*, they are so high that the lock staff have to use loud hailers to communicate with boat crews below, and an 80-foot waterfall is cascading down the sill only a few feet beyond my bows.

I ask the lock master for details—it's the second biggest single-rise lock in North America (the largest is in Tennessee); the guillotine bottom gate weighs 186 metric tonnes (372, 000 pounds) and takes four minutes to lift, and it takes just 20 minutes to fill the lock chamber and raise boats 86 feet. He tells me there is no mooring place before the small marina five miles upstream but I find a pleasant creek in what appears to be a provincial park, well satisfied with the day.

22nd July, 1992

A lovely day sailing—bright and sunny with enough white clouds to enliven the blue sky, sparkling water and sunglasses essential, the northwesterly wind light to moderate and not a sign of the promised southwesterly 10–15 knots (a fair wind for sailing upriver). The province of Quebec is on the north shore; Ontario on the south, and the provincial border runs along the centre of the river. Ontario is flatter, Quebec mountainous and further inland, Parc Dollard au Ormeau with campsites on the Quebec bank, nice houses and farms on both shores. Beating all day in a light shirt, cotton trousers, *Wanderer* clean and organised. Just like a pleasant, English summer day.

31st July, 1992. Hull, Quebec

Ottawa is a lovely city; a most attractive skyline seen from the river with the Prime Minister's residence, the French ambassador's house, the Royal Mint and public buildings on the cliff high above the river; parliament buildings on Parliament Hill and the statue of Champlain overall, and eight staircase locks climbing a narrow gorge beneath more magnificent buildings.

Inevitably, attitudes in a capital city differ from elsewhere and I was fortunate indeed in my largely chance contacts, but little did I realise that my stay in Ottawa was to be such an education.

There is an excellent new museum in Hull just along the river bank with fine collections. The Musée de Civilisation is an imposing, modern and spacious museum with some excellent displays.

3rd August, 1992. Ottawa, Ontario

If I had to select two outstanding memories of my stay here they must be the National War Memorial, which was deeply moving; and, for very different reasons, my visit to the By Market which was stupid and very amusing. The war memorial is a 'must.' It is a monument in the centre of the city, the pillar in stone, the detail cast in bronze; the soldiers exhausted, the horses spent, slipping and sliding, covered in mud, hauling a field gun through the gateway at the base of the column.

The By market, named after Colonel By, is one of the sights of Ottawa with vast quantities of fruit and vegetables, farm fresh at reasonable prices. Next to the ice cream parlour is a food stall advertising 'Beaver Tails.' To say that I was surprised to see such an item was an understatement. I asked the advice of a couple of Canadians sitting on a bench: "I'm English. Can you help me please (my first mistake)…I have never eaten beaver. Would you recommend it?" (my second mistake). They assured me the beaver is a local delicacy only available in the Ottawa area, succulent beyond belief. Surely. I had tried moose meat and venison? This was even better.

"Isn't it tough? Surely the tail is all muscle?" I ventured. But they ordered for me, ignoring my question. "Just fried in batter, plain with a touch of lemon: you don't want all those fancy sauces, it spoils the taste of the meat," they said.

I bit into it carefully, not quite sure what delicate flavour to expect from the tail of a beaver—and they fell over laughing. I'd been 'had,' for it was a pancake with a dusting of sugar and lemon inside!

4th August, 1992. Ottawa, Ontario

The beaver tail confusion wasn't the last of my cultural misunderstandings. A young woman interviewed me for *Le Droit*, a French language newspaper, but she was prickly to me throughout. In the printed article, I am told she portrays me kindly but describes me as a "loup de mer" which spoils the article for me as no one likes being called a wolf. In the evening, a neightbouing yacht invites me aboard for a beerr and there are references in French to "loup de mer" which I do not understand and the term rankles. My friend whose wife is French Canadian told

---

me years later that "in the Quebec culture the wolf enjoys a high standing, synonymous with toughness and intellignece." Quite the opposite of what I had assumed—she had actually paid me a great compliment!

11th August, 1992. The Rideau Canal, Ontario

The Rideau Canal is a chain of beautiful lakes, rivers and canal cuts, winding its way through varying landscapes, stretching a distance of 123 miles from Ottawa to Kingston at the head of Lake Ontario. The Rideau Canal was conceived in the wake of the War of 1812 as a war-time supply route to Kingston and the Great Lakes, if the Americans had attempted another invasion. It did not take me long to appreciate the hazards of sailing the Rideau Canal. There are two difficulties: the waterway heads directly into the prevailing wind, and in Canada, the prevailing winds do prevail for long periods; I beat almost all the way to Kingston.

The waterway in many places is scarcely wide enough to regain steerage before coming about again, and it is frequented by power boats with no knowledge of sailboats. In the narrow waterways of England it is normal to wave the motorboat to go under your stern on the side required. Here, this method is fraught with danger—I wave the powerboat to go under my stern, but all he remembers is "keep to the right" and as the gap gets narrower, he forces his way through, sounding his horn desperately while I lose steerage way and drift onto the rocks swearing. In the narrow sections it is safer to row.

13 August, 1992. Merrickville, Ontario (along the Rideau Canal)

For the last 10 miles I have left the houses behind and now in farm land, the river has narrowed, the prettiest country and canal so far, winding through islands, little headlands and marsh. Delightful sailing. A large number of antique wooden boats were going down to the Ottawa Wooden Boat Show and one was short of a crew so I helped him through the locks and hitch-hiked back. One of the crews, Peter Ayling, has a boatyard at Merrickville and I have an invitation to stay at his yard.

His is one of the few yards specialising in wood construction, customers allowed to work on their own boats with advice available, and a friendly atmosphere. He was surprised to find me photographing his toilet pump-out unit but I explained that it was 'professional interest' as I built most of the equipment at my marina in Cheshire including my pump-out which had several advance features on those available at the time. Several seagull droppings are discolouring the tent and one lets rain seep through slowly.

22nd August, 1992. Smiths Falls, Ontario (on the Rideau Canal, 264 feet above the Ottawa River)

I was rowing out of the last lock in Smiths Falls when the lock keepers asked if I knew there was a guided canoe trip through the local wetlands next day. For a moment, I thought they were joking so I remarked with a grin that I "didn't have a canoe with me." Before I knew what was happening they had made a telephone call, booked a canoe and reserved a ticket! It was an interesting tour too; white and yellow water lilies, great tree trunks left from the construction of the canal, water snakes: all the things I don't know about nor see as I sail past in deeper water.

One of the deep locks on the Trent Severn Waterway. The bow and stern ropes are taken round vertical guide cable and hand-held while the boat rises. Wanderer *is tied alongside a powerboat which does the work.*

The forecast this morning began with the announcement that, "For the first time this summer the temperature will be above the daily average for the time of year!"

Head winds have been standard ever since leaving Ottawa, beating all the way and short tacking to keep in the narrow buoyed channel because of weed, submerged tree trunks, and the occasional rock.

25th August, 1992

Now through the lock at the narrows. At last, I am on the summit level and the rest is downwards to the Great Lakes!

This three-foot lock was not part of the original design of the canal but was added because at the far end of the lake the labourers were decimated by swamp fever, heat, and the exhausting work of cutting the canal through solid granite. The resulting three-foot rise in lake level flooded the pestilent swampland, and meant three feet less quarrying—a clever and economical engineering solution!

The trees are already changing to magnificent fall colours, I first noticed it 10 days ago. All summer I have been told "it's been a cold year" although compared to England, it has been excessively hot.

28th August, 1992. Approaching Seeley Bay, Ontario

Past Hog Island the channel opens out into the half-mile-wide Whitefish Lake with high steep slopes on the northwest shore. Here I notice a pair of marker buoys close under the west shore, and although the main channel runs southeast, I follow them through a narrow passage between rocky sides and into a lovely steep-sided granite, completely hidden, lake. It is a lovely spot to anchor overnight as there is not a single house and it is overlooked by two mountains of almost bare granite delightfully named 'Rock Dunder' and 'Dunder's Mate.'

In nearby Murphy's Narrows there is a Wayfarer (or possibly a CL16) on a mooring but I do not linger as thunder clouds are building and growing darker. I am writing up my log book alongside the docks at Seeley Bay when an outboard ties up and the owner introduces himself as Peter. He learned to sail in a Wayfarer and saw me looking at his CL16 as I sailed through the narrows.

We discuss the best method to reef a Wayfarer and he practices on *Wanderer* for a while. Rain starts before we get the tent re-erected and I have a wet boat for the night. I curse and comment it must be Murphy's Law which prompts Peter to remark with a grin that "This area is the centre of Murphy's Law: there's Murphy's Narrows, Murphy's Island, Murphy's Bay…."

He invites me home to see his CL16, for supper and to meet his family. They are a nice family, the CL16 is a copy Wayfarer but not so well finished and the dinghy has a pleasant biblical name. As I leave, they tactfully tell me that their boat is named *The Apostle* and I got it wrong all evening calling it the *The Prophet*. He drives me back in the outboard and as soon as we leave the rain lashes down. Fortunately, I have a full set of oilskins and a peaked cap to keep the water off my glasses but Peter is soaked through within 30 seconds and he tells me this is the tail end of Hurricane Andrew.

Back aboard *Wanderer* there are sombre black clouds from horizon to horizon, the rain heavy, the wind from the southwest is beam on, the tent sides bulging. Gale warnings, heavy rain overnight with flash floods, and a small craft warning has been issued. The only cheering thought it that there are only three mosquitoes.

30th August, 1992. At Seeley Bay, Ontario

Midnight. The distant grumbling thunder quickly increases to crashes directly overhead with slashing rain driven into the side of the tent by strong winds. There must be at least a full gale in the open. I can hear the roar in the tops of the tall trees 100 yards away but fortunately the full force doesn't reach down to water level. *Wanderer* is on the wrong side of the dock—the wind hasn't gone northeast

---

as forecast but is southwesterly, so *Wanderer* is bouncing on her fenders against the windward side of the dock. Fortunately, the springs hold her in place and prevent her hull rubbing on the dock. I get up to put a plastic sheet under the tent where an occasional drip had developed under wind pressure. The rain stops at 7:00 A.M.

The forecast calls for gales of 40 knots with higher gusts and the seas on Lake Ontario are predicted to be 10–14 feet. There are banks of black evil-looking clouds marching across a dark grey sky from horizon to horizon—I'm not going anywhere today! I move *Wanderer* to the lee side of the town dock where the wind holds her off.

During the day, I repair a hole in *Wanderer's* transom, caused by the stern line snatching, probably from the wake of a passing power boat. Then I fit a mooring eye onto the outside of the stern giving a stronger point of attachment. Wind is slowly dropping. Black menacing clouds race past all day long, dawn to dusk, the wind strength and the roar never varies all day and it is extremely wearing! It is the remains of Hurricane Andrew coming up from the Gulf of Mexico according to the weather service.

31st August, 1992

I have almost overstayed my 48-hour limit at the town dock; not that I imagine it matters for there are no boats except me, an outboard, and one powerboat.

I don't expect to get further than the far end of Little Cranberry Lake today, or possibly just into the larger Cranberry Lake to anchor overnight. Cranberry Lake leads into Dog Lake with many bays and narrows, and from the chart it appears a lovely area to explore.

One reef down is ideal now and it is a delight to feel *Wanderer* slicing up to windward through four-inch wavelets. Off Track Islet there is a three-mile fetch across the lake and the waves are now a foot-high, long streaks of foam on the water, a lot of spray and an occasional breaking crest. *Wanderer* is overpowered and I heave-to on starboard tack to pull down a second reef, with very little sea-room so it has to be done quickly. The granite shore is very close, *Wanderer* is 'in irons' and won't pick up speed, so I grab an oar to pull her round but she stops; wind and waves push her towards the rocks and I am looking at a lot of damage in the next few minutes. A low branch tangles in the genoa and holds her 18 inches clear of the rock until I get sorted out. I have narrowly missed disaster.

Squalls are roaring down the lake, *Wanderer* is badly overpowered in the gusts and I have to head up to ease her through them, and soon I am having to play the mainsheet continually as well as luffing. A rest in the lee of Beaupré Island is welcome, then through the gap to meet more squalls whistling down the lake. It is a half mile to the narrow entrance to the Cataraqui River where I can see the marker on a white base. *Wanderer* is staggering and several times she takes water over the gunwale. In one violent gust I completely free the mainsail to prevent a capsize, she stops, and the wind blows her sideways with her sidedeck underwater. She comes up with a lot of water aboard and I almost decide to run back for shelter; but the squall eases a little, and the 200 yards to the river entrance tempts me onward.

Only 100 yards away from the narrow entrance of the river, another violent gust repeats the process and when she comes up the bilge water is six inches over the floorboards. I wonder if she will tack with all the weight of water she is carrying—but she does. There is a round granite boulder, 'The Round Tail' at the entrance, and a marker on a rock restricts the river even more. *Wanderer* tacks sluggishly twice in the narrows then we are through and protected a little by the trees.

The river is narrow with big granite boulders both sides; we are still feeling the squalls, and I need both reefs down. *Wanderer* beats up to the power station, through a rocky defile so narrow and winding and there is no wind, so I get out the oars and have time to enjoy the pleasant passage with the maples changing colour. In the basin before the lock there is another lovely park area. The wind is roaring in the tree tops, but there's little wind at water level.

A restless night, wind still roaring in the tree tops. Thunder suddenly peels out right overhead and wakes me. A vicious squall from the southeast through a gap in the trees at 2:30 A.M. bounces *Wanderer* onto the jetty but her fenders shove her back with a squeal, and monsoon rain sets in a half hour later. Hurricane Andrew is still overhead.

1st Septmeber, 1992. Nearing Kingston, Ontario

The dense morning fog is caused by the air temperature dropping as the fall approaches while the water remains at summer temperatures. I have had headwinds all the way through the Rideau Canal from Ottawa. It has been hard work but what a wonderful waterway.

The lock staff at the next flight have telephoned along the waterway to advise me to delay for a day as the lake is so rough that water is piling up at the lock station and breaking dangerously. It is a kindness that seems to be normal on this delightful canal.

The guide tells me that the last flight of locks (Kingston Mills) drops down into a 'spectacular' gorge before joining the river and Lake Ontario. I look forward to it.

Kingston Mills top lock is in a little bay of the lake, hidden behind a shoulder of land until very close, but the army blockhouse gives it away. My view of the last flight of locks on the Rideau Canal is indeed spectacular with all the bottom gates open, dropping down into a steep ravine to join the river to Kingston. I am tempted to stay overnight at the top but decide to use my one-day pass to lock down and moor at the bottom.

3rd September, 1992. Kingston, Ontario

My night was disturbed by bad dreams ending with a nightmare. I dreamed I was in a life boat in a storm of incredible force, the seas horrendous and only was a only a matter of time before my boat capsized. It is well-known that at the end of a nightmare, when you're falling endlessly into a dark vortex, that you die immediately if you hit bottom before waking up. So I assume that drowning results from a capsize in a nightmare storm. I wake sweating, exhausted and afraid.

4th September, 1992. Kingston, Ontario

Kingston has always been the strategic centre of Upper Canada with a long industrial history of shipbuilding, railroad and lake and river communication. In addition to its rich history, it is also the ideal place to recuperate from the strains of autumn bad weather. Not only did I relax but I 'fell on my feet' too with introductions to everyone.

The Muir brothers had built five wooden Wayfarers over the years so *Wanderer* was welcomed to their marina and could do no wrong. Andy Soper, a sailmaker was working on a neighbouring yacht whose lines seemed familiar. She is a traditional English type, of wood, beautifully kept, gaff rigged, galvanised turnbuckles, pin rails and a 12-foot bowsprit. Andy tells me she is a More-cambe Bay Prawner built

Wanderer moored alongside a Martello Tower in Kingston.

1899 in Chester, England, fully restored by her new owner and shipped across the Atlantic. Andy made a jib for her when serving his apprenticeship in England with

---

one of the famous sailmakers. He has started his own sailmaking business in Kingston and he is again making sails for the yacht—now on this side of the Atlantic. Yachtsmen are horrified when they see her 12-foot bowsprit heading into the marina.

I asked Andy's advice on proofing and he drove me to the local store where we searched the shelves and eventually found a one gallon glass jar of 'original' canvas proofing. He has insisted on taking my sails away for valeting and overhaul.

A local man named Barry Porteous showed me the sights of Kingston and took me to Fort Henry at the Canadian Military Academy to see the great fortifications reinforced by four Martello Towers in 1850 that protected this major naval dockyard from the Americans. He introduced me to the curator of the maritime museum and showed me around the yacht club.

Last evening we went down to his workshop for some whipping twine only to find the most wonderful model railway I have ever seen. Barry is a model train enthusiast. He and five others were partners and developed the railway throughout the whole basement of the condominium, but over the years the others moved or died, and now he is the only one left. It is a magnificent layout with incredible detail—sawmill, quarry, stations, lakes, boats, people—all hand crafted with different locomotive types and wagons travelling through different types of country, over trestle bridges and steel girder spans, crossing rivers and ravines. We played for an hour and I have an invitation to return any time—an invitation I am sure I will take up several times during my stay.

Lake Ontario can be rough especially in autumn. Only yesterday a gust of 40 miles per hour was recorded. I have been told that I should turn down the St. Lawrence river to see The Thousand Islands which are beautiful. However, there is a very strong downriver current running at seven knots in places and it will be impossible to get back against the prevailing westerly wind, so I shall head up the Bay of Quinte which is relatively sheltered to the entrance of the Trent Severn Canal to cross the Ontario peninsular.

9th September 1992. Trident Yacht Club, The Thousand Island, Ontario

The forecast of several days of easterly wind have tempted me to sail down the St. Lawrence to the Thousand Islands using the flow to take *Wanderer* down, and the wind to bring me up against the strong current.

There must be a hundred yachts in the Trident Yacht Club plus a half dozen trawlers, the clubhouse is on the rise of the headland which shelters the cove, and a pleasant small flower garden and lawn under the trees on the steep bluff. I came alongside a good looking trawler to ask if I might fill my water containers (I had almost run out completely), and instead received a kind invitation: "There's a lot of wind forecast tonight. You'd better stay overnight—and come for supper."

My hosts, Jack and Lilo Dirks, are a nice couple who love Canada, their adopted country. They emigrated from Germany in 1952 and Jack has built up a considerable engineering business. I am always interested to discover why so many business people work as hard as they do—and I credit business people for generating a country's wealth— and I shall always remember Jack's remarks about the ways his early experiences shaped his work ethic. Describing his experiences as part of a Hitler schoolboy battalion and as a Russian prisoner between 1944 to 1950 he told us, "It was a rough time and we were always starving; only the young survived and noone over the age of twenty. I developed a burning ambition—for the rest of my life, I wanted to be able to eat when I felt hungry."

The Dirks are very likeable and they have much the same attitude to cruising as Marg and I have; sensible adventuring, enjoyment in the planning and execution. They enjoy their seamanship, and navigate by compass, depth sounder, wristwatch and experience, without radar or Loran. Lilo does the navigation and chartwork. Their trawler is diesel-engined and capable of eight knots all day, a handsome boat weighing ten tons, with no unnecessary top weight, fitted with an upper steering position, but no flying bridge.

We chat about their experiences on the inter-coastal waterway: they had a real bad crossing of Port Royal Sound near Hilton Head with eight ten-foot seas running in from the sea on their starboard bow. They got out in the sound before they realised how bad it was, and running back would have been dangerous so they carried on, waves so short that their propeller and rudder were out of the water much of the time and it was difficult to get the trawler back on course in time to meet the next sea. The next four-and-a-half miles took them three hours.

At 2:00 A.M. the wind in the trees wakes me and I open the front tent flap then stand on the bows to watch. It is a bright moonlight night, an almost full moon with a haze round it. A great bank of black cloud from horizon to horizon rolls up from the southeast, rolling over the moon and extinguishing it, and the night is as dark as Satan's waistcoat. An even darker and denser black cloud rolls up from under the other. With it comes total darkness and the wind, and I retire inside.

12th September, 1992. The Thousand Islands, Ontario

Returning through The Thousand Islands against the current, I notice two seagulls 'mobbing' something in the water so I sail to investigate.

A black squirrel is crossing the half mile channel to the next island. Whether it was driven on this journey by a lack of food or driven out by a stronger male I do not know, but swimming steadily across the passage it has become exhausted and the seagulls have sensed an easy meal. It is concentrating solely on keeping its head above water, and I have a real feeling of empathy as I have a dread of my head going underwater; a fear so severe that I tend to swim 'upwards' not forwards. So I come alongside, pass him a paddle which he holds tenaciously while I bring him aboard and shake him off on the floorboards. He looks a scraggly thin wisp of wet fur, panting and exhausted, unmoving in spite of my close inspection.

I come alongside a private dock and reach down to put him ashore. He views me malevolently, and I reckon that I am going to be bitten. Remembering the stories of settlers catching rabies from the bites of animals I realise that I need gloves and move forward for a pair of heavy rubber gauntlets. He draws himself up to his full height and chatters at me angrily, as if to say: "Don't you dare touch me. I have dealt with bigger animals than you. Come near me and you'll wish you hadn't!"

I reach for him to put him on land and he escapes under the sidebench. I follow him. To my amazement, he disappears through the narrow gap at the edge of the floorboards and I am afraid that he will be stuck below decks. I lift the starboard rear floorboard, first removing all the equipment tied to it, and with astonishing speed he jumps my outstretched hand and goes up under the sidedeck behind the boat roller. I move all the tied-down gear. His next move is forward into the safety of the starboard underdeck bag from where he swears at me continuously.

Not wishing to sleep with such a companion I follow him. He stops between the water containers, then he escapes to the port underdeck bag, and from there underneath the port forward floorboard. Stripping all the gear from that side of the boat, I drive him out onto the top of the stern locker. Unfortunately, it's the end furthest from the shore from where he scolds me furiously. I follow him and as I grab for him, he eludes me with a lightning jump, then five quick leaps to the bows and he is gone.

I look around at the shambles of a once-tidy boat, and swear viciously. I've saved a life but was it worth it?

18th September, 1992. Collins Bay, Ontario

I leave Portsmouth Olympia Harbour in the morning with a forecast of "southwesterly 15–20 knots becoming westerly 20-25 knots this afternoon, possible thunderstorms. Tonight northwest 25–30 knots." Head winds again.

Shorter seas and much steeper. An occasional roar astern as waves break, pulled over by *Wanderer's* wake. Visibility poor, less than two miles. I pick out a red buoy, then the shadow of an island at the end of Amherst Reef and head up for shelter in Collins Bay behind Amherst Island. With wind increasing and *Wanderer* already overpowered and needing a second reef I have an unpleasant choice: either to beat up to Kerr Point and Bay and hope to find shelter—four-and-a-half miles close-hauled (approximately three hours); or 12 miles close-hauled to Prymyer Cove in the Bay of Quinte to a well-sheltered anchorage. A yacht is clawing up to windward, and making heavy work of it. *Wanderer* needed another reef, and it seems sensible to get into the lee of the land before the thunderstorms, so I turn back and run to the north shore of Collins Bay. With the benefit of hindsight, this is the correct decision but I do hate forfeiting ground made good in bad weather.

I cross the five mile open stretch with the wind blowing the length of the Bay of Quinte, and run down the land until I find a rather dilapidated wharf of stone boulders some 60 yards long on the north shore of Collins Bay giving shelter from southwest, west, and northwest.

A lovely sunny day, warm out of the strong winds now force 7, with spray coming over stone breakwater in sheets. The radio forecast has become more dire, warning of, "a severe weather warning, southwesterly 20–25 knots this morning; 30 knots this afternoon. A severe lightning and heavy rain warning has been issued: gusts inland to 32 miles per hour tonight, then becoming northwest 30 knots with gust to 44 miles tonight. I have rigged battery jump leads to shrouds as lightning conductors, and extra mooring ropes so that I can swing west, close under the wharf, then round further as the wind goes northwest. There is good protection here as far as north-northwest but if the wind veers into the north I shall have to move.

I fall asleep at 10:00 P.M. and don't wake to notice the gale, although I am told by the householders that it reached storm force in the early hours.

26th September, 1992 . Trenton, Ontario

I came into Trenton at the western end of the Bay of Quinte, and the beginning of the canal system crossing the peninsular to Georgian Bay via the canalised Trent and Severn rivers. I ignore the big marina as it is full of big power boats and not a single mast among them, and instead I tie up in the town marina next to the Memorial Gardens, conveniently adjacent to the main street. There is no reception on my weather radio and the crew of a wooden craft, *Sure Beats Workin'*, tell me they can only get New York forecasts and nothing Canadian. I'm told by several people that there is so much water coming down-river that it is now impossible to stem the strong current without a motor.

27th September, 1992 . Trenton Town Basin to Lock No. 3

The night is disturbed with a power boat leaving at midnight, loud voices in the park at a midnight party with barbecue and heavy music. Additionally, I am worrying about how to get upriver against the current—I'm wondering if I could get a tow. But it is end of season and what few boats are moving are heading south.

The rain lightly starts at 6:00 A.M. but soon becomes heavy lasting for two solid hours, until finally it reduces to a light drizzle.

The wind fills in quickly and it is soon blowing hard judging by the 'crack' of flags on the building above me. Storm clouds are moving in fast from the south. The wind has a long fetch and swell is building and will soon reflect off the steel piling into the basin and boats are beginning to roll but I realise the wind is ideal, blowing directly upriver. The dock lad in the office says there is a special telephone number for weather, he dials it and hands the telephone to me in time for me to hear: "Southeast 15–20 knots, becoming west 20 knots this afternoon, with gusts of 25 knots or more as the wind changes direction. Rain, becoming brighter this evening, with wind west to 15 knots."

It is a wet, blustery day; the rain is heavy, storm clouds are racing across the sky. I have a coffee with the dock lad, and we chat in the dry. The wind is directly upriver and would carry me over the current but again I am warned of the dangerous conditions in the lower river with this weight of water coming down, and of rocks littering the river close outside the buoyed channel.

10:30 A.M.: The rain stops, wind has veered to southwest off the land and *Wanderer* is rolling in the corner of the basin in the reflected swell. I dress in oilies, pack my wet tent and stow it against the mast. The chart shows the road bridge as a swing bridge clearance of eight feet closed, and cables 37 feet but the dock lad says the old bridge has been replaced by a new bridge of 25 feet, then adds a disturbing qualification, "well…probably 25 feet." It's not worth taking a risk in this weight of wind, so I row round to the floating dock and lower the mast into the small crutch and keeping close under the shore for what little lee there is, I pass under the end arch. *Wanderer* continually heads into the wind because the long mast overhang astern causes her to weather-cock.

Beyond the railway bridge, I raise the mast and hoist the double reefed main. A surprisingly strong current almost catches me out and sets *Wanderer* back onto the bridge and I run off downwind. The channel is on the right side of the river behind a retaining wall of concrete one-foot high, five-feet wide and a current is pouring down the other side. Very pretty, the bank covered in scrub, occasional trees all in autumn colours: bright yellow, vivid red. The training wall ends as the lock cut begins and the current is pouring round the end of the training wall and across the lock cut, so I work up level then pay off and let the current sweep *Wanderer* across safely.

The lock keeper is inside, keeping dry; outside the rain is slashing down now, and I tie under the railroad bridge for shelter. A train passes overhead—box cars, and tank wagons—and rattles on endlessly; it must be over three-quarters-of-a-mile long. The lock gate is open and I let *Wanderer* blow downwind into the lock under the windage of her mast and tie up. The vertical ropes are farther apart than in the Rideau system, so I have the problem of reaching the bow cable which I solve by tying a loose rope at the stern, letting the boat drift forward until I can tie on forward then pulling back. In spite of the foul weather, I get a beaming smile of welcome as I walk into the office to purchase a five-day pass, which cheers me up, although it is soon apparent that the enthusiastic greeting is intended for the lock keeper's girlfriend who has arrived behind me.

Wanderer blows out of the lock and I luff to hoist my two-reef main before rejoining the river where the wind must be all of 20 knots. The wind becomes dead astern as it follows the river, extremely squally and *Wanderer* takes off in a mad plane. A pair of channel buoys appear ahead on the right side of the river, pulled under by the current, the whole width of the river is white with breaking crests, caused by the very strong current running into the force 7 wind. Ahead there are heavy overfalls in the channel with standing waves, short, three-feet high, and hollow. *Wanderer* takes off in another mad plane trying to bury her bow as we approach.

With the centreboard three-quarters raised, I ease slowly out of the channel to windward being very, very careful not to broach, drop mainsail and run off under the windage of the mast. Waves are overtaking *Wanderer*, vertical faces, breaking heavily, and, for some 50 yards, I expect every one to climb over the transom, then they recede. The downriver current is over five knots and even under bare poles *Wanderer* is still gaining ground. With shock cord on the tiller, approaching the next bridge, I hold the rope tail of the forestay in my hand in case the mast touches, relying on the weight of wind to keep the shrouds tight. I lower the mast head some two feet to clear the bridge, before I can tighten up the forestay and the dinghy is entering the lock. Fortunately, the lock keeper swings the gate open as I approach for there was no way I can stop, and I blow straight into the lock chamber of a big lock between massive wood gates. *Wanderer* storms in under the influence of the squalls and I have a job to stop her. The lock chamber is half full of spindrift blown in with us. The gates close hydraulically behind and all is calm.

As *Wanderer* rises to the top of the lock, her flags snap out straight and we rise into a wild world. Now blowing a full gale from the west, it's very squally with black, threatening clouds racing across the skies, the river behind and below in spate—covered in white breaking seas from one bank to the other, It is absolutely wild out there. The lock keeper asks if I am going onto the next lock. I take one look and say, "No. I'll tie up for lunch or until the winds drop." There

---

is a long narrow channel beyond the lock bending round, so it is sheltered even if the wind goes right round and blows downriver tonight. A full gale is howling in the tree tops. The lock keeper says here the fall colours are spectacular but the gale is already blowing all the leaves off the trees.

2:15 P.M.: I walk to the end of the cut where the channel enters the next stretch of river. It is a beautiful walk above the white water of the river but, according to the chart, this is the best anchorage until I get to Lock No. 6. Certainly it would be foolish going further with a gale blowing. Clouds are racing over all afternoon, many black and heavy with threat. I write up my log and put up the tent.

6:30 P.M.: The last clouds have gone and I can see the weather front going away eastwards. The wind has dropped, a beautiful clear yellow sky, sun shining pastel yellow across the river, illuminating the tall chimney against the sky on the far bank. A walk to the top of the lock chamber to check on the wind strength then I sit on the bows just after midnight to enjoy the night and watch the myriads of stars in a clear sky.

28th September, 1992. The River Trent, Ontario

A cold sunrise wakes me—a pastel yellow glow below the skyline in the east is spreading across the whole sky. Surprisingly, I receive a weather forecast clearly from New York State across Lake Ontario, "Southwest 20 knots becoming west 25 knots and a northwest gale in the evening and overnight." Must be a freak reception because now there is nothing but static. However, I have found out what I need to know.

I have a quick wash at the lock station washroom and a walk through the village, past a charming, flamboyantly decorated wooden house, which I stop to admire, then to the convenience store displaying a notice "Midnight–10:00 A.M. Breakfasts"—the notice inside specifies coffee, two eggs, homefries, toast with choice of bacon, ham, peameal and sausage for $3.99. When I ask, I am told that peameal is a fatty, rather salty bacon and I fall for the temptation; justifying my lapse by the thought that there isn't any wind yet. It is excellent too.

At 10:00 A.M. I am away under mainsail only, leaving the genoa rolled up for better visibility. This section of canal is built into the side of the valley, lined with stone, very narrow, with a factory on the far bank dwarfed by a massive chimney. A light wind dead astern takes me to an open section where the strong current downriver increases rapidly to white water near the barrage, strong enough to pull the six foot green buoys under—the top four inches is all that appears. I notice a back eddy along the bank which sweeps *Wanderer* along the shore and behind the lock breakwater where the lock master swings the gate open as I appear and waves me in and I steer straight into the lock chamber. Two locks upstream, the lock keeper comes out to report with a cheerful grin: "They're forecasting wet snow tomorrow morning for you," and I thank him. "No boats yesterday and there'll only be a few boats from now on," he adds.

Lock No. 6 is the last lock of the series with a long run to the next barrage and big power station, but water is pouring downstream and *Wanderer* is just stemming the current and only gaining a half knot over the ground until I pick up a back eddy for the last quarter mile to the lock. Nice houses with long lawns to the river on this section. Frankford village, on the opposite shore, seems a prosperous, small town. A quarter-of-a-mile down the cut I luff in order to drop the mainsail and blow downwind under the bridge, lowering the mast two feet on the rope tail of the forestay. I hoist the main on the run, but the wind gusts suddenly and *Wanderer* luffs in spite of the shock cord on the tiller. A quick turn of the halliard on the mast cleat secures the sail half raised but the boat almost hits the stone bank as I free off. The wind drops back to light.

I devour one of the apples given to me by the lock keeper as I approach the 'emergency gate' shown on the chart. It's a swing bridge carrying lifting gear for lowering stop planks into stop grooves, needed if there is a breach in the man-made section of canal. Next, comes a one-mile-long guide wall of boulders, stone infill, reed beds and ballast, separating the channel from the river. There are a couple of gaps only partly filled by dumped stone, and water is sluicing through into the river, which has little effect on a big power boat but is dangerous to an unpowered 16–footer. I keep well clear and sail into the river where it widens to a quarter mile at Mile 9. The wind is increasing in open water, to 15 knots dead astern and *Wanderer* lifts into a plane.

The big hill which I have been heading for since leaving Picton is now astern (the canal has rounded it) and *Wanderer* is heading on into the interior. Now there is a sense of exploring the interior of the continent and it is easy to imagine a party of Voyageurs returning downriver after a successful trading expedition, with the trees changing to their fall colour.

This canal reminds me so forcefully of the canals of northwest England—first of Bollington on the Macclesfield canal and now of rounding Pendle Hill, on the Leeds and Liverpool canal. I have been warned to keep strictly to the buoys as there are rocks everywhere—the first red buoy has a rock two feet alongside—a stark reminder that this is not the domesticated English canal system.

Half-a-mile later, as *Wanderer* gets into the buoyed channel of the appropriately named Danger Narrows, the wind becomes gusty and then settles into the west—dead on the nose. The current is four knots and I tack and tack trying to beat it. I discover that I can gain against the current by beating up the north bank well outside the channel, until I hit a rock, losing all the ground I have gained. For the next half hour I am in the same place, gaining 10 yards then losing 20. Everywhere outside the buoyed channel there are rocks only 18 inches to two feet below the surface.

Fortunately, when I hit the rock I was gaining ground upstream; had I been going backwards, I would have lost the rudder; on the other tack, going across the stream when the centreboard touched, I would have capsized. I get out the oars but the wind backs and *Wanderer* draws clear of this rock littered narrows and next tack takes me into the wider river with current reduced to two knots and I am soon under the shelter of the lock approach peninsular.

It's now blowing hard from the west and the lock station flag is 'board stiff.' The lock gates are open and the lock keeper shouts down to ask if I am going through straight away as he has a big power boat waiting to lock down. He saw me beating up and held the lock for me. I apologise and say I'd like to have lunch first, and he waves cheerily and closes the gate and fills the chamber. The powerboat is enormous and fills the lock. It is an American boat from Charlotteville, North Carolina and it seems such a long time since *Wanderer* left there. The second lock keeper warns me of an approaching gale with flurries of snow. He recommends that I should stay below the lock as it's much more sheltered than above.

Wanderer is below the land in the approach cut, trees all round, looking lovely in autumn colours. This is another well kept lock station, terraces of flowers along the approach channel, with many trees, flower beds round the lock station building, clean well-kept toilets and washrooms, and I am given a washroom key overnight. Lock operating hours have been reduced to 9:00 A.M. to 4.30 P.M., and it is only two weeks to canal closure for the winter.

8:45 P.M.: A roar in the trees. At first I think it is a train but the railroad bridge is 'open,' so it must be an approaching squall. Even sheltered below the lock in the approach ravine and in the lee of the trees, *Wanderer* bounces on her fenders against the wall. It roars and whistles for 10 minutes then it is gone. What a vicious line squall: I'd have been lucky to get through if it caught *Wanderer* in the open! Suddenly, it's calm again.

29th September, 1992. At Lock No. 7

The lock keeper tells me snow flurries are forecast for tonight. At 1:08 A.M. a northwest gale slams in. There is a roar in the trees, it builds quickly and blows for the rest of the night. Below the lock, *Wanderer* is sheltered, almost no wind at water level. It is still a warm night at 1:35 A.M. so I walk up to the top of the lock chamber in my pyjamas. There it is blowing a full gale from the northwest but it's warm with no sign of snow, although snow clouds are banking up in the northwest, and a few brilliant stars are visible through the overcast. Back at the boat, I leave the front of the tent open while I make a mug of tea, then close up and go back to bed.

I receive the Canadian coastguard forecast faintly when standing on the top of the lock: "Lake Ontario: gale warning still in effect. Northwest wind dropping to 25 knots this afternoon, 15–20 knots northwest this evening." The wind is strong northwest with snow clouds but no snow flurries. It drops then climbs up the scale all morning; there is occasional sun then cloud. Large numbers of autumn leaves are falling in my boat.

30th September, 1992

Another bend and *Wanderer* is laying her course close-hauled upriver. Wonderful colours everywhere. Murray Marsh is on the left with so many different colours—golden reeds, greens, yellows, dark bulrushes, and autumn colours stretches into the far distance. The long beat to windward is due north past the shores of Wilson Island. There are a few buoys and I lay my tacks so I can read them. A fierce current is pushed by the wind and I have to make a big allowance for sideways set, the wind is gusty and varying by 20 degrees—sometimes set down and sometimes well above the buoy I aim at.

Open water at last at Percy Reach to see heavy snow clouds building, and I can see the snow falling from them, but I only get one light snow flurry. It makes me luff up and I put my back towards it but it is soon over and I come back onto course for the narrow channel through Hickory Island. Gaps in the clouds are letting the sun through. Astern it is breathtakingly beautiful: trees and land are shrouded by darkness, but the sun rays through the clouds lights passages of brilliant fall colours like a travelling searchlight. But it is cold too. I shall be lucky if there is no snow before I get in.

It has been a lovely day's sailing today but it must be very cold outside. Even inside the tent, my feet are like blocks of ice, being furthest from the heat of the lantern and nearest to the stern air vent. I make a mental note that all gaps need to be blocked with plastic bags tonight, and I must close the air vent. The forecast says that the temperature is rising to 60°F tomorrow but with general frost tonight except Lake Huron where light winds off the lake will keep temperature above freezing.

1st October, 1992. Campbellford, Ontario

I survey my pleasant surroundings: a commercial river frontage on the right, the co-op mill, a warehouse/mill with double pitched roof and decorated dormer windows on the top floor; a clock tower with minaret, two churches standing high further back; a bridge the chart says is 22 feet; and the park and tourist office.

There is a long jetty and I sail the length of the park looking for a more sheltered spot then sail back selecting my spot carefully.

The tourist centre closes at 5:00 P.M. and I arrive one minute before. "It's alright to tie up, no charge, here's the key to the washrooms." I am advised. "But there's no hydro. Sorry." "What is a 'hydro'?" I ask, mystified. When she responds that "It's what you plug in to keep your refrigerator going." I realise she means 'electricity.' She gives me a map, apologises for all the digging and construction in the centre of the town, and leaves.

I walk round the town. It has a population of three thousand; good services, bookshop, restaurants, banks, a cinema, some hardware stores—and an enormous big hole in the crossroads just as the woman at the tourist centre had said.

3rd October, 1992

A lovely riverside. Only one mile to the lock which has a 22-foot lift. The gate opens as I arrive and I row straight in. Above the locks is another long approach channel and I close-haul along the lee bank, light wind off the higher bank, occasionally only the top six feet of mainsail pulling. I ought to row but I am enjoying the sun and the colours even though *Wanderer* is stationary over the ground held by the strong current, when the light wind switches to *Wanderer's* quarter and we crawl ahead. Then comes a short stretch of flooded river to Lock No. 14, a large lift of 26 feet with a short approach channel and a power station at the far end.

Round the bend the little island hides the lock (there might be a good sheltered anchorage behind the island and I note it in case the current defeats me) and I have to row out of its wind shadow, to pick up the light breeze again close-hauled. The power station opens up on the right, then the lock, then the rapids from the barrage—and these are real rapids with water pouring down, white with broken water, standing waves across the whole width of river, spray everywhere. It dawns on me that it is going to be very tricky to get up to the lock against the weight of water!

There is a choice:

a) I keep to the left behind the islands, then cross the race from the barrage to the lock but the current must be 15 knots plus! This isn't possible as *Wanderer* will be swept downstream hundreds of yards!

b) I could creep up close under the right hand bank, but this is on the outside of the bend where the current is running fast and deep beneath the rock, but I shall get some breeze to help my rowing. There should be a back eddy in the bay halfway along but here the power station outfall will prevent any back eddy forming. I stand up and view it carefully.

Neither alternative is attractive, and I cannot follow the buoyed boat channel through the deepest and fastest flowing water as that route is impossible to me without an engine.

I edge *Wanderer* across the stream, gently lee-bowing the current, using what breeze there is, to within 10 yards of the low white cliff, then row. The current is less than I expected—probably only four knots. Rowing flat out and helped by the light breeze, *Wanderer* gains ground ever so slowly, but I can judge progress and direction by the neighbouring rock face.

A quick glance over my shoulder and the little point is only 20 yards away. I redouble my efforts, and suddenly *Wanderer* is out of the main stream from the barrage with only the power station outlet to deal with. I calculate distance, angle, and current, and row furiously, allowing the power station tail race to lee-bow *Wanderer* across until I slip round the end of the breakwater.

Suddenly, I am in still water and I can relax. I row into the lock, sweating heavily. The lock keeper high above on the lock wall says: "You got that just right! From up here I could see the edge of both streams and you came right up between them!" A nice compliment I thought as I lock through.

Standing on the barrage above the roaring sluices is like leaning on the stern rail of an ocean liner doing 20 knots! I ask about the half submerged tree growing in the rapids. The lock keeper tells me that it moves, then grounds and roots further down. It used to be on a ledge 200 yards upstream but so far it has moved twice! He gives me apples, tomatoes, and oranges from his garden. Lock keepers are a mine of useful local information!

I row past the power station inlet, then the cut narrows and the current increases, and even close to the bank I cannot make progress however hard I pull. There is no way I can row the next quarter mile, so I row in, grab a bollard, and tie up to think things out. Towing is the answer but how can I go about it, I wonder. I attach a rope to the cleat in front of the mast which is forward of *Wanderer*'s pivoting point so I can pull her in; a stern rope to pull her forward and keep her out from the bank, rudder free to swing (fixed, it would pull me in), and the centreboard almost raised so that if the rudder jams over she can still be pulled to the bank. It works a treat. At the end of the cut, it is blowing hard and I tie to a picnic table to hoist the mainsail, pull one reef down and cast off from the wooden table.

I find a pretty anchorage behind Hardy Island with the sun setting in bright yellow behind the trees. I'm hailed by a man walking down to his outboard fishing boat: "Don't anchor there—speedboats and fishermen come through fast all night long, and they won't look for an anchored boat. My neighbour says you can tie to his dock. I'll come and tow you in."

He introduces himself as Bob Scott and helps me tie up. His neighbour Charlie invites me to the house for coffee after I have put up the tent. I find that 'coffee' includes a meal. Back at *Wanderer*, there is a brilliant half moon. It's a clear night, stars sparkling in the heavens and the forecast predicts 'a real cold one.' I wear socks, my sweater over my pyjamas with the hood pulled over my balaclava hat, and all this inside two sleeping bags. A lovely sunset dies reluctantly, the afterglow reflected in the still water until three speed boats travelling very fast spoil the reflection by roaring across the spot I was anchored. "They do that all night," remark Bob and Charlie, who have walked down to check that I am alright, but *Wanderer* lays bow on and rides the wakes easily.

5th October, 1992. Rice Lake, Ontario

The thickest frost yet on deck. The chart marks 'English Hill.' I wonder why. I let *Wanderer* sail herself while I get out thick working trousers, rubber boots, oilskin jacket. I look up to find that *Wanderer* has luffed into a marshy creek so gently that I had not noticed. It is named the Ouse River. Perhaps *Wanderer* liked the name and was feeling homesick for the river Ouse in Fenland, England.

1:55 P.M.: Cameron Point is abeam and I am entering Big Rice Lake. How nice to be in open water again and feel *Wanderer* lift to the small waves and shoulder them aside as the wind increases to 10 knots. The marinas are all empty of boats.

The much bigger Sugar Island ahead is higher with less trees; an 'Indian Reserve' says the chart. I take the direct route inside the island but weed defeats me and I come onto the wind for the landing at Serpent's Mounds Provincial Park where most of the floating docks have been brought ashore for the winter. Autumn colours are at their best in the park and I wander enjoying it. The woman at the reception office is going off duty but stays to give me literature and describe the area. The Native peoples were upset by the open graves after an archeological dig and the graves have now been covered. This is Indian land leased by the provincial government; the lease runs out in two years, and it is not known if the Native community will agree to renewal after the tactless 'dig.' The last comprehensive excavation was in 1985. The graves are approximately two thousand years old. The tribes made this their summer home gathering fish, shell fish, and hunting rabbits. The descriptions on the boards tell me there was trade in silver, copper and other goods from as far as Hudsons Bay, Lake Superior and the mid-west.

I light the lantern for heat and light, strip off my extra outer clothes and heat my supper. The 'slap' 'slap' 'slap' of small waves under *Wanderer*'s stern is annoying and will keep me awake, so I turn out to remoor on the other side of the dock, bows to the lake. Already it is freezing heavily.

6th October, 1992. At Mouth of the Otonabee River (leading to Peterborough), Ontario

Passing a yacht at a dock, I notice the owner working on a marine railway to haul out his yacht and I return to find out some local information and to inquire for a boatyard to store *Wanderer* over winter. He recommends Willowbend Marina four miles south of Peterborough, and I stay for the rest of the day assembling and bolting up the rails while he cuts the plates and the bolt holes. "A general frost warning, patchy fog."

The next morning it is intensely quiet, no sound. Dawn breaks slowly with not enough light inside the tent to see until 7:30 A.M. and ice covers the decks inside the tent. I roll back the rear of the tent to find dense fog with visibility only to the next bush—maybe 25 yards.

9th October, 1992 . Peterborough, Ontario

My end of season worries—namely, where to store *Wanderer*—have evaporated. I called at Willow Bend Marina to see the Smiths. They are a nice couple and said they'd be pleased to store *Wanderer* under cover and we have coffee and cakes in the office to seal the bargain. There is a Canada Customs office in Peterborough for the essential paperwork detailing repairs.

At Peterborough City Marina there are few boats still in the water but Don Sargent off a trawler offers the use of his insurance office basement to store my gear with unlimited cardboard boxes supplied—an offer I gratefully accept.

10th October, 1992. Peterborough Marina (to Nassau Mills), Ontario

I potter about and chat with a number of people and do not get away until noon. The wind is blowing hard and I leave my two overnight reefs tied in to cross Little Lake. Once clear of the marina narrows *Wanderer* comes up into a plane to the lock on the far shore. I drop the mainsail well clear of the approach channel as I do not want to find that there is not enough width to luff, especially in this strength of wind, and tie up to the blue painted waiting section of the quay.

It's very uncomfortable alongside the quay with the reflected waves off the vertical concrete walls making a nasty 'popple.' I tie *Wanderer* bow facing into the wind but as the gate sluices open the rush of water swings her round and she crashes into the concrete heavily, rolling and pitching frantically. We rise to a short length of canal to a blue swing bridge, tree lined and spectacular colours. The keeper swings the bridge as *Wanderer* appears, and she runs under bare poles straight into the lock chamber. A lovely downwind sail follows under genoa only between autumn colours which get better and better until the great concrete structure of the Peterborough Hydraulic Lift Lock appears beyond the oranges, reds, and golds of autumn—a wonderful first view of a magnificent canal structure.

The principle of the hydraulic is simple and economical: the weight of the water in the upper chamber raises the lower one through the connected hydraulic rams and vice-versa.

I decide to head on as far as the Indian summer weather will allow before I return to lay-up at Peterborough.

10th October, 1992. Peterborough, Ontario

Two weeks ago, there was a cold snap with snow flurries and frost all day while crossing Rice Lake, but since there has been an Indian summer although still with frost on deck in the mornings. Heavy water flow and strong currents in the river have made it impossible to reach lock entrances except by using the back eddies close to shore.

Trent Severn Waterway, approaching the Peterborough Hydraulic Lift Lock.

15th October, 1992. Lock No. 22, Peterborough, Ontario

Back at Peterborough I tie up at the lock for the last night of the canal season. A full gale is blowing through the tree tops as I walk to the headland where I can look across Little Lake to Peterborough Marina directly upwind. It is blowing extremely hard with white horses, waves breaking on the beach and spray blowing ashore. I wash my socks at the lock station and hang them on the mast to dry.

The staff are boarding up doors, windows, storing equipment, removing notice boards for the winter. I take a wrong road and follow a long looped road through a housing estate. The trees are half stripped by the gale last night but there is a beautiful coloured maple on the street and I decide to photograph it on my way back when the sun is further round, but on my return the leaves have all been stripped by today's gale, and *Wanderer*'s tent is covered in leaves, most of them maple. I have a supper of noodles, smoked ham, fresh carrots, cucumber, and fruit juice. It is too hot with the lantern going even with the air vents open, mainly because the river is so well sheltered under the trees.

I was told by the few yachtsmen I met that, "If you can sail in the Saint Laurent you can sail anywhere in the world." I did not believe it at the time but I do now. It is the most frightening area for an engineless sailing dinghy and in some peculiar way the most rewarding. Dorothy Blythe, my publisher at Nimbus Publishing, described the sailing conditions of the Lower St. Lawrence as 'the impossible equation.' A description I find extremely apt.

The continual roar of water across the dam lulls me to sleep. I shall miss this sound soon.

Nothing on the weather radio: it must be the end of season.

18th October, 1992. Toronto, Ontario

While I await my flight to England, I'm staying with the Wayfarer owner I met in Bay of Quinte. He is from Slovenia in the Balkans. A charming family with a very adventurous mother-in-law who has learned to drive at 80-years-old and passed her test. Now she intends to learn to fly.

It's cold now: 20°F yesterday and snow is forecast today; but *Wanderer* is safely under cover at the friendly Willowbend Marina in Peterborough, and my gear stowed safely in boxes at a local insurance office.

A storm warning has been issued. A front will bring northeasterly winds, cold temperature overnight, snow and violent winds behind the front on Friday afternoon. Winds of 90 kilometres per hour and more in the gusts.

My over-riding memory from this year's cruise is that it was the most demanding and unforgiving sailing circumstances I have yet encountered—synonymous in my mind now with the St. Lawrence River. The Saint Laurent, as the Quebeceois call it, is 1,000 miles from the sea to Montreal. The lower river is 65-miles wide narrowing to 30 miles at Matane; the water is bitterly cold from the ice carrying Labrador current.

It is a fog-ridden, iron-bound shore with small artificial harbours every 12–15 miles but no landings between. The vertical cliffs cast a long wind shadow from the prevailing southwesterlies so if a sailboat keeps inshore she is becalmed, and if she goes out a half mile for wind she is in the Gaspé current going out to sea at four knots. The wind drops in the late afternoon but it is too deep to anchor, and in the ever-present fog the harbours are elusive.

I was told by the few yachtsmen I met that, "If you can sail in the Saint Laurent you can sail anywhere in the world." I did not believe it at the time but I do now. It is the most frightening area for an engineless sailing dinghy and in some peculiar way the most rewarding. Dorothy Blythe, my publisher at Nimbus Publishing, described the sailing conditions of the Lower St. Lawrence as 'the impossible equation.' A description I find extremely apt.

1993. Peterborough, Canals, and the Canadian Shield

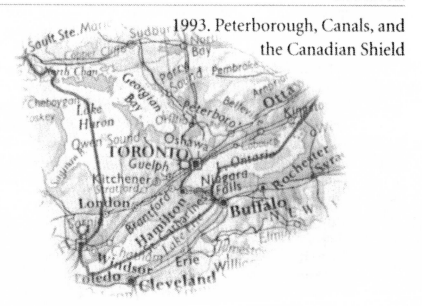

6th June, 1993

There was the usual panic in getting away from England but it gradually came to hand. I promised that I would visit the Wooden Boat Show at Greenwich before I left, as our first *Wanderer* W48 is always brought out of the National Maritime Museum for the show.

Wanderer has attended every show since they started and Marg was allowed to put up the tent and live aboard at the first event. It is prohibited to sleep in a royal park overnight and we had a special dispensation. The office staff and the day people knew about us and came round to say 'Hello' but unfortunately no one informed the night security men. So in the early hours the tent flaps were pulled open by two burly men in uniform, "Come on, out of there," they ordered and listened sceptically to our explanations. It seemed to be hours before they were able to contact someone in authority who knew about us.

A long eight-hour flight passed quickly with cheerful staff and an excellent curry meal. Letting down in Toronto was nerve-wrecking as the airplane descends into dense vortexing cloud near the ground. The wing tip disappeared, and I could no longer see the outer engine from the cabin window as the aircraft was thrown about.

A long bus ride takes me to Hamilton and the home of Alan and Joy Phillips, long-time Wayfarer friends. Joy drives me round various stores to buy food supplies, change my money to Canadian dollars, and purchase a new pair of trousers.

Alan drives me to Peterborough and then helps me launch and load *Wanderer* before returning home.

12th June, 1993

7:30 A.M.: Slept well and feeling better now I am aboard. I am enjoying being afloat and look forward to sailing immediately. For once there is no forward planning needed as *Wanderer* spent the winter halfway through the Trent Severn Waterway and I did my pre-planning last autumn, although I will have a hard slog against the current until I reach the summit. Fortunately, there will be no current until I rejoin the river near Trent University.

It is a calm, still morning and I am enjoying rowing across Little Lake to the lock on the far side when I row straight into a green navigation buoy and hit it plumb centre! The lock gate opens and I am waved straight in. "Welcome back," says the lock keeper.

The Peterborough Hydraulic Life Lock appears round the bend. It is a grand sight towering over the canal—the biggest non-reinforced concrete construction in North America by the same designer as the Anderton Boat Lift in Cheshire but this is a later development (1904) with 22-yard lift. As the caisson locks into position 80 feet above the water, the skipper of an American powerboat tied close to the outer gate calls, out to the lock keeper: "I hope you open the right gate," and there is general laughter. (I am told that in years past, it has been known for a gate to open on the way up, and usually boats grounded on the floor of the caisson before the rush of water swept them out. The fault has been rectified by fitting positive locks to all gates).

At Trent University there is no wind, and I have an exhausting pull through the bridge against the strong river current; several times I am almost driven back.

I row slowly and carefully under the next bridge as the official clearance is stated to be 22 feet (the lock keeper says the levels are a little down) and *Wanderer's* mast is 23-feet high. Stemming the current, it is easy to inch forward and *Wanderer* clears—just.

14th June, 1993. Otonabee River to Stoney Lake, Ontario

Sailing fast, an occasional gybe as the wind is deflected by the trees but the strong current is against me so speed over the ground is very slow. The stream in Lakefield Narrows is running hard and *Wanderer* crawls up to the lock entrance under sail where I luff close to a rock to drop the mainsail. I am about to push off when I remember the prevalence of poison ivy and hurriedly use an oar instead of my hands!

Lakefield is a deep lock. The lock keepers appear to be following my progress. ("I hear that you had difficulty against the current all the way from Peterborough!")

"The bridge clearance is shown on the chart as 23 feet?" I question and the lock keeper assures me that I should get under without difficulty as the water level is low.

It is a long cut, a ravine through rock for a quarter mile above the lock, steep sided, and no wind, so I row. Round the bend is the fixed bridge and I put the shock cord on the tiller, a few quick pulls to regain steerage way, release the rope tail on the forestay to drop the mast back 10 degrees and the mast head clears by a few inches. I don't bother to put in the second purchase to tension the forestay as there is another bridge five miles on, and with *Wanderer* running downwind, it carries no load anyway. The waterway widens to 100 yards and I hoist the mainsail but not very efficiently as I take too long and the dinghy luffs and runs aground gently on the rocky shore. There are new pontoon docks before the next bend and it is conveniently close to town but there are no boats, no signs indicating whether these are private or town docks. Opposite, is a beach and caravan park. The channel turns left through narrows against a racing, eddying current and *Wanderer* crawls through. On the far shore, the channel markers are easily visible to First Island, Second Island, Third Island and then out into the open water again of Lake Katchewanooka.

I approach the bridge at Young's Point at 3:50 P.M.—only 10 minutes to lock closing time so I shall have to wait until morning to go through, but there are plenty of islands for shelter. I run into a bay before the bridge, drop the five pound danforth which bites immediately and holds against the pull of *Wanderer* sailing away. I drop the mainsail and listen to the forecast. "Occasional thunderstorms this evening, 60 percent chance of rain, south-southwesterly wind 10–15 knots, gusts to 20 kilometres an hour in thunderstorms."

There is no sign of thunderclouds building but some light cloud is coming in from the south. Even with a force three breeze keeping the temperature down, I am still exhausted by the heat so I put up the front end of the tent for shade, the front flaps raised for extra draught, and I flake out for an hour then wake with just enough energy to make a mug of tea and porridge. No enthusiasm to eat until the temperature drops. I have to muster up considerable effort in order to write up my log.

8:30 P.M.: The weather is grey and cooler. I get out my cantaloupe melon but it is soft, over-ripe and tastes bad. The sky looks like rain. I could have moored in the lock approach but I suspect reflected waves would be caused by the strong current from the barrage and I don't want to roll all night on the edge of seasickness! So I anchor well clear of the navigations channel where I am sheltered to the south, although there is a half mile fetch to the southeast.

9:00 P.M.: Daylight is holding well although it is dull and overcast. We are 90 yards from shore so I hope to be out of reach of mosquitoes. The wind has almost died away but I rig the second anchor in case it is needed overnight. A couple of mosquitoes have come aboard so I close down the tent. The temperature drops at last. It has been an unbearably hot day! What will it be like in late summer when it gets really hot? There is no sign of thunderclouds building but the weather radio repeats its warnings.

15th June, 1993. Between Katchewanooka Lake and Clear Lake (Young Point Lock), Ontario

A disturbed night with a rain shower at 10:40 P.M. which gets me up to close the front air vent and to check that I had led the halliard and anchor warp so that they didn't run water onto my sleeping bag. Still too hot to sleep.

1:50 A.M.: Vivid lightning, tremendous crashes of thunder and torrential rain. The thunder is continuous. The interval between flash and bang started at 10 seconds (a two mile distance) decreasing steadily until it is overhead, and the inside of the tent is completely and continually bright from the lightning. Marg once described such thunder as "The gods banging about." I forgot to rig the jump lead lightning conductors to the shrouds and I'm not going to do so now. It is too risky with the possibility of getting struck by lightning with metal in my hands; and, I keep my head and limbs well away from the metal boom and mast. The thunderstorm continues for an hour, then moves away at 2:30 A.M. Fortunately, the tent doesn't leak at all and I relax slowly from all the violence.

At 3:30 A.M. the storm returns and it's even more violent and stays overhead for an-hour-and-a-half. It is so close and violent that I remove my watch because of its metal strap. At last, it moves away, the rain stops, there is no wind, and it is cooler. Finally, I can sleep.

7:30 A.M.: A cool, clear, sunny morning but I am so tired. If go back to sleep I'll never get up so I have breakfast and pack my tent, ready for an early passage through the lock. A check on the canal map indicates a clearance of 22 feet.

8:30 P.M.: I anchor and row across a line of rocks to get to the channel, centre-board and rudder blade kick up as the rocks are only 18 inches below the surface. A strong current is running so I have to row hard to get under the bridge. The clearance appears doubtful so I swing the mast down into the crutch and pull hard along the left hand bank in the shallows to cheat the spate.

The lock gates are open and the green light is showing but I tie up to the quay before entering in order to raise my mast and insert the additional forestay purchase as there are several miles sailing to Clear Lake and Stoney Lake (which appears from the map to be well worth exploring) and the bridge at Love Sick Lock has a clearance of 10 feet above my masthead.

I row into the lock chamber, welcomed by the lock keeper, the same man I met at the Peterborough Lift Lock last fall. One top gate is swung open to let *Wanderer* out (it is normal practice to open only one gate for small boats) then, very ostentatiously and making a great fuss, his assistants open the second as far it will go. "Lock 24 told us about your standard of boat handling!" he shouts down and there is general laughter! (Lock 24 had opened one gate to let *Wanderer* through and I rowed into the closed gate and hit it plumb centre). I was to find that the story had travelled the whole length of the canal ahead of me and every lock will insist on opening both gates fully before I am allowed to enter.

The post office and shop across from the lock is a real gem, an old-style general village store remembered from my youth, and a great pleasure to walk round. I bought stamps, extra airmail stickers, PVC insulation tapes, postcards and general supplies. Remembering some of the dangerous "Hell's Gates" I have seen, I ask the lock keeper for local advice on Hell's Gate in the next section of waterway. "It's a very narrow, winding channel between rocks just below water. It used to be very dangerous before boats had motors," he tells me. "A strong current?"

I inquire. "No, it shouldn't be any trouble to you at this time of years but it's too narrow to tack."

It is mostly open water from now on and I work out a compass course across Clear Lake—my chart work being photographed by the crew of a power boat moored astern. The crew tell me they have come up from The Thousand Islands on the St. Lawrence the same as I have, but in less time, I imagine.

I 'make a fist' of raising the mainsail—fouled ropes, kinks that won't run through the blocks, the reefing line round my feet, and when, at last, I sort it out and look up there is a twist in the head of the mainsail—the result of tiredness after last night's storms, I expect. There is a four-mile reach along the open water of Clear Lake and it is pleasant sailing past forested shores, cottages all with boats on moorings. The buoyed channel winds through a mass of small granite islets with more cottages, and one prominent building has a cross on the gable end. So I read the notice through binoculars: "St. Peter's On the Rock Anglican Church: open for services 10:00 A.M. July and August." It looks a friendly, small church and a timely discovery at the entrance to Hell's Gate! I meet the cruise ship *Hiawatha Queen* in the narrows, so I sail between the islets to starboard to get out of her way and find myself in a lovely anchorage surrounded by small trees on granite rocks with boathouses and boats on moorings, so I drop anchor and doze in the sun for an hour, then write, have lunch and do some needed maintenance.

The weather radio issues a thunderstorm watch, warning of hail and damaging winds and the need for extreme caution. The wind increases to 20–25 knots in the open but I am sheltered from the west, and the five-pound danforth has taken well hold.

It is clouding up and now quite cold with the sun behind the clouds. I add a sweater and socks for dinner of cheese and cucumber sandwiches and a large mug of tea, then hot soup. The wind increases rapidly as the sky clouds over then drops away to force 2 and I close the front tent vents for warmth and pull a sweater over my pyjamas. I wake at 1:30 A.M. to a calm, pleasantly cool night.

16th July, 1993. Lovesick Lake, Ontario

Lovesick Lake is very pretty with a mass of rocky islands before it opens out. I lock through into Buckhorn Lake with only one hour and 20 minutes to cover the five-and-a-half miles to Buckhorn Lock and only the barest breath of wind—I soon accept this is an impossible plan. This is a much bigger lake with fewer islands, and the shores are forested, but it is uninteresting, possibly because I am now rowing and suffering in temperatures over 80°F. The breeze dies completely as I row past Grassy Island, Dinnertime Island and Three Islands—three miles rowing a dead boat, the heat pouring down on me from the sun and reflected up again by the water.

At last, there is a light wind from ahead as I near the narrows at the end of Lower Buckhorn Lake and I row/close-haul through the narrow channels and out into the little bay where there is a pleasant breeze. I drop the mainsail, pulling down two slab reefs prior to rolling the sail on the boom in case I need to move in the dark. I come in to tie up at 6:30 P.M.

17th June, 1993. Buckhorn and Pidgeon Lakes, Ontario

The weather radio reception is poor so I change the waveband and the reception is slightly improved. "Light southwesterlies, hot this afternoon. Chance of thunderstorms."

I'm up early to tidy *Wanderer*, lower the mast for the 22-foot bridge, pack the tent, and finish breakfast in time for the the lock keepers arrival at 9:00 A.M. The lock chamber is full of water (left full overnight, in case someone falls in) so they let the top boats down first, then tell me to tie towards the front of the lock and other boats to follow me in. The lock keeper had a Folkboat but never had time to sail it so I sympathise and we chat 'boats.' A headwind is blowing down Buckhorn Lake, light and variable.

Buckhorn Lake is a wider lake, nine miles long with a line of large islands across the widest part (Emerald, Curve Lake Indian Reserve, Fox and Nichol Islands). All day I'm beating, light winds with an occasional pull on the oars to help *Wanderer* through calm patches. A head wind is funnelling through the narrow channel between the trees of Fox and Nichol Islands, but approaching Gannon Narrows, the temperature rises, wind comes over the port quarter as the channel turns northeast. The road bridge has 22 feet clearance again—eight inches less than my mast. It is not worth taking a risk so I drop the mainsail, roll the genoa, drop the mast into the crutch, then let *Wanderer* blow under. I raise the mast and sails but now there is no wind, the temperature is appalling with not a breath of air—it must be in the high 90s. Fortunately, the waterway opens out into Pidgeon Lake—much bigger and hopefully cooler!

A slight breeze allows a slow beat out into Pidgeon Lake where the wind dies entirely and it becomes a furnace on the water and I have five miles to row in unendurable heat and another mile up the river to the next lock! I check the chart. There is no sheltered place to anchor, but I'll put the hook down offshore out of range of mosquitoes and move if I need to.

A small yacht puts out from the shore and we exchange greetings. He advises "keep to the middle of the lake and the wind will hold until you get to

Bobcaygeon." Sure enough, in the centre there is a pleasant breeze and the temperature drops a little though it is still unbearable. The shore is featureless so I mark off buoy '339' near Long Point on the chart as it comes abeam at 5:10 P.M. 'Three Sister' buoy is a half mile abeam at 5:20 P.M. so I know where I am and I mark up courses, bearings and distances. How wonderful is the cool of the evening, after the last few days of extreme heat.

18th June, 1992. Bobcaygeon (Pidgeon Lake Yacht Club), Ontario

Waking with a splitting headache I decide to spend a day ashore—the effect of the last few days' heat. I ought to be almost acclimatised by now though!

This is a big continent, unbelievably large, and Canada is the largest country in the world after the U.S.S.R. with the greatest reservoir of fresh water. Looking at the postcards showing maps of Canada I have bought, I realise that in several years of cruising, I have only travelled the bottom right corner!

28th June, 1993. Lake Simcoe, Ontario

Lake Simcoe is 15 miles across and some 40 miles long. By English standards it is big although by Canadian standards it is only a medium-sized lake, though notorious for sudden storms and bad seas. There is an illuminated weather board at the end of the canal updated automatically to the latest forecast and when I leave at 6:30 A.M. in order to cross before the wind gets up, it reads "gusts to 35 knots." An hour into the lake the wind has increased to 15 knots so I reef down and heave-to for breakfast. The wave are short and steep and *Wanderer* is being thrown about more than I would have expected with two reefs down in the North Sea. These fresh water shallow lakes do kick up quickly.

The Trent-Severn Waterway consists mainly of long lakes connected by locks but there have been several straight canal cuts in the last sections. The lock keepers are helpful and a mine of information on the area, vegetation, crops, and history of the surrounding villages.

29th June–4th July, 1993. Hawkestone Yacht Club, Lake Simcoe

The Hawkestone Yacht Club is pretty with a really nice crowd of members, the basin hidden and very pleasant. I intended hauling *Wanderer* out for a scrub on Monday but three club members had already done it and insisted on washing her down and scrubbing the bottom ready for me to anti-foul. I have a half tin of red copper anti-foul paint in the forward locker but I can't find it anywhere and I have searched the boat from top to bottom—unbelievable in a 16-foot boat! Anti-fouling *is not* necessary in fresh water although is discourages zebra mussels, but the old paint was looking tatty. Another day of maintenance and the refitting is all done. I stay a week which is unusual for me: racing, visiting, relaxing and eating at the yacht club's annual lobster supper.

On my last day, I am privy to a tumultuous episode at the club. I returned from a walk to be met by an angry group who demanded, "Are you supporting the duck or the turtle?" Apparently, a couple of ducks had reared a family of six ducklings but the numbers gradually reduced to three and the resident snapping turtle was suspected. Two of the club officers had then witnessed him snatching another little duckling. and taking the turtle to the far end of Lake Simcoe before releasing him. I naturally said I was 'for' the duckling. It was the wrong answer and I was angrily told that ducks were a part of the natural food chain and if they reared two ducklings per year the species was in balance, whereas the turtle kept the basin clean and was a useful member; the club officers had exceeded their authority and members were getting up a petition to instruct the officers to find the turtle and bring it home.

5th July, 1993. Hawkestone Yacht Club to Orillia, Ontario

I planned on making an early start but my good intentions came to nought as I overslept. I write a 'Thank you' note for a wonderful stay and pin it on the notice board and then phone Ted Carter, a Wayfarer owner whom I have invited to sail with me to Orillia. The wind returns gently, then rapidly, freshing from the northeast. It is 10 miles to the end of the lake so I shall have a 'long-and-short' as my course turns to windward. I cast off and beat out.

It is nice to be away and sailing although it is a wrench to leave such a nice club. Ted is waiting at the end of his dock with a food box and a lifejacket. He unrolls the genoa then takes the tiller. He is a racing man and sails well, and soon has me working hard, sitting forward to balance the boat, transom out of the water to increase speed, sails adjusted properly, fitting a line to the Cunningham hole, altering the stowage weight, and moving sails in and out. We get on well and it is an enjoyable sail with *Wanderer* creaming along.

As we enter Orillia Narrows, the wind comes over the quarter and Ted mentions 'shooting bridges all standing' which he has read about in *Wayfarer News*. He is obviously intrigued and I promise to demonstrate at the approaching bridge. I remember to unclip the retaining line to the reefing drum, single up the rope tail to the forestay in advance, and the mast and sails swing down against the tail wind. (I did wonder for a moment as the wind gusted, if the mast would refuse to move and the bridge would knock it down for us). The mast and sails swing up easily under the pressure of the wind, no ropes jam in the tabernacle and we are sailing immediately with no loss of speed. I am congratulating myself on an impressive demonstration when I look up to see a railroad bridge 20 yards ahead I hadn't noticed but fortunately, it is 'open.'

A most enjoyable sail follows with Ted pointing out features ashore and afloat. There is enough wind now for spray to blow back into *Wanderer* but it is too hot to wear a jacket. Walking round town, I notice neighbourly churches on the same street, an opera house putting on a play, and a cinema showing *Snow White and the Seven Dwarfs*. At the chandlery, I am introduced to a lively Alsatian dog called Zodiac and we chase one another round the park barking at each other.

I invite Ted and his wife, Myrna to see *Snow White*, but they make their excuses. I'm sorry to see them go. Such nice people, but I feel that I dented my image somewhat with my excessive enthusiasm for ice cream, barking at Zodiac and chasing him round the park, and childhood memories of Grumpy, Dopey, Happy and the

A typical lock. Only one gate is opened for small boats like Wanderer.

other dwarfs. I walk through the park again to the bronze statue of Champlain, the great French explorer, with its fine symbolic figures of Commerce and Christianity at the base. A very pleasant waterside walk.

6th July, 1993. The Canadian Shield

Wanderer is close-hauled to windward of Chief Island in the Indian reserve, carrying full mainsail, an occasional gust pushes the lee gunwale down into the water. The wind drops to a pleasant sailing breeze, the sun comes out, thunderclouds disappear into a blue sky and *Wanderer* is laying her course. It's lovely sailing. The buoys come and go 200 yards to leeward.

There is a line of paired buoys marking the channel through the islands and a line of rocks just awash of a different colour so I sail over to look and find that the rocks are granite, not limestone. I have come to the edge of the Canadian Shield! From now on I must be careful of isolated rocks just below the surface as granite does not wash away like the softer limestone.

At the far side of the lake, my 23-foot mast touches the bridge so I drop back and tie up alongside a mooring wall for the night with springs to prevents *Wanderer* sheering about. I am eating my supper as two powerboats go through too fast and their wakes throw *Wanderer* heavily against the concrete. As a precaution, I lower the mast and row beyond the bridge in case more boats go through after dark. It is one-and-a-half miles to row to the next lock where I can be certain no boats will be moving until morning. This is a lovely canal, the scenery is completely different from the limestone area behind—less trees and more open vegetation. It must be the effects of the Canadian Shield. It's pleasant rowing in the cool of the evening as I am the only boat about.

7th July, 1993. Couchiching to Sparrow Lake Chute, Ontario

At the narrows, the current speeds up to two knots approaching the railroad bridge. There is a total change in land character. Now it is granite with more rock, less trees, but a much higher proportion of silver birch, fewer cottages, more wild rice, weed and rocks in the shallows.

In the evening, I sit on the bow admiring the colourful

Big Chute Marine Railway. Wanderer *is almost hidden on the carriage which is capable of taking of twenty boats or 100 tonnes.*

sunset. I sit out too long and get driven inside by the mosquitoes and while securing the front flaps, I get bitten viciously. The mosquitoes are hunting in pairs and biting my eye lids, ears, neck, back, feet and legs. I tie down the tent skirt then light a five-inch-long piece of anti-mosquito coil and spray the surplus insects. At 10:30 P.M. the final mosquito kicks its last. Both *Wanderer* and I are covered in blood where I have swatted mosquitoes who have already dined well and were slow taking off.

8th July, 1993

McDonald's Cut is only three to four boat lengths wide, with granite rising straight from the water to 40–60 feet. The current accelerates to two knots and this paired with unusually low water levels prompts me to ponder about what it must have been like for the voyageurs when they canoed this way, paddling against the current before the river was tamed.

Pulling easily, I sweep through at some four knots over the ground and approach the lock. It really is massive—the 47-foot lift makes it the biggest lock of the Trent Severn system. Unwisely, I moor below the lock as the slight swell from the tail race of the power station reflects from the concrete wall and sets *Wanderer* rolling enough to keep me on the border of seasickness all night.

A wonderful day of sailing—all around me are open lakes alternating with fast flowing narrows with high granite sides, no cottages and absolute silence. The stillness is wonderful after all the lawn mowers, chain saws, drills, car engines, and boat motors of the last few days! The silence is broken only by the chuckle of water under *Wanderer*'s bow, then even that dies away.

14th July, 1993. Port Severn/Georgian Bay, Ontario

I was looking unsuccessfully for the government wharf for shelter for the night and came alongside a private dock to inquire where it was. "It's gone. There's a marina in its place. Stay here overnight," says the owner. Later, when we are sitting on the dock and had somehow ended up chatting about the difficulty of understanding modern poetry, he asks if I had ever heard of the poet Robert Service, from England, who immigrated to Canada and wrote "The Cremation of Sam McGee." When I reply that I didn't know of him, he recites the poem from memory and it is wonderful:

> "*There are strange things done in the midnight sun*
> *by the men who moil for gold.*
> *The Arctic trails have their secret tales*
> *that would make your blood run cold…*"

It is a evocative, sonorous poem of the Canadian north in winter and it sums up so much of the Canadian character. It is something I shall long remember.

20th July, 1993. Monument Channel (just northwest of Go Home Bay)

Now well into Georgian Bay. This is different country—now it's old Canadian Shield granite with more bare rock and less vegetation. The coast is mostly of low bare islets sheltering the channel from the onshore waves. I was sailing from Port Severn, a tiny village at the west end of the Trent Severn Waterway, for Midland but strong headwinds prevailed (and this fresh water kicks up quickly into an ugly short sea) so I anchor in the lee of a little horseshoe-shaped island for three hours.

2nd August, 1993. Mink Islands, Ontario

A chap in Parry Sound with a nice little double-ender recommended Windsor Bay, Franklin Island saying, "It's a lovely harbour and the best kept secret on the Georgian Bay so don't tell anyone." It certainly is pretty with a narrow granite inlet extending miles with several sandy beaches (rare in the old hard granite of the Canadian Shield) along the sheer-sided shores. But by Saturday mid-day, when I sailed in, there were already 25 yachts anchored, rafted together or tied alongside the rocks. I explored to the end, had a beer with the coastguard I met back in Parry Sound then sailed out to avoid the crowds. It was too crowded. I am afraid 'The best kept secret on Georgian Bay' has been discovered, as another six yachts were motoring in as I sailed offshore to the Mink Islands.

Gardening on the granite Mink Islands.

The Minks are a string of low wind-swept granite islands some five miles out that once supported a thriving summer fishing community. I picked my way carefully through the reefs and anchored amidst the low rocks, sheltered from all directions except southeast. I was greeted by the friendly invitation of Warren Edgar who called out, "Use you anchor as a stern line and tie your bow to the mooring ring and come up to the house for tea." I went in to find the family living,

---

with no electricity, in small detached buildings of one kitchen, two bedrooms, four young children and three boats.

There were thunderstorms in the early hours with continuous sheet lightening, and thunder overhead accompanied by torrential rain. The rain went into the southeast and *Wanderer* laying across the wind to a stern anchor, bow line to the rock, rolled all night with me on the point of being seasick.

The young family are all keen gardeners which is a difficult hobby on bare granite rock! Each time they visit the mainland they return with a bucket of soil scraped from cracks which they then spread over bare rock, make compost in a crevice between two boulders, and harvest beds of wild raspberries and strawberries.

I spend three enjoyable days with the family. Warren is a research engineer and spent some time with the British navy in the Second World War developing the 'hedgehog' anti-submarine mortar, then studying the problems of balance in jet engine rotors. I found his story of the development of the 'hedgehog' fascinating, especially having seen it fitted to the last corvette in Halifax Harbour.

5th August, 1993. Snug Harbour, Ontario

It is a pleasant day and suddenly all the powerboats are gone and the public wharf is empty, except for *Sure Beats Workin'* and *Wanderer*.

Snug Harbour has the reputation for the best smoked whitefish in Georgian Bay, and Brian, the fisherman, is also well known for his help to yachtsmen in trouble out in the bay. I meet him when I buy supplies and smoked fish and he shows me his smokery. He introduces me to his cat who has a long history too—it died some years back but his daughter, a trainee vet, massaged its heart and brought it back to life; then it went blind but she treated it and now it can see and it regularly climbs aboard visiting boats and cars and hides.

This is a lovely part of the small craft route—probably the best yet as it is more open. There is a beautiful

Georgian Bay Lighthouse: A forty-mile open water crossing from Pointe au Baril to the Bruce Peninsular.

Sailing to the Edge of Fear

stretch inside Franklin Island (Shebeshekong channel) the route generally goes north so navigation is easy; just a few boats travelling at a reasonable speed and the channel is wide enough for the wakes not to be a nuisance. Once through the narrows, the buoys turn west for three miles and I leave the buoyed channel to thread the mass of islands and rocks and it is real fun to find my own way through unbuoyed channels, skirting various reefs almost awash.

7th August, 1993. Bayfield to Britt, Ontario

I have been planning to cross Georgian Bay direct to Bruce Peninsula, a 40-mile open water passage. The early morning forecast is for "northeasterlies 10 knots overnight, becoming easterlies 10 knots in the morning, then northeast 10 knots" and this is ideal for a direct crossing to Wingfield Basin if the wind holds, but I have found before that a forecast of 10 knots can mean considerably less. I get up early and mark up the chart. I had forgotten the thrill of planning an off-shore passage—it is completely different from planning a coastal or small craft route—a real pleasure even doing it in a rush. But as Murphy's Law would have it, there is no wind!

8:30 A.M.: A slight ruffle appears on the water so I raise the anchor at last. Alas, the wind rises to force two then drops to force one and it is 10:30 A.M. before I clear the outer Inlet buoy and the wind still only a light zephyr. I have to reassess if a crossing is sensible: the breeze will probably die at 4:30–5:00 P.M. leaving *Wanderer* 18 miles offshore with a long row ahead. There is a difference between being adventurous and stupid, so I call it off and lay along the shore. A lovely sail one mile offshore all morning, bright sun, and rowing until I can see ruffles creeping across the water astern and the breeze picks up. Further along the coast, I turn down Byng Inlet towards Britt.

9th August, 1993. Britt, Byng Inlet, Ontario

For the second time in North America, I use earplugs and for the second time I severely regret it. (The first occasion was at Bobcaygeon because of loud music from a pub opposite. Someone fell into the water alongside my boat in the early hours and almost drowned. He was shouting "help" and I didn't hear him!) I used earplugs again last night to drown the sound of pumps unloading a big oil supply barge.

At 1:15 A.M. I wake to flashing police car lights leaving the dock. I remove my earplugs and listen to the receding noises—something had happened but as the crowd is drifting away I replace my earplugs and go back to sleep.

This morning the crew of the neighbouring yacht are having breakfast as I walk past: "You slept well last night, Frank. You missed all the excitement." Two aluminium outboards without lights had collided at speed, head-on in the dark. One of the boats is beached 20 yards away on the shore with its bow stove in. The crash had been so bad that the big outboard had jumped into the centre of the boat: one passenger was thrown out, and the girl in the bow had injuries to her back with no feeling below her waist. One of the lads went in the Britt Inn shouting, "My girlfriend's badly hurt. We hit a buoy!"

They called an ambulance and loaded her onto a stretcher before someone noticed that the paint on the damaged bow was blue and realised there are no blue buoys in the inlet and they began to look for another boat. They found it on the other shore, beached just before it sank—the fisherman too believed he had hit a buoy so he didn't report it! We have all done silly things such as running without lights, but an accident like this makes us assess the difference between calculated risk and recklessness. I am told that the girl has a broken back.

Later that day, I took the landlord of the Britt Arms for a sail then gave a hand to clear the scrub behind the hotel. Unknowingly, I must have picked up some poison ivy and paid the penalty for many days to come with weeping weals across my chest which don't heal.

12th August, 1993. Bad River (where the coast runs east-west at the top end of Georgian Bay), Ontario

This is a spectacular area. Some 15–20 miles of water filled narrow granite ravines only 20-feet wide, sides vertical to 30 feet. The whole area drains through a narrow gap in the granite wall of Bad River called 'The Devil's Door,' only 12-feet wide, vertical to 40 feet and the powerful rapid in the doorway is called, of course, 'The Devil's Door Rapid.' The anchored yachts said I would not be able to get through 'The Door' without at least 25 horsepower because of the current but I rowed my heart out and managed to get through—just.

Next I explore the many narrow glaciated rock channels to the north and feel my way through a narrow cleft eight-feet wide to anchor overnight in a delightful little rock pool. Here, I am discovered by an American named Chuck who could not believe that *Wanderer* got through without a motor. "Join me and my wife for a bonfire and barbecue on the rocks," he suggests. "I'll go get her. She's my fourth wife!" he explains proudly. "I'm his fourth wife!" she remarks, equally proudly, when we are introduced.

10:45 P.M.: Back aboard *Wanderer* I light a piece of mosquito coil before bedding down. The line of sores across my chest are inflamed and weeping. I haven't been bitten or scratching so it still must be the poison ivy I picked up at Bing Inlet. I wash with diluted antiseptic.

13th August, 1993. Towards Collins Inlet, Ontario

The islands and bays all merge with no distinguishing features: Maitland Bank is a mass of reefs, rocks and foul ground extending one mile offshore; there are no buoys, and with low speed and erratic winds, I cannot judge the distance run. Ahead, is another area of foul ground off Green's Island, followed by White Rock Ledges. The only safe, sensible course is to beat directly to Horseshoe Bay under Point Grondine, the only identifiable feature in the area as it is outermost point of land along this coast. If the wind dies, I can anchor there among the islets.

3:00 P.M.: *Wanderer* is inside the inner rocks of White Rock Ledges and it is a relief to know where I am amongst all this foul ground. I follow a straight deep water channel on the deep water side of a line of rocks towards Horseshoe Bay, come about and close-haul out to the triangular beacon on Grondine Rock off-shore, tack towards 'The Chickens,' rocks where I am tempted by several little anchorages, especially a cove in the Hen Islands, but decide to carry on while the wind holds.

Each time *Wanderer* runs onto rock patches (rising suddenly from the depths and only just underwater) I throw round and tack out. Finally, I see the range markers on Toad Island where I free off for Collins Inlet but there are too many sudden rocks to dare risk picking my way across the reef.

Close-hauled with an occasional short tack out as *Wanderer* runs onto the reef shallows and at last, I pass the end of the reef at Rooster Rock and the range markers line up. *Wanderer* surges as she gybes onto the next range in a fresh breeze, a gybing back to follow the next range for 200 yards, then due north as the furtherst range lines up to pilot

Devil's Door, Georgian bay

me through the rocks to Toad Island, and anchor in Noble Island Bay.

I have had enough of picking my way through rocks today. Collins Inlet tomorrow for which I need an easterly wind.

For the last week, the forecasters have been predicting a wind change. When it does come I shall go across to the Bruce Peninsular. Temperatures still remain obstinately too high and I'm staggering in the heat. Temperature all week has been in the 90s compared to the average for this time of year of 71ºF. It is the hottest summer ever recorded.

17th September, 1993. Crocker Island, North Channel, Lake Huron, Ontario

After the scorching weather all summer, the temperature has crashed now. There has been frost on the deck the last two nights and during the day it is cold enough to make your fingers tingle, though the sailing has been wonderful. Yesterday was lovely with sparkling water, bright sun, unlimited visibility and a good sailing breeze.

I stayed overnight in Boat Cove on Great La Cloche Island, a completely landlocked cove ideal for a Wayfarer as it had a depth of only 15 inches in the ten-foot wide entrance. Four miles in perfect conditions brought me to Bedford Island and another seven miles to Clapperton Island where I bypass the recognised anchorage and find a beautiful little cove just behind a small point with one solitary cottage. I anchor in four feet of the edge of the marsh. Manitoulin Island, on one side of the sound is of limestone, and the La Cloche Mountain ridges to the north are white quartzite, bare, and sparkling in the sun and occasionally turning to black in the shadow of the clouds. Socks, woolies, long-johns, wool shirt, sweater, boots, oilskins and beard are now standard for day sailing and I go to bed fully dressed at night. It's time I got out my inner sleeping bag.

Whale's Back Channel, Georgian Bay

22nd September, 1993. Spragge, North Channel Yacht Club, Ontario

The Benjamin Islands are beautiful with long, flat slopes of bare pink granite running down into the water. I have a long passage beating, the seas big and breaking between the sheltering islands. The waves are rapidly getting worse and I half filled *Wanderer* during one tack when the mainsheet jams. Expecting to get less shelter from the low skerries further on, I decide to run back to a cove on the last island. But first I beat between two little islands for a rest and a bite of lunch—and there, unbelievably amongst all this bare granite, is a narrow sand beach, ideal to pull out on. There is even a convenient tree stump to attach my mainsheet purchase although there was an adjoining patch of poison ivy which I almost blunder into. I am still suffering from the effects of the poison ivy I picked up in Byng Inlet— one scab is infected and none are healing properly. I wash down with antiseptic and feel better.

It is a pleasant warm day on the beach, until the wind goes north during the night and begins to eat away the beach. By morning the water is within two feet of *Wanderer*'s stern.

27th September, 1993. Hotham Island, MacBean Channel, Ontario

Raining all afternoon and evening but I have just about got *Wanderer* dry, apart from a last few drips from the boom and folded sail. My oilskin trousers must be allowing water through when I kneel as my trousers are damp at the knees. I am writing in my log book using a flashlight in my sleeping bag.

Trees are changing colour now, and there has been no sign of fall colour until a week ago. I am exploring Oak Bay at the end of a narrow channel in the midst of pouring rain. The colours are spectacular even in the rain—bright ferns deep bronze, slashes of scarlet, red maples, brilliant red scrub, yellow poplars, grey-green mosses on black and grey and red granites, golden reed beds alongside. I thread my way down this gorgeous, winding channel, even prettier the second time, especially the mosses and lichens—light and dark greens, blue, slate grey, the ferns are a magical bronze, mingled with trees, lichen, reeds and wild rice.

Now I am working back from the hospitable yacht club at Spragge to Little Current and then on to Killarney to leave *Wanderer* for the winter. Today the forecaster announced that "Fall is here." Rain is pattering on the tent but inside I am warm, dry, comfortable and well-fed. I have been shivering as I am not equipped for cold weather sailing, but I suddenly remember that I have my new cold weather clothing stored away which I have never used. My next job is to get it out.

2nd October, 1993. Little Current to Killarney via Lansdowne Channel, Ontario

At Spider Bay Marina: A full gale from the northwest blows until 2:30 A.M., then it drops to 15 knots and backs to west-northwest. *Wanderer* is occasionally chafing her bows on the dock as the wind drops so I have to get up to readjust her stern line.

The long range outlook calls for snow flurries and strong winds of 38 miles per hour to the middle of the week so I decide to get away first thing so as to get into shelter before the afternoon increase in wind. It is two miles to Strawberry Island Lighthouse then I can duck into Heywood Island (three miles away) or straight across to Lansdowne Channel (six miles) where *Wanderer* will get a lee for the northwest, and then I can keep in the lee of the La Cloche Mountains.

7:00 A.M.: The tent is dry so I pack it away in the stern where the weight aft will improve running.

9:10 A.M.: Fenders taken in, two reefs in the mainsail, sheets rigged to the genoa in case I need to run under genoa only.

There is a lot of wind in the open and I am glad I put in two reefs. A broad-reach down the channel past the town harbour wall towards the swing bridge. A stronger current than I expected sets towards the bridge—probably one-and-a-half knots by the way the buoys are leaning. I can stem the current using either sail or oars but nevertheless I am cautious about getting too near the bridge and I give three 'toots' of my foghorn well back. I can hear the bridge engine start immediately, the traffic stops and a gap appears as the span slowly turns. A green light and then a friendly wave from the bridge keeper as we pass through.

The lighthouse on Strawberry Island is prominent two-and-a-half miles away and I am tempted to shake out one reef under the land, but instead half unroll the genoa to keep *Wanderer* balanced off the wind, and her speed increases to four knots. The white lighthouse is shining brilliantly as the clouds blow away and the sky clears.

Beyond the lighthouse, the wind builds gradually from 'fresh' to 'strong' and speed rises from four to five knots. Heywood Island is three miles away to starboard but Browning Cove on the island is invisible as the forest blends with the background. There is a long fetch as *Wanderer* crosses the sound and the seas become high as the wind has been blowing from that direction all night. A compass sight enables me to identify the white quartz headland of Creak Island from five miles out. *Wanderer* is now surfing on the front faces of the swells, which occasionally break at her stern as her wake pulls them down on her, but the pull of the half-reefed genoa at the bow keeps her running straight. In the lee of Heywood

Island the seas decrease for a time for which I am grateful; then they build quickly where the wind funnels through the gap between Heywood and Partridge Islands at the entrance to Lansdowne Channel. Snow clouds have been building behind but they pass either side.

11:10 A.M.: A big swell is running into Lansdowne Channel and I know I ought to pull down my mainsail and run under only the genoa for safety, especially as the dinghy is running dead downwind and sometimes by the lee, but I carry on to get under the land in order to reduce the swells before gybing. These gusts are too strong and the swells to big to gybe safely, so I tack round quickly and plane down Lansdowne channel on the other gybe, running very fast, before gybing heavily approaching the great quarry. Beyond Quarry Point the wind jumps from west to northwest so I am on a broad reach across to Killarney Channel.

The wind is now as much as I can handle but *Wanderer* is making great speed and swells are building again in the open. I take a last look back at this lovely cruising ground with its predominating quarry island with the high quartzite shore of the white La Cloche Mountains behind. Grey snow clouds are heavy astern and below these, areas of grey have obliterated the land. Is it snow? The sun disappears as the snow clouds tower above. It is now a raw, cold day as *Wanderer* runs up Killarney Channel to the Mountain Lodge to tie up for the winter. I thoroughly enjoy my lunch, admiring the totally grey scene as a few snow flakes begin to fall.

I find that I don't want to end the trip yet—maybe there are a few days of Indian summer yet to come?

3rd October, 1993. Killarney, Ontario

It is the end of season and I am in a pleasant wood cabin in Killarney Mountain Lodge, with my gear all over the floor. Annabelle and Maury East, the hardworking owners of the hotel, both with a wonderful sense of humour, were sure that I would freeze overnight in *Wanderer* and insisted that I move into the hotel. They were right, of course, as there is no sign of an Indian summer and the extended forecast speaks of wind, snow flurries and increasing cold through next week so I asked if I can pull out here for winter storage and maintenance. "No problem. Stow your gear in the dormitory," they responded.

As soon as the frost melts off the deck and rigging, I spend the morning removing sails and tent in another cloudy, cold but dry day. I empty the forward buoyancy and most of the stern compartment, then the cockpit equipment into boxes and now it is raining with occasional snow flakes.

I eat on the 'staff' table with Ron and Joan (who operate the lodge yacht), Jonathan the air pilot, Stephen the resident biologist, and the two accomplished, intelligent East daughters who occasionally make known their disapproval of my chauvenistic English modes of expression.

5th October, 1993. En route to England

On the flight home, I reflect that this cruise has been my first experience of extended fresh water sailing. Fresh water has many advantages—there is no corrosion to the boat or equipment; oilskins are not vital except to keep the wind off as the fresh water dries quickly under the sun (whereas sea water always leave a damp salt residue); navigation is easier without tides; and the water of the Great Lakes is clean enough to be used to top up water containers.

The drawbacks of fresh water is that it is thinner, the waves kick up much more quickly. But I do miss the unique challenge of tidal sailing.

I am already anticipating eagerly the next leg of my journey—sailing the great inland fresh water seas of the Great Lakes.

CHAPTER SEVEN

1994. The Great Lakes

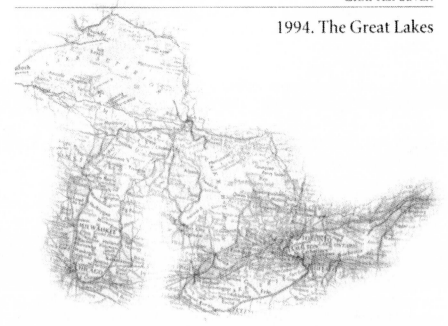

12 th June, 1994. Toronto, Ontario

When I phone my host Bill Sager from the Toronto airport at midnight I find he had not received my arrival details but he gets out of bed to collect me without protest. Cruising a small dinghy in such a large country is a fine way to make such dedicated friends.

14th June, 1994. Killarney, Ontario

The staff of Killarney Mountain Lodge had removed *Wanderer* from the stables and trailed her to the edge of the water on Sunday and I am able to start straight away on the fibre glass repairs left from last year. I am soon rained off by torrential downpours (often described in Canada as "light showers"), so I took the mail bus to Canada Customs at Sudbury—it's a 120 mile round trip—for my cruising permit.

17th June, 1994

The temperature has been 104°F and very humid. Unbearable!

I stowed my food, gear, and equipment and began my sail yesterday. Glad to be afloat at last. There has been a lot of fog the last few days because of the sudden temperature rise, and mosquitoes are out in quantity and they still love my soft English skin!

My friend Maury East has warned me to keep a good lookout for black bears which are numerous this year. They are powerful, fast, well-armed, and can be very dangerous, especially mother bears if a person inadvertently gets between her and her cubs. Males are very unpredictable. He added another warning, "If you get into trouble, don't try to walk out—you won't make it" and he arranged to fly me over the area to show how inhospitable the Canadian Shield country really is.

19th June, 1994. Snug Harbour, Lansdowne Channel, Ontario

I have been listening to guitar playing on a yacht anchored 100 yards away. The sound is lovely drifting across the water. The crew saw a black bear chasing off another last evening, and they tell me the speed bears move through thick undergrowth is unbelievable; they flatten everything in their way.

My cruise this year will take me from Georgian Bay (sometimes called the 'sixth Great Lake') via North Channel and into Lake Superior the largest deepest and coldest of all the Great Lakes, then along the northern (Canadian) shore. It is said to be spectacular, beautiful, magnificent and lonely. Several Canadian Wayfarers have cruised there over the years, and I have promised to return to Killarney in the next few days to cruise in the company of Don Davis, the master of Canadian Wayfaring, and Tim France, Wayfarer Cruising Secretary, so I will be able to benefit from their first-hand experience.

17th June, 1994. Covered Portage Cove, Ontario

This is a lovely cove surrounded by white quartzite cliffs which glisten and reflect the sun. And only one yacht is anchored under the cliffs; how different from last autumn when there were 28 boats here. Our three dinghies then move to the neighbouring cove which is smaller and more sheltered for cruising dinghies.

Summer arrived with a bang three days back; the temperature rising suddenly to the low 90s and my shoulders are raw and blistering under my shirt as I haven't acclimatised to Canadian weather yet.

The mosquitoes are now out in full force biting hungrily, aided by blackflies. Blackflies are a new experience for me and a very unpleasant surprise. They bite so gently under shirt cuffs and trouser legs that the victim is unaware until he notices a ring of blood running copiously down his wrists and ankles.

23rd June, 1994. La Cloche Mountains (north of Fraser Bay and Landsdowne Channel), Ontario

The Canadians, with their greater crew weight, could carry genoas to windward and had an easy four mile crossing of Fraser Bay. I had fallen behind when the wind veered and even after pulling two reefs down I had a hard struggle to get into the lee of the land before turning into Baie Finn, a true Norwegian-type fjord running some nine miles into the La Cloche Mountains. It was even more spectacular than I remembered from last year with the spectacular white cliffs reflecting the sun. We spend our time rambling, camping and gunkholing before I wave goodbye as my Canadians friends return to Killarney.

24th June, 1994. McGregor Bay, Ontario

The word 'uncharted' describing McGregor Bay drew me like a magnet. I had been told that I could buy a map at the post office…if I could find my way there. It is a mass of small granite islands and immediately I was completely lost. This is cottage country and cottagers are rumoured to dislike visiting yachts, but some 20 Wayfarers are racing regularly in the bay and I have an introduction to one of them.

Eventually, I find an occupied cottage and am pointed in the right direction and a local man in his outboard leads me through several miles of complicated channels to within sight of the post office island. The postmaster, Jeb, supplies the only map of the area, a copy of a private island survey done in the last century, and tells me where to anchor and what to see. I visit the community church, a lovely little wooden building next to the post office, and anchor behind a low rock beach, sheltered and out of everyone's way.

26th June, 1994

There was rain all night in bursts, occasional squalls across the low beach but without any real weight in the gusts, and after breakfast I allow myself one-and-a-quarter hours to sail to church in the light winds. I ask a young man in the church doorway if he is a visitor too. He says he is in a sense, and explains that he's the new minister and this is his first service. It is a lovely little wooden church, rustic-type pews, no ornamentation apart from a beautiful wood and a plain glass east window in the shape of a cross. The congregation almost completely fills the church.

One of the worshippers who saw me sail into the church dock, tells me that he owns one of the 23 Wayfarers in the Bay, but unfortunately he cannot raise his mast because of a injured arm so I volunteer to rig it for him after the service—an offer gratefully accepted. Another chap Tom Brown served in corvettes in the Second World War on the North Atlantic run and we chat about the *Sackville* in Halifax.

Crossing an open stretch, I set *Wanderer* to sail herself, the tiller steadied by a shockcord. While I am taking compass bearings for my turning point through the islands, *Wanderer* crashes herself onto a reef—down wind, doing three knots—and the centreboard kicks up to the horrible sounds of crunching and gouging fibreglass. She is hard on and almost out of the water, the rocks are extremely slippery and I cannot lift her over. Quickly I down the sails, and I heave her round towards deep water to sounds of more damage. Worse, this rock has been split by winter ice and *Wanderer* ran along the razor sharp edges, which must have cut through the hull.

I am kicking myself, swearing viciously at my stupidity when an outboard motors across to ask if he can help and tells me that he has been aground on this reef too in his Laser. I thank him and pole off with an oar and return to "post office island" where I may be able to haul out in case I have to carry out repairs immediately.

"It's the oldest rock in the world; it doesn't bend and it doesn't break; and we have all done it," Jeb the post master sympathises as I remove all the gear to examine the inside of the hull. The self bailers are watertight and surprisingly there is no hull leak, so I can safely continue and pull out on the beach at North Channel Yacht Club at Spragge to repair and anti-foul.

27th June, 1994. Cruising McGregor Bay, Ontario

An early morning sail through delightful scenery restores my sense of propor-tion, and I enjoy the hundreds of picturesque granite islets, the bigger ones each with its cottage. Calling again at the post office, Jeb recommends I sail to North Bay and anchor in the narrow fjord that runs south. "It is beautiful, with vertical cliffs and a landing at the far end," he remarks.

I work north, carefully following the channels now that I have a map, after my experience of running *Wanderer* onto a reef on Saturday. My only difficulty is a narrow cut marked 'Bad Current' where the wind is funnelling and already heavy, and I have to pull down the first reef. The gut is longer than expected, scarcely wide enough to regain steerage way after each tack before hitting a training wall just awash on the west side. Ten tacks and I am safely through. As Jeb said, the fjord is superb, the scenery spectacular. I anchor at the far end but it is too hot to stay long so I swallow a quick sandwich then beat out with rocks towering over me on both sides. A worthwhile visit.

I have supper with the Browns whom I had met at church. They have invited a few friends including the young minister and it is a delightful, friendly evening. They press me to stay in their guest cottage overnight. I prefer to sleep aboard *Wanderer*, but when I cast off so many mosquitoes descend on me that I return and ask if I might change my mind!

28th June, 1994

7:00 A.M.: I walk down to the dock to say 'hello' to *Wanderer*. Suddenly, I stop. A packet of noodles is torn open and scattered over the floorboards, then I notice the lid is off the cool box and contents pulled out. Cheese has been opened and partly eaten, bread pulled out of the haversack, the sachets of chocolate drink emptied, every envelope of 'Lemsip' opened and licked clean, apples nibbled. Racoons have been aboard! And clearly, they have had a wonderful time! The porridge box is empty—I have been hoarding five envelopes of my favourite 'peaches and cream' instant Quaker Oats for a special occasion but only one packet has been opened and eaten. Surprisingly, the rest are missing so presum-ably the raiders have carried the other five home! I find it very funny. I have been told that racoons will steal any type of food and are very dextrous but this is my first experience of them.

I have breakfast with the Browns and they seem to feel responsible for the thievery of the island's raccoons so, in spite of my protests, have stripped their house for me to make good the loss.

I am less sure about cruising Lake Superior since last night. Everyone agreed the scenery is magnificent but it is deep, cold, inhospitable, rough, and foggy!

7th July, 1994. John's Harbour, Whalesback Channel, Ontario

There are only a few boats about these days. I have been at North Channel Yacht Club the last few days repairing the damage done when I carelessly ran *Wanderer* onto a rock. Sand beaches are almost non-existent amongst all the granite rock but I knew there was a wide beach at North Channel Yacht Club at Spragge and they have an enviable reputation for being helpful to cruising boats.

Benefiting from my recent experience with raccoons, I remove fruit, food haversacks and cooler box from *Wanderer* and put them inside the clubhouse and replaced hatches so that the raccoons cannot get inside to nibble. There are lots of volunteers at the sailing club to help stow my gear and help roll *Wanderer* up the beach, and we pull her over so that the sun shines on the bottom of the hull to dry the damage and accelerate the curing of the repair, and I hold her down with a bucket of water tied at the masthead. Oars, tent, clothes, inflatable, and anchors are piled on the beach. There's a long deep gouge under the bow and someone on the other side says, "Here's a four-inch gash right through the hull on the port side." I cannot understand why there has been no leakage, until, looking inside the boat, I realise that a single reinforcing layer of foam and glass weave between the tabernacle and the front bulkhead has kept the hull water tight. What amazing luck!

The owners of a nearby trawler-yacht loans me a long electricity cable, a hair dryer and, from a nearby yacht, comes an angle grinder whilst I unpack my glass mat, resin, pigment and tape, and dry the damage with the hair drier. My neighbour, another Frank, cuts out the damage then recommends using epoxy as *Wanderer*'s materials are now several years old, and no gel coat is needed as epoxy is waterproof. Hours later, exhausted from working in the full heat of the afternoon sun, I stagger to a stop and make a cup of tea in the kitchen, then flake out in the dock master's camper overnight.

8th July, 1994. North Channel Yacht Club, Ontario

This morning, while waiting for the anti-foul paint to dry, the dockmaster Bob, an émigré Englishman, showed me his delightful garden. He is a great enthusiast and it is as close to an English vegetable garden as is possible in the extreme climate of Canada—three types of tomato, two types of cucumber, three sorts of beans, broccoli, cauliflower, red cabbage, butter beans, red lettuce, romaine lettuce, butter crunch lettuce, spinach, swiss chard, parsley, tarragon, basil, strawberries, peppers and flower beds, including sweet peas, gladioli, lilies, blackcurrant, radish, and onion. I follow him round admiringly, but I am too tired and there are too many clouds of mosquitoes following me, to appreciate it fully.

12th July, 1994. Beardrop Harbour, North Channel, Ontario

A lovely sunny evening as I write up my log book. The early morning forecast had been enticing, suggesting it will be too cold for the mosquitoes! This evening's forecast has been updated to 'strong gusts' so I come into Beardrop Habour for shelter.

There are some dozen masts behind the rocks which shelter the cove from the east and as soon as *Wanderer* appears someone in a trawler yacht shouts across the anchorage, "Hi Frank. Have you repaired that hole you put in your hull yet?" and everyone in the anchorage turns to look. It is a most embarrassing and public comment upon my seamanship! The vice commodore of North Channel Yacht Club tries to rehabilitate my dented reputation by waving me over for food, and suggesting that I might give a talk to his yacht club next year for their 25th anniversary.

The wind hasn't dropped as usual this evening and sullen looking clouds are now spreading in from northwest beyond the granite, and the tree tops are obscuring the sun. The sun's rays illuminating the clouds from behind give an ominous feeling of apprehension which is reinforced by the lurid mirror reflection in the water. It is cold!

13th July, 1994. North Channel, Ontario

Clara Island is the last of the string of islands that make the eastern part of North Channel so delightful. From here on there is open water to St Mary's river leading to Sault St. Marie (commonly referred to as 'the Soo') with much fewer sheltered anchorages and a constant headwind blowing downriver. Turnbull Island was explored today. It is the prettiest anchorage in Whalesback Channel—an area deservedly noted for its pretty coves.

The little creek at the west end of Clara Island has only two feet in the entrance, with numerous sunken timbers and deadheads inside. It is very bad holding ground—soft mud and my five-pound anchor drags three times in spite of rowing in. I change to the 13 pound with its 10 feet of heavy chain but this drags twice although it holds better at the third attempt. It will be unreliable if it blows, but the forecast is for settled weather tonight. The anchorage is acceptable only because it is a good takeoff point tomorrow for Blind River six miles away.

The next morning I find the anchor rope is caught on a light branch which pulls easily out of the silt—it was the only thing that held *Wanderer* overnight, as the 13-pound anchor pulls home easily.

15th July, 1994

I'm about to cast off from the marina at the town of Blind River when I hear someone say, "Hi Frank." I turn to find the two Tweedies, friends from Douglastown, New Brunswick, whom I had met three years ago on the Atlantic coast when they showed me that wonderful gunkholing area, the Miramichi. They are returning home from visiting their son in the Yukon (a drive of some 4,000 miles) and they have been looking into coves and harbours, having heard I might be about. It is an amazing coincidence as half-an-hour either way and we'd not have met.

15th July, 1994. Mississagi Bay, Ontario

Rounding the long reef out from Jolliette Point exposes *Wanderer* to a nasty short sea that has built up from the long fetch from the west. I thrash up into the next bay, overcanvassed and with spray flying. The bay is filled with marsh, so I sail between the rocks, slowly and carefully, into the next bay. This has boulders and reefs to seaward, marsh at the upper end, but a longer fetch than I like so I sail further in to a delightful area of small islets and bare rock.

A charming, lovely area, but littered with rock just awash and numerous 'deadheads' set to foul my anchor line and it is rather more open than I like to south and southwest, so again I let the wind drift *Wanderer* through a reed-lined gut into another creek which is protected from every direction. Now there are rocks and reefs to break up any swell from the lake, and reed shelter from all other directions.

The five-pound danforth bites immediately so I brew up and have supper in the loveliest anchorage that I can remember as I watch the sun go down, reflected in the water. The narrow pathway of water winding between the islets and reeds has becomes golden, reflecting the sun, and the whole western sky is pastel yellow. The wind drops to five knots but it has served me well.

16th July, 1994. North Channel, Ontario (halfway between the towns of Blind River and Thessalon)

I have exactly ten minutes to write postcards as it is now 9:05 P.M. and in 10 minutes, the mosquitoes will move in. So by then I must have my tent rigged, plastic bags blocking any gaps round the shrouds and mast, otherwise they will make a meal of me.

Last night, watching the sunset, I was a couple of minutes late closing down the tent, and I paid in full. I was heavily bitten and by the time I had finished spraying insect repellant I counted 108 bodies on the side decks and there must have been many more under the seats and in the bilges that I couldn't see!

　　　　　　　　　　　　　　　　　　　　Sailing to the Edge of Fear

19th July, 1994. Bruce Mines, Ontario

Heading for 'The Soo' but there is no wind so I stay a day for a look round. Bruce Mines was the first successful copper mine in Canada circa 1840 and there is an excellent reconstruction of the mine showing the method employed and the equipment used.

Lloyd Smith, a local sailor, takes me to see a caterpillar of the Monarch butterfly feeding on a milkweed plant opposite his sister's house, and the green crysalis on the house wall—each autumn these delicate young butterflies travel an incredible 2,000 miles to Mexico feeding only on the milkweed plant and return next spring—one of the great mysteries of navigation. His sister tells me she has asked the council not to spray the roadside any more as it is the only patch of milkweed locally. She suggest that I must see the famous 17-foot canoe in the local museum and lets me read an article by Joe Youcha about it in *Wooden Boat* magazine. There are a couple of memorable quotes and one particularly hits home: "It is in the nature of all of us—or is it just my own peculiar makeup—which brings, when the wind blows, that queer feeling, mingled longing and dread? A thousand invisible fingers seem to be pulling me, trying to draw me away from the four walls where I have every comfort, into the open where I shall have to use my wits and my strength to fool the sea in its treacherous moods, to take advantage of fair winds and to fight when I am fairly caught—for a man is a fool to think he can conquer nature."

Thessalon is a delightful town with lawns of mown grass sloping down to a well kept river and I enjoy my walk round. Henry Hudson's replica ship is due next weekend for an open day but unfortunately I shall miss it. Both marine and land forecasts are predicting thunderstorms for the afternoon but I hope to be in shelter by then, and anyway the promise of a favourable southeasterly is too good to miss.

Three hours later, the wind freshens to give exciting sailing without being dangerous. I goose-wing the genoa and *Wanderer* enjoys herself, occasionally trying to surf on the front faces as the waves steepen.

But already the horizon is black where the land of St Joseph's Island must be, and the vivid multiple lightning flashes highlight *Wanderer*—even from seven miles away on a bright sunny day. To the southeast where the wind comes from, the sky is clear and I relax as I am sure the storm will pass me by. Suddenly, the thunderclouds storm in from the west and all hell lets loose. The world goes black, an unimaginable torrent beats the seas flat and I am a lone witness of the Wrath of the Gods.

I come into harbour like a drowned rat.

24th July, 1994. Sault Ste. Marie, Ontario (at the junction of North Channel, St. Joseph's Channel, and Lake Superior)

The temperature is much cooler now after the excessive heat and humidity, thunderstorms and torrential rain of the last few days. On the chart, I had noticed a circular lagoon on the outskirts of Sault St. Marie completely sheltered with a narrow entrance, and in pouring rain went into the Algoma Sailing Club (sail boats only). Jack Goldie, who turns out to be a Catholic priest-in-training helps me tie up, phones the commodore for permission to stay, and greets me by saying, "Isn't that a Wayfarer? I've just been reading a book from the library on Wayfaring by Frank and Margaret somebody but I can't remember their name." I keep quiet. We drove into the city for a coffee and donut in torrential rain, which lasts less than 30 minutes but floods the streets to a depth of 18 inches.

I moved to the marina, conveniently located in the centre of town in Bondar Park (named after Roberta Bondar, Canada's first female astronaut) and close to downtown. Jack Goldie has a Herreschoff 18-foot catboat and I promised to show him how to hove-to and reef afloat. It was a long beat against the strong current but there were no other boats about and it was pleasant to be afloat.

Off the marina, I hove-to and demonstrate how to pull down the first reef. We discuss the various ways of reefing, then Jack hoists full sail and repeats the exercise. The current is carrying us downstream and *Wanderer* is nearing the shore so we got out the oars to row through the wind, and hove-to on the opposite tack. Jack pulls down the second reef a couple of times, tacks towards the shore, and we eat our sandwiches. "We are calling the Coast Guard to get you towed in," shouts a woman running down from City Hall. "Don't worry. They won't be long." We try to reassure her that we are not in trouble and row back to the marina entrance.

The marina staff are anxious: "We were about to come out for you," and they explain that they had watched us stop with sails shaking, trying to lower our mainsail, then getting out oars and putting them away again, and having more trouble with our sails. They assumed it had been a broken motor.

26th July, 1994. Agawa Canyon, Ontario

I took to the railroad this morning on the Algoma Central & Hudson's Bay railway. The A.C.& H.B. is deservedly known locally as the "All Curves & High Bumps." It is a fascinating four hour journey northward through the ancient rock of the Canadian Shield where every bend brings a new view—steep grades, high timber bridges over small rivers, deep narrow cuts blasted through solid granite hills, impossible curves where the sides of the carriages scrape the rocks—and occasional tantalising views over Lake Superior. There is a one-and-a-quarter hour stop in the Agawa Canyon for lunch before returning, and I climb the wall of the canyon to the observation platform. It's an impressive view: vertical granite walls 300 yards apart, the canyon winding through the mountains, the river far below stained dark brown with tannin from the bark of the forest trees.

I have been reading the sailing guides. *The Great Lakes Marine Weather Guide* notes the extreme conditions of Lake Superior; it is the deepest and coldest of the lakes with heavy fog, often experiencing vicious winds, with strong thunderstorms. After more reading, I reluctantly change my plans and turn south towards Lake Michigan.

7th August, 1994

I have cleared customs into U.S. at Drummond Island. Yesterday, I lowered my Canadian courtesy flag and raised the U.S. one as I sailed across the dotted line on the chart. This was not strictly necessary until after I had cleared customs, but a nice courtesy I thought to both countries who had been so kind to me. I get a little tense about clearing customs but this customs officer has the reputation of knowing boats and understands that yachts are dependent on unpredictable winds and weather, which eases the process.

After two days at Drummond Island, I sail through De Tour Passage out into Lake Huron to find a great swell running in from southeast from the open water, probably from a gale beyond the horizon, so I slip round into the mass of islands for shelter overnight. It makes me realise with a jolt that I am now sailing a lee shore. I do not like lee shores —and this one needs extra care.

9th August, 1994. Les Cheneaux Islands, Michigan, U.S.A.

Today a good run of 21 miles. I started out early and took *Wanderer* to Les Cheneaux Islands. These islands ('Les Cheneaux' meaning 'the channels') ought to be the ideal cruising ground with long channels running southeast–northwest, but every island has big holiday cottages along the shore with small racing yachts and lovely varnished wood launches in boat houses, and cruising boats are discouraged and sent along to anchor in Government Bay. The forecast next day was for winds going northwest-north and Government Bay is big and necessitates moving as the wind shifts. I had almost reached the marina in Cedarville when the wind slams down out of the north and I have to heave-to in order to pull down two reefs in horizontal gale-driven rain. A yacht entering the marina disappears in the murk then re-appears alongside to ask if I am alright and if I would like a tow. It is kind of them.

From Cheboygan on the south shore I have been told there is an Inland Route, some 40 miles of river and lakes connected by locks, which goes through to Lake Michigan. It looks interesting on the map but no one seems to know much about it.

14th August, 1994. Mackinac Island, Michigan

Very cold the last 10 days. At night time I now need extra clothing; I'm wearing socks inside my sleeping bag. Last night's temperature was 38°F and daytime highs mostly in the 60s. I have been in Mackinac Island for three days. It is a high and attractive island, with a big fort above the colourful Victorian style town, and no mechanical vehicles are allowed. All transport is horse-drawn—even the garbage truck, and they employ a man to follow the horses round with a brush and shovel. It's a full time job and I wonder if it is well paid. It makes me wonder how the great cities managed before the automobile.

I have been trying to sail to Cheboygan, 12 miles southwest across the straits but I have been defeated by several days of strong winds and thunderstorms. Mackinac is an uneasy harbour—always disturbed by wakes from the constant ferry traffic, even boats in the marina roll heavily, and any gale from the southeast blows straight in and yachts have to run for other shelter. The island is very popular in the cruising season, with boats anchored in the outer harbour sometimes queuing for several days to get into the docks where there is a maximum stay of four days. But they fitted *Wanderer* into a corner.

I intended to leave this morning, the fourth day of my stay, but there is a gale in Eastern Lake Superior coming this way, and a small craft advisory has been issued for the Mackinac City area.

15th August, 1994. Cheboygan (15 miles east of the junction of Lakes Huron and Michigan), Michigan State

I am now back in mainland U.S. after two summers in Canada.

17th August, 1994

This evening, I was beginning to wonder if my hand had lost its cunning. Or, more accurately, if my judgement was still sound. This "inland route" is a lovely waterway through marsh and reed, narrow and winding, occasionally a few small groups of houses appear, but mainly trees, bushes, and meadows where the trees have been cleared by settlers in the past, and a strong downriver current.

I enter the river at 4:00 P.M. with a dying wind, thunder and rain clouds building, and several miles to row against the current before the only marina. The forecast is for the wind going northwest tonight at 25 knots. I almost anchor in a marsh creek at the entrance but I decide: "No, I'll be able to find somewhere to tuck into up the river."

I row and row but there is nowhere to stop. Two hours later as it begins to rain I come across a little side stream only 12 inches deep, less than 10 feet wide and dark brown with cedar tannin. It is no more than a drainage ditch across the meadows but there are low mud banks on both sides of the entrance and a few reeds to damp down power boat wakes.

I poled *Wanderer* stern first through the mud for 20 yards and tied her to a bush, bows to the river, and towards tonight's forecast northwest 25 knots.

This part of the waterway reminds me very much of our Norfolk Broads; it is very pretty, and perhaps I am a little homesick.

20th August, 1994. Crooked River Yacht Club (inland route from Cheboygan), Michigan

Spectacular thunder and lightning, unbelievable rain the last two nights. This is a lovely waterway. I am at Crooked River Yacht Club at mile 33, rain and thunder is beating the side of the tent now as I write in my log book. I have been reading about how the Native Indians used to portage their canoes across the narrow ridge to Little Travers Bay and I have been planning to do the same.

I am beginning to realise that my planning of a direct crossing of Lake Michigan is suspect, and I return to basics: Lake Michigan is too wide to cross directly and too narrow to safely lay to a sea anchor if caught out in gale conditions in the middle. Beaver Island, situated in mid-lake, has a good harbour, therefore I need to cross to the Beaver Islands, and from there to the Garden Peninsular shore. However, Beaver Island is well north of my portage to Traverse Bay so I still have a long lee shore with no shelter before I can start the crossing. I do not like the long lee shore and I am becoming more cautious of this fresh water now I have seen how quickly it can kick up. One possibility is to wait in Traverse Bay for a favourable wind; another alternative is to return down the Inland Route to Cheboygan, go west through the Straits of Mackinaw, and overnight in the rocky peninsular of Waugoshance, so reducing the open water leg to Beaver Island to 20 miles albeit against the prevailing westerly wind.

According to the Indian River Route Guide I have reached the head of navigation, but my road map shows the stream continuing to a small lake almost touching Lake Michigan. I poled *Wanderer* upstream through beds of water lilies when round a bend I am faced with a difficulty: a road has been built across the stream over a four-foot diameter culvert. I was tempted to haul *Wanderer* out of the water and across the road on boat rollers but I hesitate as it is a six lane interstate highway and it seems possible that the police might arrive while *Wanderer* is crossing and might not be sympathetic. So I never reach the watershed where the Indians portaged.

I am quite happy to return 38 miles to Lake Huron for I have enjoyed the inland route working through the locks, and I have made a lot of friends whom I would enjoy revisiting. And it would be downwind all the way.

28th August, 1994. Waugoshance Point at the entrance to Lake Michigan, Michigan State

I had a good sail yesterday from Mackinaw City 15 miles along the first sand dune coast I have seen. A lovely sail today, light northeast wind with warning of thunderstorms this afternoon and evening, some of them violent. There are beaches now on which I could pull out, but I gamble that I shall be able to find shelter behind one of the islets at Waugoshance Point. The chart does not show depths but I feel my way through reefs where the shallows will break any swell. Wind, heavy rain, lightning, and thunder slam in from the south just after I anchor and get the tent up and the wind was whining in the rigging as I clip the lightning conductors to the shrouds. Now I am warm and dry inside the tent.

So this evening I am anchored in a shallow rock pool half-a-mile short of the point, listening to a full gale roaring outside, and looking at the tumult of gale-driven seas breaking on the shallows and crashing on the reef 150 yards away. Awe-inspiring. I never get used to the noise.

The forecast warns of another day of strong westerlies tomorrow.

29th August, 1994. Beaver Island, north end of Lake Michigan, Michigan State

From Waugoshance Point it is 18 miles upwind to Beaver Island and in spite of an unpromising forecast, I snatch a passage safely, close-hauled to Hog Island Reef buoy some five miles south of Hogg Island and then short tack through the shelter of the rocks and reefs under Hog island until I can lay St. James harbour on the other tack.

Beaver Island in the middle of Lake Michigan is the ideal place to break the long 75-mile passage from the Straits of Mackinac; it is also a fine spot to spend a few days. The islands of the archipelago are ideal for exploring with a shoal draft boat. The harbourmaster recommended that I explore Garden Island and a shallow cove on the west side of Hog island.

Garden island has an ancient Indian cemetery with many 'Spirit Houses' still intact above the graves. At the north end of the island lives the last of the area's Native Indians, now in her 80s, teaching Indian medicine, herbal cures, Indian customs and folk law. She is intelligent, charming, and she tells me she has white blood from her Yorkshire-born grandfather, and she hopes to be buried in the Indian cemetery with her people when she dies. On the west side of Hog island is a shallow cove, less than two-feet deep and I have to navigate by the satellite photograph as, surprisingly, it is not shown on the chart. The area is littered with reefs but this poses no problem to a Wayfarer with an eight-inch draught—and it's pretty indeed.

There is much to do on the main island. I made friends with Carl Felix, a retired master boatbuilder from Maine who makes quality models of ships, schooners, boats, and aircraft. His latest venture is Viking 'Dragon' longships beautifully finished to scale, and three-feet long. His customers are the large number of Scandinavian families who have settled in the mid-west who wish to put the ashes of their dead in a Dragon ship for a traditional Viking funeral.

I am wondering how to cross to the mainland against the prevailing westerly with the days shortening, and the autumn calms of morning and evening. Navigation is always difficult beating against prevailing winds and the morning and evening calms plays havoc with planning, and for the latter part there is a long rock peninsular under my lee. I do not like these long hops with nowhere to put into if the weather turns bad. While sheltering from the rain all day today, I relax by sewing minor tears in the batten pockets and re-stitched the luff of *Wanderer's* mainsail.

The Beaver Archipelago are indeed a jewel and the islanders friendly. I was just getting to know local people and have accepted an invitation to the harbour master's 50th birthday party, when I noticed the weather bulletin posted in the harbour office promises the rare occurrence of a favourable northeasterly for the next day so I sail immediately for Gull island 10 miles away to anchor for the night.

2nd September, 1994. Gull Island to Parent's Bay, Garden Peninsula, Michigan

I roll overnight off the beach at Gull Island. Still I cannot receive the weather for Green Bay, though the forecast for Travers Bay come through clearly but Travers Bay is well astern so it is of little use. I shall have to assume yesterday's forecast is still correct and I'm away rowing at 4:15 A.M. A brilliant starry night gives just enough light to see the shadow of the land but there's no moon. I pack

Wanderer in the dark, careful not to let anything roll overboard. I have a feeling this is going to be a long and difficult day.

I row down the lee (east) side of Gull Island, heading far out to skirt a couple of reefs where the rudder blade rattles up and down on unseen rocks. Off the south end of Gull Island, I see a darker ripple of rock only a few feet ahead and pull round sharply, rowing a quarter mile out before the rudder blade will stay down, then I sail on a back bearing from a clump of bushes silhouetted against the star-filled sky. The sweeping beams of light from the lighthouse at the north end silhouette the island and suggest that I am not entirely alone out here. I row on to my course of 285 degree magnetic to start crossing with an occasional glance at the compass by flashlight.

A 'Laker,' a blaze of light, crosses my course ahead makes me nervous. Astern, a vertical strip of red light rises between the trees of Gull Island. It looks very odd and I watch mystified as it rises, turns yellow, then white. As it rises it becomes a sliver of a crescent and I realise it is the newly risen moon. At least I now have something to steer by instead of lighting the compass card with a flashlight every few seconds.

I'm awake by 5:30 A.M. and it's still black, the stars are brilliant. No sign of the pre-dawn light yet. A slight breeze fills in giving 1 knot but it is easier than rowing! I had forgotten the pleasures of night sailing calm sea, a black night, clear brilliant stars and a light breeze. Normally, I would enjoy it but am worrying about crossing Lake Michigan - short days, a bad reputation for kicking up quick, calms morning and evening and Fall weather approaching.

By 7:00 A.M. I am sailing as light variable winds fill in but no sign of the fair northeasterly at all. Headwinds force me 10–30 degrees below my course so eventually I tack, headed again so tack back after an hour, then there are calms. It is a 22 mile crossing to the nearest headland and I am getting nowhere and I half expect to be beating all night, but the wind helps by shifting to southwest and freshening, and I anchor during the evening at Parents Bay. Thirty miles completed after a long and frustrating day.

3rd September, 1994. Washington Island, Green Bay, Wisconsin

Only when I come to the breaks in the islands and check back on my reckoning do I discover that I anchored last night in Portage Bay, not Parent's Bay as I thought —four miles south of my estimated position. Nothing to be proud of but an understandable error in the light variable winds.

Another 30 miles completed today south down Garden Peninsula to Washington Island. I am very conscious of the fall weather just around the corner and have been pushing on. Another 30 miles to my Wayfarer contact at Bailey's Harbor.

6th September, 1994. Porte des Mortes, Wisconsin

It always delights me how *Wanderer* rides so easily as the seas increase. Crossing the main passage to Door County mainland, a short sea is building in the middle because of the long fetch through the Porte des Mortes channel, and I take one reef down and roll the genoa. A coastguard boat is towing a yacht up under the land for shelter. She looks an able yacht, sail covers on, riding well and I am unable to see any obvious damage through my binoculars. *Wanderer* is going well, shouldering the seas aside and, stupidly, I begin to feel superior.

10:45 P.M.: In Europa Bay, planing to leeward of low rocks just awash, *Wanderer* suddenly stops wallowing in the troughs. I look up to find the mainsail has blown out, split from luff to leech, held up by only the doubling of the material at the leech. I scramble it down then unroll the genoa and limp into the shore which looks like sand but is stone and too steep to pull out, no one is about to help, and the bottom is of great flat rock slabs which won't hold an anchor, and it is a lee shore.

Fortunately, there is an old abandoned jetty sticking out for 100 yards, so I roll up the genoa and row. In its lee, it is comfortably calm, sheltered from the wind and waves by the jetty and it's ideal for sewing the sail. The anchor bites and holds, hooked over the end of a slab of rock.

By mid-afternoon I have enough stitching to give strength to the panels, the luff and leech doubled over and bound to give strength. The forecast is "northwest 10–20 knots for the rest of the day, but going southwest tomorrow." So I need to get as far as possible using the rest of today's fair northwesterly as the repaired mainsail won't survive beating to windward tomorrow.

A cruising man, no matter how careful, sometimes needs luck and I have certainly had my fair share today: the mainsail could have blown out when crossing from Beaver Island yesterday, or today when fine-reaching south along the rocky lee shore of Garden Peninsular. Instead it happened when there was a ruined jetty conveniently to leeward for shelter to carry out repairs.

Rowley Bay is five miles wide, point to point. The village is too far to windward so I go to windward of the stakes of a 'fishpond' (it would be called a 'fish weir' on the East Coast), then free off for the next headland.

North Bay, a deep indentation in the coast, is shallow with numerous marsh channels and it looks ideal for 'gunkholing' but my concern is to reach Baileys Harbor, where my Wayfarer contact may be kind enough to lend me a mainsail. In a fresh wind, *Wanderer* is reaching at five knots and I am carefully favouring the mainsail when a sudden gust causes me to release the sheet enough for the sail to flog and another tear appears four inches above my sewing. I swear at myself: it was careless of me with only six miles to go. The imposing tower of Canna Island is prominent on the next headland (it is an island with a causeway to the shore) and when the leech tears apart in the next gust I scramble the sail down and, under genoa only, work into the cove behind Canna for the night. A holiday family volunteer to deliver a message to Bailey's Harbor and Gordon Hegenbarth arrives two hours later with his mainsail with an offer to store *Wanderer* over winter. How generous.

9th September, 1994. Bailey's Harbor, Wisconsin

Wisconsin is a farming state, and I feel at home here. The main crop is fruit, in particular cherries.

Wanderer is now ashore at the home of the Hegenbarths who invited me to 'come visit' when I was on Lake Michigan. Gordon is a retired accountant and Susan an artist, a nice couple who are prepared to store *Wanderer* in their garden and all my gear in the cellar until next June.

Gordon has been explaining the rules of American football to me before we watch two games of the Green Bay Packers his "local team and the best football team in North America, Frank" but I seem to have a mental blockage when it comes to understanding the game.

I have been looking at the possibilities for next season—either south to Chicago and into the Mississippi system—but distances between harbours are greater on Lake Michigan for an engineless boat, with nowhere to duck into if the weather turns bad; or possibly explore the bay of Green Bay where a waterway goes south almost joining the upper reaches of the Missouri river leading far west.

"Where to next?" I ask myself, flying back to England. I am only now getting used to the vast distances of the United States and Canada. The cruising grounds are endless, and fascinating, and it would take a lifetime to see all that I want to.

APPENDIX

Nautical Terms

Bearing of an Object Relative to the Boat   **Boat Heading Relative to the Wind**

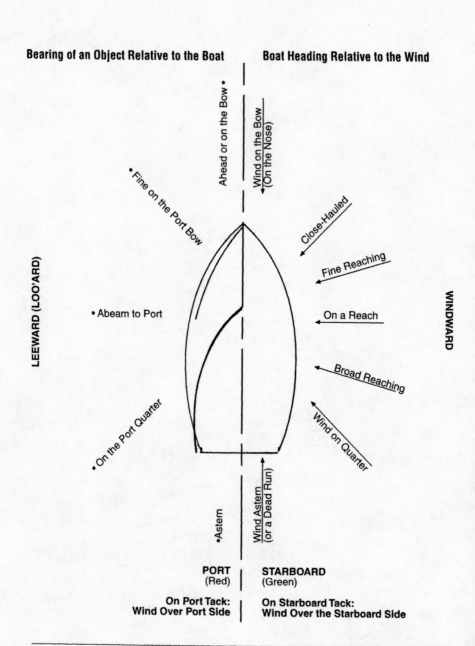

Ahead or on the Bow •

• Fine on the Port Bow

• Abeam to Port

• On the Port Quarter

• Astern

Wind on the Bow (On the Nose)

Close-Hauled

Fine Reaching

On a Reach

Broad Reaching

Wind on Quarter

Wind Astern (or a Dead Run)

LEEWARD (LOO'ARD)

WINDWARD

PORT
(Red)

STARBOARD
(Green)

On Port Tack:
Wind Over Port Side

On Starboard Tack:
Wind Over the Starboard Side

Appendix B

Parts of a Wayfarer

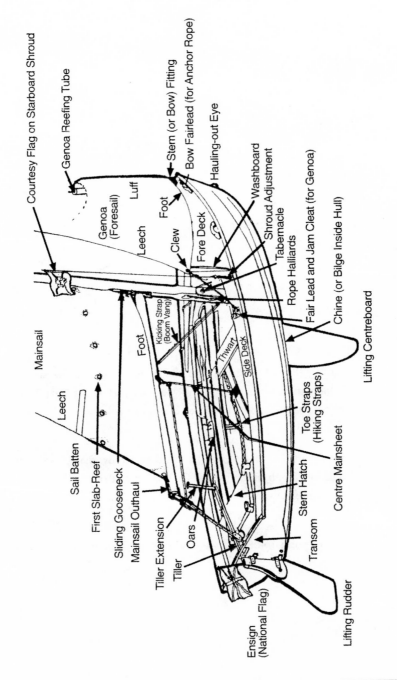

APPENDIX C

Heaving-To

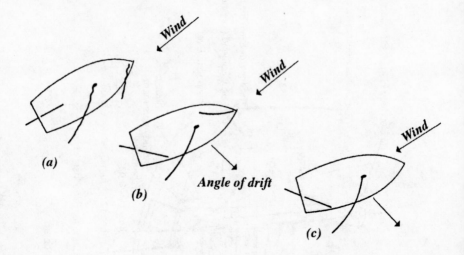

a) Losing speed by luffing into the wind or freeing the sheets, usually in order to reef. Not very satisfactory as the boat is not under control and steerage way can easily be lost.

b) Heaving-to in order to reef, navigate, or eat. By freeing the main, backing the jib, and tying the tiller to leeward, a boat will heave-to comfortably, drifting slowly across the wind.

c) A boat will also heave-to under mainsail only, but it takes more time to lose steerage.